BRAND THINKING AND OTHER NOBLE PURSUITS

DEBBIE MILLMAN

FOREWORD BY ROB WALKER

ALLWORTH PRESS
NEW YORK

ALLWORTH PRESS BOOKS MAY BE PURCHASED IN BULK AT SPECIAL DISCOUNTS FOR SALES
PROMOTION, CORPORATE GIFTS, FUND-RAISING, OR EDUCATIONAL PURPOSES. SPECIAL EDITIONS
CAN ALSO BE CREATED TO SPECIFICATIONS. FOR DETAILS, CONTACT THE SPECIAL SALES
DEPARTMENT, ALLWORTH PRESS, 307 WEST 36TH STREET, 11TH FLOOR, NEW YORK, NY 10018
OR INFO@SKYHORSEPUBLISHING.COM.

19   18   17   8   7   6

PUBLISHED BY ALLWORTH PRESS
AN IMPRINT OF SKYHORSE PUBLISHING
307 WEST 36TH STREET, 11TH FLOOR, NEW YORK, NY 10018.

ALLWORTH PRESS® IS A REGISTERED TRADEMARK OF SKYHORSE PUBLISHING, INC.®,
A DELAWARE CORPORATION.

WWW.ALLWORTH.COM

COVER DESIGN BY RODRIGO CORRAL
INTERIOR DESIGN BY RODRIGO CORRAL DESIGN
LETTERING ON COVER BY DEBBIE MILLMAN
EDITED BY JEREMY LEHRER

LIBRARY OF CONGRESS CATALOGING-IN-PUBLICATION DATA IS AVAILABLE ON FILE.

ISBN: 978-1-62153-247-7

PRINTED IN THE UNITED STATES OF AMERICA

For Simon Williams, with gratitude and love

Contents

Foreword
by Rob Walker

Strictly speaking, brands do not exist. You can't
extract them from the earth, craft them in a
workshop, manufacture them with industrial
robots in a state-of-the-art facility, or fabricate
them with a 3-D printer. You can't put one in your
pocket, grow it on a farm, put a fence around it, fling
it through a window, or leave it at a restaurant by
accident. You can't even download a brand. A brand
is nothing but an idea.

Wait: Don't ideas exist? Well, sure. But
only by way of a kind of mutual agreement. That's
the case with any idea, such as Christianity,
participatory democracy, modernity, or market
capitalism. Speaking of capitalism, the fact that
brands do not exist does not mean brands are
worthless; indeed, they have value that can't be
denied—unless, of course, you don't believe in
the idea of money. This is why the stakes around
branding are so high in today's marketplace,
and thus why so many genuinely smart people
enmesh themselves in the business of figuring out
how to do it right.

Debbie Millman has rounded up a rather
impressive cross section of such practitioners to
discuss and debate, among other things, what it
means to do just that. The result is a consistently
insightful collection of conversations about

branding, one that should be illuminating to new students of the form as well as hardened practitioners and everyone in between. I'm forever meeting people who think "a brand" means nothing more than a logo, or that it merely encompasses TV ads; perhaps now I can carry around this book, and hand it over by way of explanation.

Probably everybody has his or her own definition of brands and branding—you'll certainly find it's been defined in a number of ways in *Brand Thinking*. My view is that branding is the process of attaching an idea to some object, or to a service or organization. That idea can be fairly straightforward: This brand of oats (or car or hammer) is of dependable quality. Or the idea can be extremely ambitious: This brand of mobile phone (or denim or yogurt) possesses and reflects a maverick and creative worldview.

Creating these kinds of associations is a complicated process, involving design, anthropology, advertising, public relations, semiotics, and, of course, the often-overlooked factor of tangible reality. (If your airline's planes fall from the sky on a regular basis, that defines your brand, no matter how cutting edge your social-media strategy, award-winning your advertising, or appealing your logo may be.) All those disciplines, and more, are represented in the interviews that follow; you'll read the views of professionals within companies, those who advise them, journalists and thinkers who write about them, and gurus who aim to extract larger points from all of the above.

Often the views expressed vary and even clash, as well they should. Branding is the sort of topic that practically demands disagreement if it's going to be talked about seriously. But while I might have different opinions on this or that subject than some of the interviewees do (actually, I'm not even sure I'm willing to go along with the implications of this book's title!), I arrived at the end of the collection having learned quite a bit. You will, too. Because this book is no rote anthology of boilerplate lectures. It's more like a buzzing dinner party, where you never know who is going to say what.

Millman is the ideal host to choreograph these discussions. This isn't just because, as president of design at Sterling Brands, she is an esteemed professional herself, or because she has established a track record of conducting thoroughly researched and provocative interviews in her Internet radio program *Design Matters*. It's because on some level these aren't interviews at all: They're conversations. She's *engaged* with her subjects, she listens, she pushes back, she shows surprise, she gets people to move past their standard talking points. Reading the resulting conversations is like following her through the party, eavesdropping as she works the room.

While a distinct optimism runs through the book, there's also enough friction at the edges to keep it lively, and challenging. As much as the reader learns, he or she is also, finally, left to think through the numerous issues and draw original, individual conclusions. For starters, you'll likely end up crafting your own definition of brands and branding from the many variations offered here. Wally Olins sets the tone by pointing out, "It is ludicrous to think that advertising is the only way in which an organization can communicate who or what it is." I'll leave it to you to discover Olins' definition in the pages ahead, but first, a few other perspectives: "Brands are a ubiquitous part of our culture. Everyone interacts with them, everyday," Brian Collins points out in one of the dialogues. "Brands are totems," argues Cheryl Swanson in another. "People who are honest about branding understand that the Catholic Church is, by definition, a brand," asserts Seth Godin in a third.

A striking number of thinkers in this book connect the brand idea to the tribal instinct, and some connect elements of branding to the nature of human-ness itself. And you'll even find some challenges to the practice: "We don't need to have branded water," Dori Tunstall states flatly in her conversation with Millman.

I came to my own definition as a result of stumbling upon "the brand" as a subject of journalistic interest, rather than stalking it as an aspiring strategist. That is, I came to it as one of those people—just like those who frustrate me today—who initially shrugged off branding as some trivial matter of symbols and slogans that didn't amount to much. Years of reporting and thousands of written words later, I've obviously changed my mind about that. I've learned a lot, and thanks to books like this one, I'm learning still. "Brands exist in the minds of people who interact with them," Brian Collins observes in his interview. I couldn't agree more. And for better or worse, this is exactly why branding matters.

Rob Walker is author of *Buying In: The Secret Dialogue Between What We Buy and Who We Are.*

Introduction
by Debbie Millman

For at least 4,000 years man has marked cattle with red-hot branding irons to prove his ownership. Literally millions of designs have been originated—some romantic, some dignified, some even comical—to distinguish herds. . . . There is a true story behind every brand, frequently a tragedy, a comedy, a tender romance, more often a proclamation of hope.

—Oren Arnold, *Irons in the Fire: Cattle Brand Lore*

Whatever satisfies the soul is truth.
—Walt Whitman

My entire life has been shaped by brands. I became aware of their transformative power, albeit unconsciously, when I was a little girl and first discovered packages of Goody barrettes hanging on the dazzling spinning display case in my father's pharmacy. I'd ogle these colorful accessories and imagine that the act of donning them would remake me into a prettier girl, though I had no real reason to believe this. Nevertheless, I was bewitched by the abundant array of hair accoutrements until my teens, at which point my yearning transferred to what I considered "cool" brands: Levi's jeans, Reebok sneakers, and Lacoste polo shirts.

Nearly thirty years later, I look back on my all-consuming need for branded goods with both nostalgia and pity. I bestowed such power on these inanimate things! I believed that by the sheer virtue of acquiring these objects, they would magically convert me into a dramatically different person— the person I longed to be.

Contrary to the way we think of brands now, the word has not always signified the imprimatur of a manufactured product. The word "brand" is derived from the Old Norse word *brandr*, which means "to burn by fire." From this 11th-century Northern Germanic origin, the word has blazed a mighty path into the vernacular of 21st-century modern life. Ancient Egyptians marked their livestock with hot irons, and the process was widespread in Europe during the Middle Ages, not to mention in the American West centuries later. Such branding helped ranchers, both ancient and contemporary, to separate cattle after they grazed in communal ranges; in addition, herders with quality livestock were able to distinguish themselves from those ranchers with inferior animals. The dynamics of brand reputation helped build better businesses even back then, and the role of the brand—a barometer of value—has continued ever since.

In 1876, after the United Kingdom passed the Trade Mark Registration Act, Bass Ale became the first trademarked brand in the world after submitting its now-quintessential red triangle for trademark status. The act gave businesses the ability to register and protect a brand marker so that a similar icon couldn't be used by any other company. In addition to clinching trademark number 1, Bass's trailblazing history includes its appearances in Édouard Manet's 1882 masterpiece *A Bar at the Folies-Bergère* and Pablo Picasso's 1912 painting *Bouteille de Bass et Guitare*, ostensibly providing the brand with the cultural distinction of "first product placement."

The timing of Bass's cameo in these seminal paintings is hardly coincidental, as brands proliferated and became significantly woven into the fabric of day-to-day life in the late 19th and early 20th centuries. Faster and more efficient transportation catalyzed the creation of both national and global brands. The Industrial Revolution led to significant improvements in manufacturing and communications. This led the way to the first mass-marketing efforts by commercial artists and advertising agencies.

A little more than a century later, we are living in a world with over one hundred brands of bottled water. The United States is home to over forty-five thousand shopping malls, and there are over nineteen million permutations of beverage selections you can order at your local Starbucks. Is this a good thing or a bad thing? The observations Naomi Klein made over a decade ago in her seminal critique *No Logo* are still resonant today:

> Openings of every sort—in schedules, in urban space, on clothes, in events, on objects, in sightlines, in democracy, in philanthropy, in cultures, on bodies—are all inscribed with an impression of the market. Things once thought free from this—even opposed to it—the museum, public space— find it ever more difficult to retain autonomy in the face of corporate culture and its sponsorships, educational initiatives, and so-called civic gestures.

Those who do not share Klein's antipathy will inevitably counter her stance with the argument that free-market economies are just that—free—and a plethora of choice is what fuels freedom and innovation. Then they might point to brands such as TOMS Shoes and Newman's Own, a design studio like Alex Bogusky's FearLess Cottage, or movements like John Bielenberg's Project M as evidence of designers and marketers advocating change via brands or branding. Perhaps then, the question of whether this behavior is good or bad is secondary to the imperative of understanding why we behave this way in the first place. Why do humans create tribes? Why do we have a drive to telegraph our affiliations and beliefs with symbols, signs, and codes?

Scientists and anthropologists tend to agree that humans are, in essence, pack animals, which explains why we feel safer and more secure in groups. And psychologists such as Harry Harlow and John Bowlby have proven that humans feel happier and better about themselves when our brains resonate with those of other like-minded humans. Perhaps our motivation to brand, and to be branded, comes from our hardwired instinct to connect. Perhaps not. In either case, what is indisputable is the breakneck speed at which brands have grown over the last century and the number of people who have literally and figuratively bought into these brands. The prospect that this trend will slow down is remote; as a result, the underlying causes and outward expressions of these activities and practices are worthy of thoughtful discussion.

In these interviews with some of the world's leading brand thinkers, I have had the privilege of investigating the central issues relating to our fascination with brands. I have spoken with key players who have designed and continue to design seminal brands—as well cultural commentators who provide unparalleled insight into branding and its influence on culture. Wally Olins, one of the forefathers of modern-day branding, shares his eloquent, pointed views on the complexity of the endeavor as well as on design research and the inadequacies of so-called branding consultancies. Procter & Gamble's Phil Duncan discusses the choreography of P&G's move to purpose-driven brands. Bruce Duckworth considers the role of wit in branding, while Smart Design's Dan Formosa reflects on designing cooking tools that will satisfy expert chefs, novice cooks, and arthritic hands. Design educator and anthropologist Dori

Tunstall talks about enlightenment in one breath, "water as commodity" in the next. Brian Collins discusses how the best brands tap into and embody archetypes. Throughout these conversations, there are recurring themes, and there are moments when one participant expresses a point of view that is in direct opposition to his or her colleagues'. The variety of opinions provides a foundation for continued discovery and debate.

Branding is a history in flux, and my hope is that this collection of conversations can provide a time capsule of the second decade of the 21st century. Coca-Cola is seeking to create new experiences through redesigned vending machines; nations and niche products are striving to brand their own individuality. Where we'll be in twenty years is uncertain. Legendary designer Karim Rashid acknowledges that even his own predilections have changed during his career: "I've made couches that are very expensive, and they embarrass me now." Technology is changing so quickly that the Facebook and Twitter of today may be the has-been MySpaces of 2030. And consumer habits are subject to shifts too. Technology has been a fundamental part of brand building in recent years, but as Malcolm Gladwell observes, "just because teens are obsessively using Facebook at sixteen doesn't mean they'll be doing so when they're forty."

While the conversations sometimes stray from the issue of branding, the discussions help us understand the forces that shape our identities and the way in which we relate to the culture at large. Though some observations may seem esoteric, it's inevitable that our ideas about who we are and how we relate to the universe help us decide between Patagonia and Prada when we shop. The spirited interviews in this book reveal the cultural and economic—and spiritual—framework underpinning this often mysterious process.

Wally Olins

*Chairman, Saffron Brand Consultants;
Cofounder and Former Chairman,
Wolff Olins*

---

*What is it about Wally Olins that makes him so
extraordinary? Setting aside the fact that he is
the godfather of modern branding, it could have
something to do with the vigor and clarity of his
thinking. He has a matter-of-factness combined with
a logical precision that makes his conclusions seem
inevitable and obvious—though they're anything
but. Olins is direct, and doesn't mince words. There
is no wishy-washiness in his answers, only definitive,
direct-from-the-source pronouncements on the state
of the world, history, and branding.*

*Olins is sharply opinionated, but he's not
dogmatic. Take his view on design research. As others
might, he doesn't dismiss it outright, nor does he elevate it
to the status of unassailable icon. It is, he acknowledges,
useful for certain situations and purposes—but not for
making decisions about the future. "Finding out what
people feel about things that are happening today is
extremely useful," he says. "Trying to get people to tell
you what will work tomorrow is useless."*

*Part of his charisma has something to
do with his jovial, old-world, British charm.
Another dimension derives from the breadth of his
experience—he worked in India at the start of his
career, cofounded and headed up the seminal firm
Wolff Olins, and now is chairman of Saffron Brand
Consultants. He has an honesty—both with himself
and with others—that is invigorating. Talking with
him was an extraordinary thrill.*

There are recurring themes throughout our conversation: communication and identity being the main two, with some added exploration into organization, advertising, beauty, and seduction. He has a keen insight into the future, predicting how a brand will become ever more place-centric. He imagines that he might like to work for the European Union one day, "provided the leadership is worthwhile, which it isn't at the moment."

Olins is ever charming in his outspokenness. There is an incontrovertibility to him that is exhilarating. This is an aspect of his success and his ability to be at the forefront of his field. As he observes, "It is very important for me to produce work that is conceptually ahead of its time."

How did you get your start in branding?

I was working in advertising in India, heading up what is now Ogilvy. I began to realize that when we talked about an organization's advertising, there was a huge amount of material that the organization employed to present who it was, yet the organization was not able to articulate some essence very clearly. I remember looking at airlines and thinking there was not much difference between one airline and another. What *was* different was the way people behaved in the airplane. And there wasn't much difference between one hotel and another—again, the difference was how it felt inside the hotel. Gradually, I developed the idea that advertising—in other words, the communication aspect of an organization, in terms of its written communication and visual communication—was only one very limited aspect of its identity.

Slowly, I began to ponder whether an organization could present itself in a more coherent, cohesive way. The more I considered it, the more I believed that some parts of what the organization did were more powerful and important, more effective and influential than the advertising it did. Let me give you an example. At that time, India was a very socialist country. There was a steel plant being put up by the Russians and a steel plant being put up by the British. Both plants produced steel, but the atmosphere and the environment were so completely different in the two that it was quite startling. This is what gradually pushed me toward the idea that an organization's identity consisted of a lot more than the way it communicated.

I began to get more skeptical about the power of advertising. To me, it didn't represent anything truly deep about an organization.

Do you still feel skeptical about the role of advertising?

No. I think that advertising serves a significant tactical purpose. But advertising is not the totality of organizational communication. It is ludicrous to think that advertising is the only way in which an organization can communicate who or what it is.

You've been described as a person with a very distinctive look. Would you consider that an aspect of the "Wally Olins" brand?

I don't think about my own brand. I don't know what is so distinctive about my look. I used to wear bow ties, and I don't anymore—I don't wear any ties. I have spectacles that I quite like. But I don't know if my look is particularly distinctive. Maybe I am particularly hideous. I doubt whether I am particularly beautiful. I don't deliberately set out to "brand myself"—not at all. But I think I know what my strengths and weaknesses are.

What are they?

I think I am very impulsive. I think I am very direct. I use language very well. I think I can be very persuasive. I believe very much in what I do. I think I am good at reading people.

How do you do that?

I get very close to people. I talk to them, and I get them to talk to me. I listen to them and I encourage them. And when they perform badly, I tell them. I mean I *really* tell them. And when they perform well, I tell them. I mean I *really* tell them. And I work with them, and I listen to them. I think those are my strengths. I wouldn't say they are my weaknesses. I have plenty of those.

For example?

I don't particularly like working in large organizations. I like working with small groups of people. And I think I probably have favorites. There are people I really like, get along with, and work very closely with. And there are people I am not so interested in. I think that is a considerable weakness. I am also uninterested in and careless about money.

Another weakness I have is that I get bored quickly. I am not very good at sustaining a long-term interest in a job. I like to deal with the people who are going to be responsible for doing it—the senior people—and work with them on the ideas and see the ideas come to life. I like other people to execute the ideas, and I like to move on to the next project.

Why don't you care about money?

I don't know. I wish I did care more about money! I could have made far more money with the companies I've worked with. I just don't pay enough attention to it. I don't care about it enough.

What has taken precedence over money?

I think one of the most important things to me is the quality of the work. It is very important for me to produce work that is conceptually ahead of its time. You can't always do that, though, because it doesn't always suit the client.

I've heard you described as outspoken, abrasive, and difficult. Is that something you find problematic?

I think I am outspoken. I think I can be abrasive. But I don't think I am difficult. I am sitting next to my PA. [*Speaks to assistant.*] *"Miss, am I difficult?"* She says I am not, but perhaps she says that because I am here. Maybe you should talk to her privately afterward. But no, I don't think I am difficult. I have quite a short fuse, and I do lose my temper. But I always apologize if I am wrong. In fact, I apologize whether I am right or wrong.

I certainly do not suffer fools gladly. But I don't think I am that difficult.

You mentioned earlier that you think one of your strengths is being persuasive. How do you think you honed that skill?

I don't know. I suppose you are born with it. But also, when you are in the front line, and you are trying to work with clients and you are trying to explain something or talk with people who have never done something before, they don't even know what you're talking about. So if you are trying to pioneer something entirely new, and you want to be successful, you've got to be persuasive. I am not really very timid. I don't curl up in situations that are new or challenging. And I am not intimidated by people.

What is your definition of "branding"?

How much time have you got? Fundamentally, branding is a profound manifestation of the human condition. It is about belonging: belonging to a tribe, to a religion, to a family. Branding demonstrates that sense of belonging. It has this function for both the people who are part of the same group and also for the people who don't belong.

The roots of branding are profoundly related to the nature of the human condition. A tribe is a brand—religion is a brand. When it manifests itself in a modern, contemporary form, you are likely referring to branding that began in the late 19th century. Then you are probably talking about this in relation to fast-moving consumer goods. But that is a distortion of what branding is. That type of branding is a manifestation of differentiation. It is an attempt to differentiate one fast-moving consumer product from another. When the functional differences are negligible or hardly exist—for example, in terms of price or quality—there is a requirement to create an emotional difference. That is how branding began in relation to fast-moving consumer goods.

When branding moves into service, it becomes much more complex. From that point of view, a brand is a product or service with a distinct personality. And that distinctive personality is what enables people to differentiate one brand from another.

But, in my opinion, this is an extremely superficial way of looking at branding. As soon as you place branding in the realm of retail, in the realm of service, it becomes infinitely more complicated. Consider the behavioral characteristics of flight attendants, or the experience of getting on an airplane. That is what distinguishes one airline from another. It isn't the aircraft, it isn't the product—it isn't the time it takes. It is the environment, the seating, and the way you are treated. These things are much harder to manage. They are infinitely more complicated, and the traditional consumer goods businesses— P&G, Unilever, and companies of that kind—are completely incapable of understanding how much more complicated a service or retail brand is.

One of the major reasons that branding has gotten the reputation of being cosmetic and superficial is that it is related to the way in which branding manifested itself historically in the late 19th and 20th centuries. But that is now changing. I don't know whether the word "branding" will retain its superficial connotation, but certainly the activity has become much more complex.

In your definition of branding, you said that it was
"a manifestation of the human condition." How so?

It is not very difficult to find examples. Consider Native American tribes, or Aboriginals. Every tribe, and every member of a tribe, distinguishes themselves from other tribes by tribal markings, by dances, by language, and by visual and verbal signs of differentiation. That enables people who are part of the tribe to see that, and it enables those who are not part of the tribe to see that too. Whatever you feel about the tribe is precisely manifested by the way the tribe presents an idea of itself.

Let me give you a very specific example, which relates to the 21st century and not the Stone Age. I was on a cruise with my wife, and there was an old Dutch lady at our table—even older than me—and she hurt her knee. She told us all about it. [*Speaks with an accent.*] "Ja, I vent down to the doctor, and I knocked on the door. There was a young man there, probably nineteen or twenty years old, wearing jeans and a T-shirt. And I said, 'Can I see the doctor please?' and he said, 'I am the doctor,' but I didn't believe him. So then he left and he came back two minutes later with a white coat and a stethoscope around his neck. And I said, 'Ahh! Now you are za doctor.'"

That is a manifestation of branding. That is a *classic* manifestation of branding. Because he had the marks and identity, she was able to see that he was the person with whom she could make the medical relationship. That is classic branding.

So, is it all cerebral?

No. It's not cerebral at all! It's visceral. We don't even know we are doing it. She did not know. She did not work it out in her head. She just saw, and absorbed, and knew.

The commercial, anthropological, and sociological branding process that professionals engage in now creates visceral distinctions to evoke immediate responses in people.

Let me give you an example that is not commercial: the red cross. The red cross, and the organization it represents, is about saving people.

You can see it on a flag or a vehicle, and it signals total vulnerability. It will not attack you, even if you are on a battlefield—this is what makes it completely vulnerable. It can't defend itself. But this also makes it completely invulnerable! Unless you are an extremely antisocial human being, you will not attack it. The symbol allows you to recognize the brand. Nowadays, we call them logos—but they are symbols of what lies beneath.

You talked earlier about religion being a brand. What do you think religious zealots would feel about that?

It doesn't remotely matter to me what religious zealots feel. I am entirely secular. I completely understand—at least I think I understand—why they feel the way they feel. A lot of people need faith and need belief, and symbolism is a very important component of this. I don't mind whether they think religion is a brand or not.

If branding is a manifestation of the human condition, do you think that we are hardwired to organize the constructs of our lives utilizing these symbols and these ways of organizing ideas? Why do you think people need to do this? Does it have anything to do with a yearning to belong to something greater than ourselves?

I don't know. I need to belong. I need to belong to my family. I need to belong to all kinds of things. And when I belong, telegraphing this affiliation demonstrates loyalty, affection, and the durability of my relationship. It is just part of what we are and how we do things.

In an article in The Economist, *you commented on cultural critic Naomi Klein's claim that consumers are "being manipulated by big corporations and their*

brands." You felt that it was quite the contrary—that
consumers in fact had the power over brands. Could
you elaborate on the role of the corporation in regard
to consumerism?

> I think that the job of a corporation is to seduce as many people as it can to buy its products or services.

Is "seduce" a good or a bad word?

> It has implications of being a bad word, and that is why I deliberately chose it. Corporations don't want to be disliked. They want to be loved. Therefore, they position themselves in order to attract people to buy their products. Most people will go to considerable lengths to deny this. Advertising people and other people in my business will say, "No, we don't seduce, we just tell them the truth, we tell them facts, or we put a slant on what we say." Let's face it, the truth is that even *people* try to be as beautiful and as seductive as possible in order to attract other people. Corporations do this so that people will come to them and not somebody else.
>
> But if you create an expectation that goes way beyond what the individual actually gets, it will end in tears, and they won't come back. Because people are not that stupid.
>
> Today, corporations purport to be different. They talk about working with their stakeholders to give back to society. In reality, the effort is just a form of enlightened self-interest. However, true "corporate social responsibility" is extremely difficult to measure. In fact, I doubt it can be measured at all. But that wouldn't stop people from trying to measure it, or pretending that they can.

Do you think that corporate social responsibility is really an altruistic desire to do good, or do you think it's a reaction to what consumers now expect from corporations?

It is a bit of both. There have always been corporations who have been genuinely socially responsible. Look at Hershey's, for example. In the 19th century, Hershey's built villages and towns for their employees. Cadbury, Lever, and the Krupps did the same. There have always been organizations that have been genuinely concerned about the welfare of their employees. But most—let's say 95 percent of organizations—are not. What corporations are saying now is, "It is in our interest to appear to be socially responsible." But for the most part, that effort is a veneer.

Michael Eisner has said the term "brand" is "overused, sterile, and unimaginative." Do you agree?

Yes. I think the word "brand" is not just overused, I think it makes the branding process seem cosmetic and superficial. The current usage of the word reduces the complexity and significance of its actual meaning. I am not suggesting that anyone who puts a logo on a Hermes handbag needs to have an anthropology degree, or needs to be aware that what they are doing has an anthropological dimension, but I believe that the business of branding is much, much more complex, deep-rooted, and fallible than people believe it is. And it is not merely a commercial phenomenon.

You've been quoted in numerous articles about the antibrand, "No Logo" movement. One of the ironies I find in the antibrand movement is how willingly its proponents use the tenets of branding that they so publicly disparage. Why do you think there is so much passion in the antibrand movement?

I think that's very easy to understand: People confuse the symbol with the reality. What people are really attacking is the capitalist system. Brands are the symbols of the capitalist system. Brands represent the visual manifestation of the capitalist system. They are symbols of entrepreneurship. When someone attacks a brand, they are attacking a symbol, whereas the reality of what they are attacking is the capitalist system. I am not saying they are right or wrong. I think—as do many other people—that the capitalist system has terrible faults. But there isn't any other system that anybody knows of that is much better.

What do you think are the faults of the capitalist system?

This takes us a long way from branding, doesn't it? The capitalist system enables people to use their energies to be successful. In doing so, it is almost inevitable that this success is likely going to make somebody else less successful. In the competition that arises, many people are going to behave in a way that others will regard as amoral, if not immoral. That's the nature of the system. Nobody has managed to make anything better and get it to work. Communism sounds fine in principle, but in practice it's an absolute disaster.

One of the questions listed in the FAQ section of your personal website [wallyolins.com] is, "What advice would you give to someone starting out in branding?" And your response is, "Are you sure you want to?" Why the question to a question? Why does the answer seem so cautioning?

Was I dodging the issue? There are a lot of jobs that are on the surface very glamorous and exciting. It is very glamorous to feel that you can travel all over the world and advise this company or that company—or even governments. But when I talk to young people, I always ask them if this kind of work is something they actually want and can derive satisfaction from. It's a very, very demanding business.

It is also a very cyclical business. It's a hunting business—not a farming business. You can never ever stop. You can never relax. You can never say, "Okay, I got this, I am going to keep this, I am going to be doing this same work for ten years." It's not like that. And that means it's very tough. A lot of people like this, and a lot of people don't. It is also extremely demanding creatively. You need to be able to break through orthodoxies and conventions that most people accept.

Why do most people accept them?

They accept them because they don't think about them. Very few people have those kinds of capacities.

What kinds of people have those capacities? Is there a specific archetype?

It is easier to find the type among creative people. They don't have to be particularly good designers, but they have to have great strategic capabilities. They have to be able to think very strategically. As far as consultants are concerned, there are too many McKinsey, Bain, and BCG people, among others, who are fed the rubbish that if you can't analyze it—if you can't chew it up into numbers—it doesn't exist. What I really, hugely, and antagonistically dislike is the attempt to quantify the unquantifiable. And if you are a branding consultant, you have to accept that there are a lot of things you just cannot quantify.

Like what?

The value of a brand, to start with. How much is it worth? Or, more nonsense: when you get an idea and have to prove it will work. How the hell can you do that? **You can't sit in a focus group and ask people if it will work. They wouldn't know what you are talking about, and they're incapable of telling you what they want.**

A classic example of this is Jaguar. Senior marketers at Jaguar used focus groups again and again and again to tell them that all the cars Jaguar produced were lovely. Consumers told them they should never do anything different. And so they produced the same car again and again and again, and people stopped buying it.

In order to be truly imaginative, you must possess an unusual level of self-confidence and creativity. Most branding consultants today—and most of the big branding consultancies—wrap themselves up in analyses, in jargon, in pretend statistical data that is comforting and gets them well-paid but is meaningless. I deeply reject all that and find it to be a contemporary version of witchcraft.

Why do you think this is the foundation of the way that many brands are built now?

Because people love numbers. No matter how phony they are. If Dickens or Shakespeare were writing today, you could not test their work in a focus group. If you are going to create something that is truly a breakthrough, you have to rely on your intuition and your judgment. Most organizations employ people to manage brands who are unable to do that. It is beyond their imagination. So they seek solace in these phony statistics and rubbish analyses. And the branding consultancies working with them create complex, mostly meaningless jargon to give comfort to people. And what do they end up with? Slogans that are not meaningful: "Tomorrow's answers today." [The company AkzoNobel's tagline.] It's garbage.

Do you think market research perpetuates mediocrity?

No, I don't. I think a great deal of market research is extremely useful. I think finding out why something didn't work well is extremely useful. Finding out what people feel about things that are happening today is extremely useful. Trying to get people to tell you what will work tomorrow is useless. I don't denigrate market research when it is used properly. I think it's very valuable. I think that finding out how consumers act and react and what they do and feel when they see things is useful. I think that trying to predict the future proves valueless—again and again and again.

Nobody, not one single organization, predicted that texting would work. Not one. Nobody thought seriously that the SMS system would be of any value. With all the research, you have example after example after example. I think market research is extremely valuable when it is used properly. But you must not use it to tell you what to do.

Is there any particular category or brand you would like to work on in the upcoming years of your career?

The European Union. They need a kick in the ass. I wouldn't mind doing that. Provided the leadership is worthwhile, which it isn't at the moment. But the EU doesn't know where it's going or what it's doing.

What would you recommend that it do?

The EU has to have very, very clear economic goals. Not just pie-in-the-sky goals. The EU has to create a feeling of unity within the countries that belong to it. That they share something. There are lots of things they don't share.

But first, they must isolate the elements that they do share. A good example is the culture of Europe. A profoundly significant initiative would be to try to contend coherently with European history. Every nation within Europe currently writes its own history. This history is usually denigrating to its next-door neighbors. The idea that we are all part of one organization, even though we have separate identities in other respects, has not taken root.

Do you think a unified symbol would rally that mentality?

I think the only requirement of a symbol is that it have substance underneath: The first thing to do is to try to establish the substance. The style comes after the substance. Only then can the style help the substance, and vice versa. It's a mutually reinforcing program.

What do you anticipate for the future of brands and branding in upcoming years?

One of the things that seems increasingly important is brands from cultures that we didn't take seriously a couple of years ago. I'm particularly talking about India, China, and Brazil—the BRICs.

Increasingly, we will see brands, or, if you like, cultural phenomena, coming from countries that previously we did not take seriously. Just as the West dominated the world politically, so it dominated the world culturally until very recently. And as the political hegemony of the West shrinks, we will see the emergence of major brands from China, India, Brazil, and so forth. I am not saying this is good or bad. It might mean more choice, which can be a bit confusing.

The second thing that is going to happen is a phenomenon relating to more and more places becoming the equivalent of city-states, like Dubai, Abu Dhabi, Singapore, and so on. With more and more of these small countries around, we are going to have an accretion of provenance branding—of the brand as a manifestation of place and of "where I come from." The place is going to become very, very important.

You see it with some products like wine, now, which you can't distinguish except by place. The distinguishing characteristic of any wine is where it comes from. Is it Chilean, Australian, French? That is going to happen to a lot more products, and with nations, cities, and regions that are trying to attract direct investment, tourism, and other business.

What do you think that means for the possibility of unifying people with brands, or for the influence of globalization?

Just because the world is becoming more global does not mean that individual citizen countries are going to accept that they don't have any personality. The tide of globalization is going to lead to an increasing attempt to shriek and scream, "Look at me—remember who I am!"

This from the organizations and countries that would otherwise be completely enveloped by it.

Globalization and place branding are not contradictory. They are not mutually exclusive. They actually encourage each other. When you move in one direction, you get another move in a contrary direction.

With globalization and the increasing dominance of the Internet, people seem to be reading books less. Do you think that bookstores will continue to exist?

Of course they will. Television didn't kill radio; film didn't kill theater. There will certainly be huge changes. But one medium doesn't kill another. Each new medium actually makes the previous one better. Radio no longer resembles what it was before television. Television no longer resembles what it was before the Internet. All these things will change, but they give us a multiplicity of choice.

As culture continues to evolve, do you think that there will be more brands in the future, or less? With the increase of mergers and acquisitions, some consultants have suggested that there will end up being one fast-food restaurant, one brand of cola, and one giant superstore.

I don't believe that for a moment. If you do, then you don't believe in human ingenuity. There will always be opportunities for people to create things.

Always. As soon as we create a monopoly—or even a near-monopoly—we get lazy, we get complacent, we get fat, we get greedy, and we get selfish. And then someone notices all the lazy complacency, and they go off and create something new.

Grant McCracken

Anthropologist, Cultural Commentator, Consultant

In conversations in my professional and personal life, I am always seeking ways to explain the importance of design. I've had the idea lately that the design and branding fields should enlist Grant McCracken as spokesperson. Grant comprehends the complexity of what designers do even when designers don't understand it themselves. There are few people on this planet who match his eloquence on this topic, and he is an impassioned champion for the role that design and branding play in business and in culture. He's a one-man band of design advocacy.

In McCracken's view, designers are invaluable to corporations because, simply stated, designers create and interpret culture. That is their essential function, and the corporation desperately needs them for this purpose. Because, in general, corporate leaders are clueless about culture. And designers are masters of it—of how to give it voice.

But there is a problem. Designers and brand thinkers haven't explained this well enough, and they don't realize their own cultural significance. The boss is using them in a way that doesn't acknowledge or recognize their full potential. And if they are to fulfill their role as culture creators, then they have to comprehend the responsibilities of the task—which Grant describes in our conversation.

What I particularly savor about our discussion is the specificity that Grant brings to his understanding of design, branding, and culture. Having been present when businesses start to conjure a new product or service offering, he has an appreciation for the possibility that is tangible when the corporation is at its most nascent. I've witnessed these moments myself, and they are magical. Secondly, he gives essential guidance to designers about the requirements of their responsibility. Not only should they better articulate their role to their colleagues, but they have to improve their own vocabulary and their understanding about the process of design and branding. "What we want to do is specify this process and give it a rigorous grammar or mechanism that can solve the problems at hand," Grant says.

Grant is the go-to guy for cultural analysis and criticism relating to the bustling world of commerce and cultural creation. He provides unparalleled incisiveness, and he is essential reading. Whether you're looking for a better understanding of the bewildering ridiculousness of forced sincerity by store salespeople, why comfort food has become more popular, the dynamics of celebrity endorsement, the skill of "noticing," or the underpinnings of Dove's Campaign for Real Beauty, Grant is your man. In his 2008 book Chief Culture Officer—*a manifesto on the importance of culture to business strategy and success—Grant outlines his view of why businesses need to be more attuned to the zeitgeist, explains how to do it, and examines who's good at it. This isn't just pie-in-the-sky theorizing—in his consulting work, Grant gives the download to companies such as IBM, Coca-Cola, and Kimberly-Clark.*

Grant is that rare breed of person who has the theoretical and historical breadth you can gain with an academic background—he has a PhD in anthropology, and has taught at MIT and Harvard. He's certainly not one to shy away from an academic treatise, but he can also talk and write about these issues with down-to-earth clarity.

McCracken believes that the objects and products we select from the ceaseless conveyor of newness are precisely the tools we use to find new relevance and understanding of our world: "This fascination with objects—yes—it certainly has its problems, and yes, we are obsessive and overhopeful when we care about design," he explains, "but it's critical to the way in which we manage to live in the world we live in."

Let's start by discussing the writing about design you've done on your blog. In one post, you wrote, "Designers are very good at thinking about provocations. After all, they are in the imagination business. They are trained to look at existing systems, spot where stasis lives, and think of ways to make things new. What designers are not so good at, in my humble opinion, is figuring out what happens next, what comes after the provocation." Why do you feel that way?

This is a general problem not only confined to designers. We're a culture that's always been committed to transforming itself. Claude Lévi-Strauss has a great quote in the book *The Savage Mind*. In essence, he says, "We're a culture that is always looking for that other message, always looking for that new arrangement." That's us, that's Western culture. In the last twenty or thirty years, this deep cultural inclination has become a professional fascination for many of us. It's become a professional obligation as well, for business purposes. People have concluded, "Innovation is the name of the game here, and we need people who are good at innovation." And that task has fallen increasingly to designers. That's the business side. On the social side, we've had people who say, "If we live in a culture that's responsive to change, let's see if we can come up with innovations that will change the world."

Do you think that designers have an obligation to figure out what happens next?

I think they do. Otherwise, we're looking at the risk of design work that is merely a gesture of goodwill. These gestures fill our hearts with gladness. But if we do a sober anthropological assessment of these gestures, we see that the good inevitably dissipates and is gone within a month or so. And worse than that, no structural change is achieved. On the social side, I'm not sure this provocation that is so dear to our hearts and engaged in by so many people has a very good return on investment. I would argue that this is true on the business side as well. Designers are engaging in acts of aesthetic, visual, and cultural provocation that don't always result in the kinds of change that their clients are eager to generate.

Do you feel that anybody who is in the business of provoking should also be in the business of solving?

Yes, but solving is never easy. I think there should always be a follow-up to the moment of provocation. And that provocation depends upon a deeper knowledge of culture and of the social world than designers sometimes exhibit.

That is somewhat ironic, given how many people talk about designers being problem solvers.

Right.

Several years ago, the brand strategist Brian Collins stated that rather than being problem solvers, designers should be "problem makers," and they should be provoking people to think about how to do things in a new or a better way. This idea has created some uncertainty in my own mind about what the ideal role of the designer should be.

Here's my feeling: Designers—or indeed anybody who's interested in business change or social change—need to make a knowledge of the culture and the social world in which they work the first condition of their provocation. Designers and brand consultants assume that they know about culture, when in point of fact—at least from my anthropological perspective—they don't. You and I have had this discussion for several years, and at the risk of being a bore about it, this is a topic I bring up with tedious frequency.

My feeling is that there is an architecture of cultural meanings and social rules in place that governs whether our actions will be effective in any way. The more completely you understand those cultural meanings and social rules, the better you can craft a provocation, and the more likely that provocation is to have some kind of structural effect. I've spent my professional life trying to get "the corporation" to take culture seriously. I have great admiration for designers for many reasons, but when called upon to defend how they create value for the corporation, they could have said, "Without us, you don't have access to culture." But they haven't.

Do you think that designers just assume that people know that they're bringing culture to the conversation?

If so, I think it's a rash assumption. The corporation uses the assumptions of economics, and Adam Smith, the forefather of our current system, is quite happy to proceed as if culture is not an important piece of the proposition—he feels we can just ignore it. I would be nervous if I were creating and designing brands, and I had to say to my team, "Listen, there's a good chance that the corporation doesn't get that this is part of the way designers create value for the corporation. So we have to tell them."

I would wear this on my sleeve if I were a designer.

Honestly, this is one of the reasons I'm so high on designers: I see them as vehicles for the corporation to take culture seriously.

But once designers identify themselves in this way, and once the corporation defines and engages them in this way, then we have to make good on the promise! The design journalist Bruce Nussbaum has talked about why design matters, and he says, "Design gives people the ability to be one with the consumer culture—to be anthropologists and sociologists and deeply understand the myriad of cultures around them. It has a set of tools and methods that can guide us towards a much better way of doing things."

So, here we have Bruce Nussbaum, who is one of the people responsible for the rise of design and design thinking, emphasizing this point of view. This is something the corporation now takes seriously and has embraced in a big way. He's saying design matters because it's a way of giving the corporation access to anthropology, and sociology, and knowledge of culture. But this feels like more of a promissory note than an accurate description of where we stand.

Do you think that this might have anything to do with the semantics of the design field? Let's face it, the word "culture" doesn't feel as scientific as economics, anthropology, sociology, or neuroscience.

It's certainly a term with a checkered past. It has simultaneously stood for *X* and *not X*. But in many ways, this is appropriate. We now have a multiplicity of meanings in our culture, whereas everything used to be much more monolithic. So it's appropriate—or maybe merely tragic—that the term "culture" itself should have this multiplicity of meanings. To speak from my own provincial background, anthropologists have been working on the term for the past one hundred years. On the anthropological side, you've got the postmodernists who have hijacked the notion and damaged it badly. In certain academic situations, it's hard to even talk about culture. This is a willfully destructive behavior on the part of the academy, for which there is no good explanation. So you're quite right to say the term's surrounded by confusion, ambivalence, and difficulty. But I do think we can—and must—use it in a disciplined way.

What fascinates you about our culture?

I guess it's that old line about the weather in Ireland. If you don't like it, wait a few moments and it will change.

Ha!

It's the endless creative power. Some years ago, I wrote a book called *Plenitude*, which was an attempt to understand how and why our culture produces so much innovation. Most cultures are pretty good at preventing change, and they're pretty good at papering over change when it occurs. What makes our culture so interesting from an anthropological perspective is how good we are at creating change, and how good we are at living with that change.

Where many cultures would say, "That will do, thank you very much, just quit it with that technology stuff," or "Stop that religious reform," or "No, this youth culture will not reshape how we think about the world," we say, "If you can make a compelling argument, and win enough minds, and if you can transform various parts of our world sufficiently, then the moment belongs to you." Culture is just so fantastically conducive to innovation. I think we were very badly misled by the Frankfurt School and intellectuals who identified materialism as the source of difficulty in Western societies.

We care about an ongoing narrative of design in objects, in ideas, and in experiences because they provide opportunities for us to participate in a new understanding of an incredibly turbulent world. Design serves us for both cultural purposes and adaptational purposes. When we embrace a new experience, object, or concept, we bring ourselves into the ambit of the new, and we can begin to understand what the new is. I think this stream of objects gives us a way we deal with a world that courses with novelty and change. I know that I'm swimming against the current here and that, with the encouragement of the Frankfurt School, intellectuals argue against this, as do people like Naomi Klein. There's a very long list of people who are prepared to say, "It's exactly the fascination with objects that is what's wrong with Western cultures."

There is only a very small academic voice that says, "Actually, this fascination with objects—yes—it certainly has its problems, and yes, we are obsessive and overhopeful when we care about design, but it's critical to the way in which we manage to live in the world we live in." And one of the very few voices providing a counterpoint here is the French historian Fernand Braudel, who, in his seminal book, *Capitalism and Material Life, 1400–1800*, asked, "Can it have been merely by coincidence that the future was to belong to societies fickle enough to care about changing the colors, materials, and shapes of costume, as well as the social order and the map of the world—societies, that is, which were ready to break with their traditions? There is a connection." He looks at world cultures, and he notices that the ones that are productive—like Western European cultures—are subject to fantastic change. He notices that they care about fashion. He suggests, "Either there's no connection here, or this might be the secret of their fantastic ability to change, and to adapt, and to survive that change." He urged us to listen.

You've talked about small signs of trouble in the design and branding community, and you've argued that we might not have it right at the moment because the concept of brand is so changeable that it will always exceed our grasp—and this problem isn't often acknowledged by designers and brand consultants.

I think when we create brands, we're engaged in a process of "manufacturing" and "managing" meaning. We're saying to ourselves, "In order for this brand to work effectively in the world, we must create a combination of exquisitely chosen, crafted, combined, and then managed cultural meanings." There are different levels of meaning associated with any given brand, some of which are absolutely new to a moment, and others that are continuously there over time. A brand is composed of these meanings. These meanings are being carefully chosen and crafted. And then they're managed, because we're swapping meanings in and out to make the brand adapt as the world makes new demands of us. This model suggests we need a systematic accounting of these cultural meanings.

Sometimes I hear designers speaking in generalities such as, "We had to freshen the brand," or, "We had to make it more dynamic," and so forth. What I don't hear designers say is, "We chose this brand, *this* particular meaning and *that* particular meaning, and we got rid of *that* meaning." We can be much more particular—we *must* be much more particular—about the meanings that we think matter. What I'd rather hear from designers is, "These are the twelve cultural meanings at issue here, and this is where the world is—this is what the world wants. This is how we've crafted the brand out of these twelve meanings. This is how we've combined them, and this is how we'll manage them over the next six or twelve months."

Instead, a lot of creative people are using the old model that says, "Just trust me." And I think the corporation is ferociously unhappy with the notion of "just trust me."

And if that's the way we respond to the sneer on the face of the CEO, we're asking for trouble. If nothing more, a shift from the old model will further the aim of surviving in the world of the corporation. But we should want to do better than that for our own scholarly and intellectual purposes.

Look, there's no question that all of us do our best work when letting our unconscious creative powers speak through us, right? You wake up in the morning, and the elves have clearly been working through the night creating a solution to the problem you were working on. And bang, there it is. And so what we want to do is specify this process and give it a rigorous grammar or mechanism that can solve the problems at hand. We want to take inspiration wherever we can find it. And it's not like we have a choice in the matter, right? It just visits us and there it is.

On the other hand, I don't think there's anything wrong with examining inspiration and figuring out why it's so compelling. Everyone looks at the fruits of this process and thinks, "Damn, that is compelling." But we can do an analysis that says, "Here's what the moment of inspiration did. It assembled these cultural meanings in this particular package for this particular group at this particular cultural moment."

I'd like to read you a quote from an article that you wrote: "Branding is a process of meaning manufacture that begins with the biggest, boldest gestures of the corporation and works its way down to the tiniest gestures. This is one of the reasons that design matters. The look and the feel, the fit and the finish, the beautiful, the sensual, the tactile, design is an essential medium of the brand message. Good design captures, commandeers, takes control of every interface and interaction between the consumer and the brand, right down to the little sound that packages make when we close them. Click. This is a brand message." Why do you think that branding begins with the biggest, boldest gesture of the corporation?

I was recently doing some work for Coca-Cola. One of their big ideas is optimism. This is a huge idea. It's what we might call "a Macy's parade float" of an idea. It's vast. Most corporations control big ideas to the same degree as a Macy's parade float is controlled. People with ropes try to handle it, and it's difficult to do. But Coca-Cola knows what they're doing, and they know that manifesting their vision from large gestures down to the tiniest gestures is a very potent idea. They know how to make it substantial, actual, and both present and compelling in the world. They know how to translate it from its absolute generality into very particular engagements with, for instance, the vending machine. Our notion of America is, to some extent, crafted by the Coca-Cola Company. Certainly, our notion of Christmas, or at least of Santa Claus, is crafted by the Coca-Cola Company.

In what way?

Before Coca-Cola began using Santa Claus in their commercials, Santa was a variety of physical shapes, and he dressed in any number of colors, primarily green. The succession of Coke ads over many decades has fixed his image as that of a large, jolly man in red and white. He's dressed in red and white because those are the colors of the Coca-Cola Company. What's most interesting about this is that, in fact, Coca-Cola has actually invented part of Western culture. That's the good news. The bad news is . . . they've invented some part of Western culture. I've been in the room when people at the company said to themselves, "Well, the fact that we invented Santa should be good for something—for marketing purposes. Surely, we can leverage that." Everybody thinks about it for a moment, and then they say, "Actually, no." The moment the Coca-Cola Company takes credit for or tries to leverage this contribution to Western culture is the moment that they suffer cataclysmic damage to the brand.

This is a perfect example of the corporation acting as a cultural actor and creating cultural meanings. They can release these ideas into the world, but they don't get to own them anymore afterwards. This flies in the face of the Frankfurt School and Klein-ian notions that dictate that corporations are guilty of the manipulation of taste and thought and are the creators of "false consciousness"—the notion relating to how consumers are supposedly controlled by corporations. If only it were so simple. It clearly isn't. Sometimes, a corporation makes powerful meanings, and when it does, those meanings are taken away from its control. And the rest of the time, the corporation is desperately trying to catch up to a culture that's moving very fast.

The opportunity for control and manipulation may have existed in the 1950s, but it certainly doesn't exist now. Designers nowadays get to sit in a room when the corporation is at its most conceptual, and they get to try to identify the biggest proposition a brand can make. In that moment, they're focused on identifying a cultural meaning that's going to make a brand more tangible in the world. That's thrilling. That's the corporation at its most intellectual, most conceptual, most freethinking. As you and I both know so well, those are some of the really exciting moments in branding.

Let's go back to the Frankfurt School for a minute. You've said that goods help us make choices. They help us make our culture concrete and public. How do they do that?

I wrote an essay about this in my book *Culture and Consumption II*. In the essay titled "When Cars Could Fly," I describe how midcentury modernism penetrated popular culture after World War II. At that time, people investigating these early notions of modernism that had been kicking around since the 19th and the early 20th century were suddenly in the mainstream. People were thinking about themselves as creatures who are moving out of the present into the future. They attained extraordinary speed in transportation and culture, and they evidenced a kind of recklessness. You can see how the whole notion of mobility became alive and well and began dominating American culture. Science also created new possibilities, which cascaded into technology, which then cascaded into personal gadgets, which then get expressed in the push button, most of all—a kind of iconic apotheosis of technological development.

All these transformations helped us play with the very notion of what time is. Time, and how we experience time, is always a cultural creation. Most cultures are taught—to put this very simply—that time is circular. Subsequently, you can see the world being played out in a circular way. What's interesting about Western cultures is, at some point, we said, "You know what? We're not circular. We're an arrow. We're not looking for a return. We're not looking for circularity. We're looking for a crazy, relentless projecting of ourselves into an unknown future.

If time is a cultural creation, wouldn't that mean that the future is a cultural creation?

Yes. It feels like we're in a moment of repudiating the modernist impulse that says we're happily abandoning the present as we rocket into the future. I think the whole return of retro design—the artisanal movement, and the coveting of everything handmade—is evidence of this. It's as if we're struggling to create a new notion of time, and this movement is a way of saying, "We want more continuity than we had in the middle of the 20th century. The future comes plenty fast enough. Our world is quite reckless enough, thank you very much. We want continuities, and we want a world with manageable proportions." In a manner of speaking, we're recovering modernists. I think a lot of design that works today has a beautifully handcrafted, delicate, and historically rooted quality. Designers are able to help us craft a new notion of what time missed.

Do you think this return to the handcrafted will end,
and we'll swing in a different direction? Can you
predict what might be fashionable in another ten or
fifteen years?

I think we're learning to live with dynamism. There is a certain amount of clutching to the present and familiar that's going on right now. The world is coming toward us with speed and fury, and, as you always do in situations when you're drowning, you grasp at anything. I think there's a certain point at which you go, "Okay—we just need a new modality here. We need to be fluid in our response to a fluid world." I think when we learn the arts of fluidity, and the instincts of fluidity, and then those of historical continuity, we will be able to understand and create these new modalities.

That's pretty optimistic.

If you look at the history of Western culture, it is the triumph of a certain kind of optimism over a certain kind of pessimism. The pessimism mostly comes from people who think of themselves as elites. They proclaim that this new innovation— whatever it is—is really going to screw things up. Think of the suffrage movement. At the turn of the 20th century, people were pontificating to oppose it and saying all sorts of nonsense. We can read the letters to the editor that say, "Give the vote to women, and all hell will break loose. Western civilization cannot survive this." Then women get to vote, and it turns out nothing happens. Actually, things get more interesting.

The same things are being said by the opponents of gay
marriage and the "don't ask, don't tell" policy.

Perfect example. Cultural transformation is not easy. The cost is high, and sometimes there is a whole generation that pays for the moment of cultural change.

We pay dearly if we don't respond to culture, and we pay dearly when we don't respond to change.

But generally speaking, I think we're more adaptable than we think.

You've written about the inalterable rules of culture. Do you think there are still things that are inalterable?

Yes. I think that responsiveness is inalterable, and the fact is that we'll find a way to reconceptualize culture. Look at the 20th century: It's all about democratizing every kind of thing. One of the questions here is whether the designer's genius for seeing the existing pattern and imagining new and more interesting patterns won't at some point disseminate from the design community into the world. And that is already happening. All of us are getting better at the kinds of problem solving and pattern recognition that designers are so good at.

Phil Duncan

*Vice President and Global Design
Officer, Procter & Gamble*

---

*As vice president and global design officer of
Procter & Gamble, Phil Duncan is responsible for
the brand and design of thousands of products
distributed all around the world. He has a design
team numbering in the hundreds. With such
a large organization, and with such extensive
responsibilities, Duncan has mastered the art of
management; one necessary part of his job is to lead
and inspire his team to do stellar branding work.*

*His management must involve empathy, an
ability to relate to people of all backgrounds, both
in terms of consumers around the world and on the
design team he leads. Duncan has mastered that, a
quality he developed early on when he was a young
high school student involved in activities as diverse as
glee club, swim team, and tennis.*

*Duncan talks in this interview about key
moments in the brand experience. The "first
moment of truth" happens when a consumer decides
to purchase a particular brand. From there, the
relationship evolves depending on whether the brand
meaningfully speaks to the consumer's values and
aspirations.*

*In this realm, P&G has entered the arena of
"purpose-driven brands." The company's approach
has evolved over time, and finding authenticity for a
particular brand has been a process of discovery. But
connecting a brand with a mission is, Duncan feels,
essential. "I believe we have a powerful responsibility*

to do something constructive with the affinity we have with consumers," he says. "The main idea of purpose-driven brands is about recognizing, embracing, and celebrating the fact that brands can enhance people's lives and help them to feel better about themselves."

Duncan's own career trajectory reveals the way in which we never know where things will go. Duncan started off as a freelance designer working on early Macintosh computers and using PageMaker for layouts. He wanted to learn more about the business of design, so he began an MBA program at Ohio State University, where he was a solitary fine arts person in a sea of business and accounting folks. Through a fortuitous happenstance, he was accepted into P&G's summer internship program, where he worked for Marc Pritchard, then an associate advertising manager and now P&G's global marketing officer.

After four years at P&G, Duncan went on to Landor, where he became one of the consultancy's youngest managing directors and built up the company's Cincinnati office, and later, its European division. Eventually, he went back to P&G.

In our discussion, Duncan shares invaluable advice on the crucible of consumer seduction represented by packaging. He speaks with great clarity on how to convince clients to sign on to innovation and what innovation means. And he praises the essential work of great design firms: "Their thinking capability matched with their creative capability represents some of the greatest talents when it comes to brand building, bar none."

As vice president and global design officer of the biggest consumer goods company in the world, you have quite an extensive in-house design group. How do you inspire your team to do great work?

First and foremost, I think it's the responsibility of a leader to have a sense of a vision. But it's also important to build that vision with your colleagues. Over the course of the last twenty years, I've had the privilege of working with truly brilliant designers and great account people who have taught me an inordinate amount. But in order to inspire them to greatness, I must be able to instill a sense of possibility in them and enable them to see those possibilities. You set the bar high, and the people who work for you also know your personal standard. I always aspire to build strong relationships with my colleagues, and through this, you create a dynamic in which they want to work for you. They want to do work they're proud of, and they also want to please you. I try to give them a sense of possibility, of inspiration.

I can't do it as much as I used to, but I always loved to walk around and visit the teams, and begin impromptu discussions about how they are and what they're working on. Through this, they see that I'm approachable and that I'm the kind of person who can break down barriers for them. I think a lot of people often build barriers around themselves, thinking that the solution to a design problem can only be of a certain variety. Well, why? So I like to challenge them.

What did you want to be when you were young? What did you imagine your life was going to be like?

This job was certainly not in the wheelhouse of my career options when I was growing up. I was a geek growing up. I was gangly, skinny, and gawky. I had diverse and unusual interests. The thing that defined me—a quality I find in a lot of people who work in our industry—was the ability to float between many different groups in school. I played tennis, and I was on the swim team—so I could hang out with the sporty group. But I was also in the equivalent of the glee club—the chorus. And I was involved in the art and architecture classes, and that provided a whole different set of connections for me in middle school and high school.

I'd say the first career I considered was architecture. It seemed like a smart choice. My dad worked for the same company for thirty years, so his mantra was, "Find something you think you'll be good at. That's what you'll be for the rest of your life."

What did your dad do?

He worked in marketing at Cincinnati Bell Telephone. My mom was the artist. She was a painter and an etcher, and she introduced me to the fine arts. She continually took classes at different universities around Cincinnati in an effort to keep exploring and growing. In our house, we had paint, woodcuts, and all sorts of other things that were part of her passion as well—which was certainly influential on me.

It seems to me that if you had that kind of cultural range in high school—art, glee club, sports teams—you must have been able to understand people and to connect on a lot of different pathways. You must have had a lot of empathy.

Absolutely. I think it serves an individual well. I've always felt like I can walk into most environments and figure out how to relate to the situation. In a company the size of P&G, there are a vast array of dynamics that you step into. As the global design officer in an organization of 127,000 employees, your calendar is booked for several months out. So when the team finally gets you in their midst, they're expecting the gospel. Sometimes you just want to walk in and say, "This really is not good!"

Or, "This is brilliant—keep going! You don't need me for the next hour or so."

It's been interesting from a career standpoint to learn how to build upon that element of empathy for different individuals. Clearly it's also useful for understanding people around the world, in terms of different consumers, and how they're going to look at brands. I wouldn't have ever thought that I was gaining this proficiency through my experiences in high school. But it absolutely set me up well.

You studied graphic design in college, then you went on to get an MBA. Those are fairly disparate areas, so you must have experienced a ping-ponging back and forth between different ways of thinking.

Yes, I joke that I had a vision that someone would write a great book called *A Whole New Mind*—the manifesto that Daniel Pink would write twenty years in the future. Knowing this, I began to prepare myself many years ago.

Were you a hands-on designer?

Yes. And I really enjoyed the hands-on aspect of designing. This was in the era, around 1987, when people had gotten their first Apple computers and were using PageMaker. Things were starting to evolve off the board and into technology, and I found it very interesting. But I felt that something was missing for me. I was doing a lot of freelancing, and I worked for a small agency for a while. I had some projects here and there that let me be a little more expressive.

I felt like I didn't have enough knowledge of the business side of the work, and I hit a crossroads. I was living in Lexington, Kentucky, which was not exactly the forefront of design. At the time, I had a family friend who was a professor at the business school at Ohio State. He encouraged me to come up to campus, and I had a great visit. I thought, "I could do this—this would be fun." So I decided to apply.

Why did you feel so unfulfilled in your design work?

I felt like there was a part of me that was incomplete. There was so much I hadn't been exposed to. I felt that, as a designer, I only had half the knowledge I needed to do the kind of work I wanted to do.

How did you feel about going back to school?

I remember the first day of classes: I was in an accounting class, and I had never taken accounting. All I knew was "debit on the left, credit on the right." That was the extent of my knowledge.

I sat down next to a gentleman who, as it so happens, I still keep in touch with. We introduced ourselves to each other. He told me, "I was an accountant at one of the big eight accounting firms," and then asked, "What did you do?" I replied, "Oh, I was a graphic designer."

Was that the first time in your life that you really felt scared?

Yes, this was the first time I had put myself in a situation where I thought, "What have I done?" The first year was incredibly difficult. All the students took the same courses, and everyone knew where you ranked academically. When employers came on campus to interview, they knew exactly where you stood in the class. I realized how smart the people were around me, and I questioned how I, with a fine arts undergraduate degree, could succeed, considering that I was in a class with folks who had been undergrad accounting majors and employees at big eight accounting firms. I thought I was doomed! At Ohio State, a certain percentage of every class had to fail, and a B minus was failing.

How did you manage?

Ironically, I think this is where my empathy helped me. I found that I understood the rules of engagement very quickly. In many of the classes, about half of your grade was based on classroom participation in the case studies we were doing. I quickly realized that if I had a question, there were likely thirty other people in the room who did too. But they weren't raising their hands to ask it. I decided that I was going to. I began to understand the parameters around me and tried to make the most of them. Because I immersed myself and tried to understand the dynamics of the class and of all the people around me, I found I didn't have to focus only on competition, GPAs, and the tension of graduate school. Instead, I was able to devote myself to learning, and I ended up getting the best grades of my life. That was what got me into P&G's summer internship program. My first interview way back then was with Marc Pritchard [P&G's global marketing officer and global brand-building officer], who, after all these years, is now my boss.

Wow! That's serendipitous!

The summer I was an intern, P&G had a position called the "associate advertising manager," and Marc Pritchard was the associate advertising manager on hair care, and I was working on Prell. Good old Prell! I had to present to him the work I did in my summer internship program in order to determine whether I would get an offer to come back. For me, this was when I began to understand the fundamentals of brand building, particularly from a marketing angle. It gave me amazing insight into the tremendously talented individuals who, at the time, were running P&G's billion-dollar businesses. Those four years during my first round at P&G were invaluable in the development of who I am today.

What did you find most interesting about brand management?

I felt that brand management was at the intersection of creativity, strategic thinking, analytical thinking, and design thinking. I saw it as a fascinating arena in which to leverage both sides of my brain, in terms of creativity and my newly honed business acumen. It was the first job I felt that I could flourish in. At the time, P&G was an organization with a "promote from within" mentality, and it was the pinnacle of the summer intern programs around the country. I think P&G and General Mills are the two most coveted intern programs in brand management. For me, to land an internship at P&G was incredible. But there were some people who were really anxious to bring someone on from Ohio State. I was the last person hired into the intern class that year. My letter from the HR director stated that there were going to be fifty-seven of us. But the "57" was crossed out, and someone had handwritten "58"! So, clearly, I was the last applicant accepted.

One small scratched-out number changed your life. Now that you have this long-term relationship with Marc Pritchard, have you ever asked him why he picked you?

Not explicitly. One of the things about Marc that I appreciated even back in 1993 was the very simple philosophy he shared with me about how he judges people. P&G brings in a lot of smart people, so there's no question about their capabilities. Naturally, Marc would look at people's leadership and relationship abilities. But he also looks to see if, at the end of the day, he would be willing to go have a beer with that person and spend some time together outside of work. I kept this criteria in mind while hiring people, and if I could say, "Yes, I would," then that's a pretty good indicator of someone that I would like to have on my team.

And now it's twenty years later.

And he takes all the credit for me coming back.

*As he should! When you first left P&G, you went
straight to Landor. Had you been working with Landor
while you were at P&G?*

On the periphery. I was in brand management
at the time, and they were working on some
programs in hair care, but I was not directly
associated with them. But I was aware of their
work and was blown away by their ability to think
strategically, push the creative envelope, and yet
be on point with a solution. They were able to see
things differently and come up with unexpected
solutions. They could take a creative brief and
turn it into a much bigger idea than what was
articulated on the page.

At the time, I worked with a design director
named Vicki Arzano. She now runs a design
firm in New York called Toast. I remember my
interview well. There I was, this Midwestern
boy who was a bit green behind the ears, and she
looked me in the eye and said, "I hope you realize
this isn't some cushy ad job!" It absolutely blew
me away, and I knew in that instant it would be
a privilege to work there. That was another of
those moments in my career that formulated who
I would become. She was the design director
in New York and the most senior woman in the
organization, and eventually, I was working with
her from Cincinnati, responsible for building the
relationship with P&G.

She set up the ground rules: She said to me,
"You don't just fax me the brief and tell me the
client needs it by four o'clock. I need to know what
your vision is for the work. And then you need to
engage me as your hands to create that vision." That
profoundly impacted me, and we built a fabulous
relationship on that. I was so appreciative that
she gave me the latitude to say, "Vicki, here's the
Crest brand"—or whatever it was, and I would
share inspiration with her that I had found in

magazines, photography, or elsewhere. She set
her expectations high, she worked hard, and she
led by example. But it was hard. I had to help build
Landor's Cincinnati office from scratch. But I loved
taking something from nothing and helping to
create it.

Did you ever worry about failing?

Oh, completely and absolutely! I kept asking myself,
"What did I leave? What have I done?" My dad, who
had worked for so long at one company, told me,
"You left P&G? Are you crazy?"

*It's interesting how our parents never considered
that the criteria for a job included how happy or
fulfilling it was.*

My father's mantra was, "Stick with it and you'll
learn to like it."

*If you were worried initially, when did you feel that you
had made the right decision?*

I think it was a moment when I was in Cincinnati,
doing a joint partnership with an agency that
we would eventually acquire. We were working
together, but the cultural sensibilities in the two
companies were very different. It was extremely
challenging. I was in my midthirties. When it
looked as if the acquisition was going to happen,
Landor began interviewing for a managing
director for the office. I wanted that job, but kept
my thoughts to myself, as there was a concern
that the office needed some "gray hair" to lead the
agency. The CEO sent down the lead candidate so
the senior management team in our office could
meet him, and largely, they didn't like him. I
remember scheduling a conference call with the
then CEO when our whole team said, "With all
due respect, we're actually not thrilled with this
individual." At that moment, I realized I deserved

the job. I had built the business. And at that moment, I crossed over my hesitation and put my intention out there. Suddenly, I had courage in my convictions. And I got the job. I was probably one of the youngest managing directors in the company at the time.

Did you ever worry that you weren't going to get the job?

Once I put my interest out there, no.

Was it a moment of aberrant courage to do so? Were you surprised with yourself that you did that?

I was surprised. I typically didn't ask for things like that. I let my history, my work, my team, and my ability speak for me. At the time, I wasn't articulate enough to be able to say, "This is what I'm going for." But I also knew I had the full support of my colleagues.

How so?

I didn't explicitly ask them, I just knew.

What was the first thing you did after you got the job?

I wanted my team to feel like they were doing great things. After I became managing director, one of my goals was to be the biggest office in the network. At that time, Landor's biggest office was in San Francisco. So I got my team together and we set out to beat them.

How long did it take?

It took about three years.

And it's still the biggest office now to date? You left it in good hands.

Yes. After that, Landor sent me to Europe to build the business there. Their European business—particularly the Paris office—was really struggling. Within two years, we turned it around to record profit.

Having worked on both the agency side and the client side, do you think there are things CEOs could learn from design firms?

Great design firms must be able to create solutions that can last for many years. Their thinking capability matched with their creative capability represents some of the greatest talents when it comes to brand building, bar none. What we create in our work—whether it's a package, or whatever it might be—it can't speak, it can't move, it can't dance. It has to embody so much of the brand. The design firm has to be able to make the right choices around what's going to be the most critical thing that will break through to consumers to build that relationship—that familiarity yet distinctiveness that connects with consumers.

The design agencies house these individuals who are trying to create design solutions for the long term, and who have to consider all these interesting aspects of the brand that are going to be expressed through very few elements. To be honest with you, that's really hard. But when it's right, it's brilliant, and it will last. So deepening CEOs' awareness and appreciation of that process and the designers' role would be great.

Any advice for how design firms can create brilliant work?

A design firm needs to bring some interesting, innovative ideas on how to validate the work, so the client is convinced the proposal is the right approach. One strategy is to show the work in the context of an unusual competitive setting. If the designers show their work in the context of brands that have done breakthrough work in other categories, they can demonstrate how their design is picking up that same feeling and will be able to break through in its own category.

How can designers create solutions that can last for many years?

Innovation. In the context of branding, I often define "innovation" as that which connects the familiar with the unknown. Because if the brand evokes connections that are completely unknown, then people don't know how to respond to it; they can't build empathy toward it. It's too odd. They would be left thinking, "How does it relate to my life? Into what part of my daily regimen am I supposed to incorporate this thing?" So when I look at great innovation inside or outside of P&G, it has always been about taking the familiar and connecting it with an unknown context. That then requires some curiosity and inquisitiveness on the part of the consumer, which leads them to explore. And that's when the brand becomes really endearing to them.

How do you define the word "brand"?

A brand is something you have an unexplained, emotional connection to. A brand gives you a sense of familiarity. At P&G, we talk about the great emotional connection that resonates with consumers when they see a brand on a shelf and decide whether they want to bring that particular brand into their lives. We call this "the first moment of truth"—that moment when you decide whether you'll invite that brand in and let it be a part of your life.

Do you remember the first time you had that experience with a brand?

When I was growing up, I was more fixated on objects than I was on the brand. I had to have a bike with a banana seat, for example.

Why did you want a banana seat?

It was distinctive and different.

*But what was it that made you decide that was what
you wanted? Did you see other people with it?*

It was new and distinct, and I knew that I would be
the object of envy in my neighborhood.

An object of envy?

Yes. People would covet my banana seat. But I
didn't really care what brand it was—the social
influence the seat wielded mattered most to me. I
think this is when, for me, branding became about
recognition and attachment. Now, I think that
brands are a reflection of one's personal compass.

In what way?

In earlier years, I think branding was a lot about
a recognition and an attachment to a person that
you aspired to or held up on a pedestal. So we went
through an era where brands focused on an association
with a celebrity or an inspirational individual.
**Now I think we've evolved,
and brands now have the responsibility to enhance the
communities in which they exist. By virtue of that, once
a brand is in a community, it can quickly be built up or
shut down.**

And branding is no longer about "I'm going to tell
you why Pantene will make your hair *x*." It's about
how Pantene can enhance women's lives. Marketers
can no longer inflict their personal opinions of the
brand on unsuspecting consumers. People are more
attentive than they've ever been about the brands
they allow to become part of their lives, because the
brands are so reflective of their values as individuals.

*This goes back to the notion of "purpose-driven"
brands. How do you determine the purpose the brands
at P&G are going to have?*

We were asking our brands to have a purpose, but
at first our initial approach to this was "purpose

as cause." There was this "purpose" work where, for instance, we were going to provide clean water for underserved communities around the world. And yet the specific brand might be—and this is an invented example to show you what I mean—about enhancing home decor through fragrance. So this kind of a purpose wouldn't be authentic for the brand. It was disassociated from the essence of the brand. But I think we've quickly evolved in a smart way. We now understand that people buy into a brand purpose with their heart, but they buy a brand based on its benefit. Everything about the brand has to work together and be congruent.

How has this affected the type of work that you do?

I believe we have a powerful responsibility to do something constructive with the affinity consumers have for brands. The main idea of purpose-driven brands is about recognizing, embracing, and celebrating the fact that brands can enhance people's lives and help them to feel better about themselves—whether it makes them look better, do a task better, or even gives them the opportunity to do good in the world.

There have been brands that have enhanced my life just by making me feel better about myself.

Even in a down economy, the ability to afford a CoverGirl lipstick can improve someone's psyche. Virginia Postrel would be the first to celebrate the notion that even in moments of great hardship, the maintenance of one's emotional psyche is critically important.

Ultimately, I think a brand should help you feel better, look better, or be better. Brands should help you reach a destination or a goal. I think there are some brands that people use because they fulfill a strictly utilitarian need. Other brands help people in lovely and interestingly small ways. Take one away, and I'm not sure anyone would fall over and declare, "If I don't have my valued paper towel, my life is going to fall apart." But without these small, but important, benefits, life would be different. When you put them all together, you have something very powerful.

Dori Tunstall

*Associate Professor of Design
Anthropology, Faculty of Design,
Swinburne University of Technology;
Organizer, U. S. National Design
Policy Initiative; Former Managing
Director, Design for Democracy*

*If I wasn't working at a job I loved—or had the
flexibility to take a very long sabbatical—I would
pack up my bags, move to Australia, and study design
anthropology with Dori Tunstall.*

*Dori is an anthropologist of design. She studies
and interprets design in terms of the complex role
it plays in our culture and our identities; with that
understanding, she seeks to help designers and
organizations communicate their messages as
effectively as possible.*

*Talking with her is like having a one-on-
one conversation with a favorite, much-beloved
professor—which, for those lucky enough to
study with her, she is. Listening to her insights on
design, culture, social hierarchies, enlightenment,
human evolution, worship, and garage sales is an
unbelievable buzz. I could listen to her discuss these
topics for hours on end.*

*When you talk with Dori, you see the extensive
tapestry that forms the complexity of her own
knowledge: books she's read, research she's done,
topics she's taught, her own ruminations and "eureka
moments"—all of it is conveyed in conversation.
She doesn't seem to forget much, and she shares
with her interlocutors an incomparable scope of
knowledge and the delight she has in discovery. There
is an undeniable magnetism in her examination,
equal parts playful and studious, of the defining*

characteristics of who we are as humans, of the core principles that define how we structure, perceive, and create our world. Conversation with Dori feels like an essential intellectual—and at times spiritual—repast.

What I adore about Professor Tunstall is her ability to make seemingly esoteric issues grittily relevant to the real-world endeavor of design and branding. She segues easily from the hierarchies evident in bee society to the success of President Obama's 2008 campaign graphics, and both fit in to her analysis of how we create meaning and structure in our lives and how these in turn relate to our essential aspirations. She's keenly aware of the milestone shifts that led to our current culture of branding, as she references in her discussion of sugar. She is not a dispassionate observer of these transformations, critiquing as she does the commodification of necessities such as water. She draws a throughline from the primal urge that drives us to create all the way to the endeavors and aspirations of modern branding. She is postmodern in her Heisenbergian certainty that the experiments we conduct—i.e., what we look for—shape the reality that we investigate.

Dori can make connections between social theory and design, between religion and creativity. As an anthropologist, her musings are never overly obsessed with aesthetics. She has a very strong sense of the sacred, and the way in which worship is a key human activity. She has a mythic sense of the human being's origins, possibilities, and the way that this drives our need to connect to a group identity. Precisely because of that, our current "rituals of consumption," as she says, are no longer making us happy.

Our conversation covered extensive ground, and I admire Dori's ability to coin quotable and immensely relevant gems, among them, "Design translates values into tangible experiences." In the space of a few sentences, she weaves from design to technology to worship. Even when my questions came out of left field, she was never off guard but rather quickly and easily responded, happy to investigate the areas we discussed. Even if she seemingly veers from a discussion of branding per se in her comments, her central concern remains our identities and aspirations as humans and the culture that gives rise to the design that we've created and are now creating.

Like some of the other brand thinkers I talked with, Dori is not merely an optimist about the power of design, but she is doing her best to support its altruistic potential. In her work for organizations like Design for Democracy and the U.S. National Design Policy Initiative, she has continually sought to use design as a tool for social progress. To that end, she recognizes the value of new technologies, and the design of them, in supporting the drive for social change while also helping us better grapple with the crises that confront us. "Values like equality, democracy, fairness, integration, and connection are values that, to some extent, we've lost," she says. "Design can help make those values more tangible and ultimately express how we can use them to make the world a better place."

Design anthropology is the focus of your study and teaching, so I felt the natural first question would be, what is it?

What is design anthropology? Well, there's a theoretical dimension and a practical one. The practical dimension includes trying to figure out how to understand people and how to design products, communications, and experiences in ways that resonate with people. The theoretical response is about trying to understand how the processes and artifacts of design help define what it means to be human.

The processes of design define what it means to be human?

Yes. Design translates values into tangible experiences. Anthropology helps you understand those values and how the process of making things actually defines us as semi–uniquely human. Design research attempts to understand design and the design process in order to improve it.

Did you invent the term "design anthropology"?

No, it's existed professionally for the past twenty to twenty-five years at places like Xerox PARC [Palo Alto Research Center] or in Denmark, where it came out of the field of participatory design. Professionally, there are probably about ten to fifteen people who are called "design anthropologists."

At the beginning of the noughties, a large number of anthropologists engaged in design innovation and high-tech consulting. Design anthropology is bringing these people back into academia to train the next generation. Students often ask me how they can become a design anthropologist. But the path that I took is impossible to follow anymore. Design anthropology is an established field in industry, but it is just now feeding its way into academia.

*When you were younger, before you found your way
to design anthropology, did you have some inklings of
what your career would be?*

I wanted to become a medical doctor—a neurosurgeon.

*Really? So, you've always been interested in how people
think and live.*

Yes. When I was deciding between whether I
was going to go into anthropology or whether I
was going to continue in chemistry and biology, I
realized that if I became a neurosurgeon, I would be
a great neurosurgeon, but I wouldn't be a very good
human being.

Why not?

With neurosurgery, you understand people,
but you understand them in terms of small
connections of synapses. You don't see them
as people. Your focus is very narrow. Also, as a
doctor, you're primarily dealing with people in
traumatic situations. This requires you to maintain
a certain distance. With anthropology, you can
study just about anything related to humans, and in
doing so, you can establish very deep connections
to and with people. Ultimately, I had to make a
decision about the kind of person I wanted to be.
Do I want to be a person who understands people
in a very narrow—albeit important—way, or do
I want to understand people in a more intimate,
playful way? I chose anthropology.

*In your effort to understand people, what have you
learned? What are the essential things that make
us human?*

It keeps changing. Way back when, we were
defined as humans because of the fact that we made
tools. Then we learned that chimpanzees can make
tools, and now we know birds actually use tools as
well. Then we wondered whether being human

was about language, and then we realized it wasn't about language either. We have discovered that whales, dogs, and elephants have complex language systems as well. I recently read that what defines being human is our ability to transform things from one energy state to another.

We can turn sand and water and limestone into concrete. We haven't discovered any animals capable of accomplishing this with the same level of intention.

And we can make an omelet.

Yes. What really fascinates me about people is our capacity to love and hate, as well as how we feel and engage, and our ability to deal with change. If you look at human history, you can see how much the everyday lives of humans have changed throughout different phases of development. Since the time when we discovered agriculture, everything changed. And when we started to build cities, everything changed. Our ability to adapt to so much change and to also be the force for change—both good and bad—is extraordinary.

How much do you think evolution has played a role in our development, and how much do you think our interactions have?

The "nature, nurture" question.

Yes.

The problem with being an anthropologist is how much time I spend being an integrationist. Meaning you can have, say, a genetic predisposition towards weight gain, but that's not the entire story.

So it's not entirely my mother's fault?

If you grow up in an environment where you eat vegan and vegetarian food, then that genetic predisposition to weight gain might not ever get fully expressed. The genetics provides us with preconditions. We have to breathe oxygen, but what we do with that essential life function impacts how we interpret those preconditions: Smoking, for example, would fall into the category of "nurture," though obviously it's not good for us. So, nature and nurture work hand in hand. I get frustrated when there is a scientific argument—and most of the time you're reading it in a column in *The New York Times*—that states, "A genetic predisposition to cancer does this, this, and that," and then people say, "Well, my parents and grandparents and great-grandparents had cancer, and I don't. This doesn't make any sense." But again, it's because nature and nurture work together, and that is what allows us to adopt to change.

Biologically speaking, there have been some major changes in our evolutionary history, but for the past two thousand years, there haven't been significant changes to our genetic code. Yet there have been tremendous changes in our environment, and we are separating ourselves from nature. I think the next step of the environmental movement will not only focus on building better technical solutions, it will also include the realization that we can no longer see ourselves as separate from nature. After all, flowers respond to the sun—why shouldn't we? There is no separation. The way our bodies are built is defined by the environment. The cells that populate our skin come from the environment. The air that we breathe is from the environment. We're not separate. It's only in relatively recent times that we've created this separation. One of the original reasons humans worshipped was to recognize that we are one with nature.

*Do you think that worship is another indicator of the
difference between humans and other species?*

There's been a lot written about the evolution of
creativity. One hypothesis is that creativity comes
from our need to make things special. And this
relates to worship because worship allows us to
identify things in order to make them special.

**We know very little about the
symbolic life of animals, but one of the most fascinating
aspects of human beings is our great capabilities to
create and interpret symbolism, as well as our ability to
make abstractions concrete. In many ways, this is the
genesis of creativity.**

The notion of making things special and the
identification of something as special or unique—
and the relationship to that thing as special and
unique—are the heart of worship and the heart of
creativity itself.

I also think they're the heart of brands.

Yes. One of my favorite books to teach with
is *Thinking with Things*, by Esther Pasztory.
She writes about how different levels of social
integration—in other words, the intimacy and
scale of human organization and interaction—have
different aesthetic values. These different "levels"
include small-scale bands of hundreds of people or
less, villages of thousands of people, chiefdoms in
the range of thousands to ten thousands, and states
at one hundred thousand people and more.

Pasztory maps out our different aesthetic
values based on our level of social integration and
our need to map our cosmology onto the landscape.
For example, think about Aboriginal Australians
and the dances that they do. These dances are all
about mapping their cosmology onto the landscape
so that the Aborigines' connection to everything is
made visible and shareable.

That explains our inclination for symbolism and iconography, but where do you think our tendencies to create hierarchies in our societies come from?

All social animals are like this. If you think of all our other close relatives—the chimpanzees, for instance—they all have hierarchies, which we describe in terms of the alphas, the betas, and so forth.

From an anthropological point of view, why is there a need for different hierarchies of power?

There isn't a functional explanation. Evolutionary anthropologists have theories about how this may work, but even as we learn more, we realize how little we know. I'll give you an example. In popular language, we describe someone who is bossy and self-important as acting like a "queen bee." In the past, we interpreted the queen bee's greater size and longevity vis-à-vis the worker bee "drones" as if she sits around all day laying eggs and telling the others what to do. Yet the more we learn, the more we realize that bee society is more "equal" in the sense that everyone has a specialized role to play to maintain the colony. If the queen doesn't lay eggs, the "foraging" bees don't do their dance language to communicate where the pollen is, the "building" bees don't build nests, the "nurse" bees don't care for the young, the "undertaker" bees don't clear out the dead—and the entire colony dies. We are learning that all the bees act instinctively to maintain the life of the colony, not because a queen bee tells them what to do. This shift in thought about bees should parallel our shift in thought about hierarchies in general.

Another example relates to how we study chimpanzees. Historically, most of our focus has been on aggression and hierarchy. Now, much of the emphasis is on the role of empathy and how chimpanzees learn with one another. This is because our values are changing, and that shift is changing our views of what's important to look at.

Sure, there's a lot of hierarchy in many different cases. But it may just be apparent to us because we're identifying with what we're looking at, and thinking that it, too, must be hierarchical. This becomes a way to justify our own modes of being. At this moment in time, we've decided that empathy and cooperation are the more important. This is now the way in which we will talk about all of the animal kingdom.

Do you think brands create hierarchies?

Humans like to think of themselves as special and different from one another. Some people like to think of themselves not only as special and different but also as better than others.

Why?

We almost always used "things" as a way to identify ourselves and to identify others. Let's start with the human body. In traditional cultures, the art of tattooing was about social coding. A certain number of tatoos meant you've been married. Another number of tattoos meant that you've had children. This many tattoos meant that you've killed a lion. Nowadays, we have a tremendous emphasis on dress and makeup and in our rituals of buying. I use the word "rituals" very specifically. But our rituals of consumption are no longer as satisfactory to us.

How come?

Because they are empty of human relationships. There was recently a wonderful study done on garage sales. When people go to a garage sale to buy something, they actually feel very satisfied about the interaction. Most of the time, it's because the object they buy comes with a story—a very real, personal story about where the object fit into someone's life. Whether it's real or not, you connect with that person through the object. So when you take the object, your purchase of it is more satisfactory. Whereas right now, when you go now to a store, there seems to be a lot of emphasis on branding that tells authentic stories in order to . . .

Sell more stuff?

Yes, to sell more stuff, but I'm not cynical about that. It's really an attempt to figure out how to make connections through the objects that people are buying. This is why it can actually work very effectively. It goes like this: "I buy from Starbucks because they tell me this little story about where the bean comes from. And this relationship and the fair trade and the overall vibe make me feel better about the purchase—even though there's a part of my brain saying, 'Hmmm, I'm not so sure about this.'"

Does that translate into a willingness to buy a $4 cup of coffee? I'm not so sure.

We see these transactions as part of our own identity, but they're really not tied into a deeper, more intimate group identity. A brand that does this successfully is Harley-Davidson. Harley-Davidson is a great brand because people actually connect with and through it. If you go on a Harley-Davidson road tour, your interactions with people, your interactions through the brand, through that experience, tie you together in a way that feels very satisfactory. Especially given that we are living in a society that makes these types of connections more difficult.

Earlier in our conversation, you spoke about how, as a species, we are able to make abstractions concrete. I'm wondering if, with brands, we take things that are concrete—this brand, for example, or this coffee, or this

sneaker—and then use that brand to project abstractions?
For example, this coffee makes me more chic just by the
sheer virtue of carrying it. Or these sneakers make me feel
fit by the plain fact of wearing them. This then telegraphs
to others who might be wearing those same sneakers
that I'm like-minded. Then a kinship can develop. So, I'm
wondering if a brand can boomerang from an abstract
construct to a concrete one, and then from concrete
construct to a projected abstraction.

Definitely! What becomes really fascinating is when people take a brand and do interesting things with it to make it their own.

For example?

Look at the logo and imagery for Obama's presidential campaign and how people were able to riff on it. One of my students looked at all of the variations. The different groups included Kids for Obama, African Americans for Obama, and Women for Obama. There was even a group called Pirates for Obama.

As she examined these variations, my student realized that part of what made the logo effective was the tangible way that people could connect with this movement, this potential for change and hope, through the identity.

People actually made it more closely aligned with who they were, while still allowing it to retain its inherent integrity. It was a fascinating process of starting with one's own personal experience—be it dissatisfaction or despondency—and then connecting it to an abstraction that conveyed hope and the possibility of change.

It made the abstract personally tangible for so many people. So, it wasn't just about hope and change for some general group of "people," it was hope and change for pirates.

This is the way that these groups gave the identity another form, and then put it back out into the public. People responded to it, and built their own communities, Pirates for Obama among them. These individual abstractions inspired feelings of openness and possibility. There were formal elements of the logo that made it easier to do this and wouldn't have been possible if the design had featured a version of a red, white, and blue flying flag. That people were able to do this with a logo and a brand is really magic.

Is that ability to create this specific dynamic connected in some way to our ability, need, or tendency to worship?

Worship is really about the call and response for connection. In the process of worshipping God, what you are doing is establishing a connection through song or dance or prayer. What people may not recognize is that in that process, they are letting go of seeing God as an "all-powerful being." What they are doing when they are worshipping is having a one-to-one chat, a heart-to-heart about "what's going on with me, what's going on with you, what's going on with the world." During the process of worship, you ignore the sense of separation that you may feel in the other times of your life. The process of worshipping is the process of connecting.

I wonder if there was ever a point in time when we didn't need to worship because our connection to God was so intrinsic. When Adam and Eve were in the Garden of Eden, there was no disconnection from God. What happened?

Eve ate the apple.

Yes! There was the split! But again, the call to worship is really the call to connection. Depending on whatever it is that you're worshipping—whether you're worshipping Buddha, Allah, Jehovah, or God—it's really about connecting with a sense of enlightenment. Enlightenment means, in most cases, that you no longer recognize the difference between you and anything else, because everything else is an illusion.

And yet we also participate in religions that have so much exclusivity to them. And rejection. And judgment. Why do we do that?

That's what happens when Christianity meets the Roman State. When religion meets the state, it becomes about hierarchy and separation. And you end up with the priests in the middle. The idea becomes that you can't directly connect with God. You have to do it through an intermediary. And that intermediary will use and abuse that power as they wish. So, it's not so much about what's inherent in belief and what's inherent in worshipping, it really is about how those beliefs get folded into the social structure we've put in place.

And the relationship ends up being about power, and using belief as a technology of power rather than being focused on anything inherent in worshipping. Our desire to be led is tied to the desire to connect, and sometimes we are led astray or led to do things that disconnect us from others, as opposed to connecting us with them.

I recently read that there are over one hundred brands of nationally distributed water in the United States. Why do you think we need to create that many?

We don't need it. That's an illusion. We don't need a hundred brands of water—in fact, we probably don't even need to be selling water. This is an interesting transition, in and of itself. The right to clean water was something we once considered inalienable. Yet the right to clean water and the right to clean air have become commodities. We don't need to have branded water. Once the decision is made that water is a commodity, then you begin to have hierarchies and differentiation, and then people begin to say, "Whoa, you need to have Poland Spring water because it's clearer and better than Evian," or "What do you want with French water anyway?" or "It should come from Fiji because it's an island in the middle of nowhere and thus it's more pure."

Whereas, if we invested all the money in keeping our lakes and streams clean, then we wouldn't need to have branded bottled water. Culturally, this all goes back to the 1920s during the shift from commodities to branded commodities. The force of competition along with the force of mass services and mass products made branding necessary. Sugar didn't need to be branded when only the most wealthy and elite of the French aristocracy could afford it. The brand of the king was more important than the brand of the sugar. But once sugar became cheap and accessible for everyone, those who wanted to profit from sugar needed to distinguish themselves from the guy down the street who also wanted to profit from it. The same goes for the plantation in Haiti versus the plantation in the Dominican Republic.

I read an interview with you in which you said, "Design has the power to help humanity versus the unbridled consumerism that it currently contributes to." How can design do that?

Between the work that I've done for Design for Democracy, the work that I'm doing to help with the U.S. National Design Policy Initiative, and the work that I'm doing on culture-based innovation, I'm trying to use design and design technologies to make values more tangible and apparent to people. Design is not all about mass consumption and unbridled capitalism.

Values like equality, democracy, fairness, integration, and connection are values that, to some extent, we've lost. Design can help make those values more tangible and ultimately express how we can use them to make the world a better place.

Why this groundswell about making the world a better place?

I think it's exhaustion! The environment is in peril to a degree that we can now see. We can visualize the destruction of what we're doing in a way that we couldn't before. We can see the damage, and because we're responsible for it, we're feeling very pessimistic about it. The next generation doesn't feel as responsible. They're looking at the problem as an opportunity. They have a natural sense of optimism.

It's been interesting to see how new technologies make the process of connecting with one another more efficient. Building momentum is now easier. In the past, a young group of idealistic people wouldn't have been able to break through existing structures to make their voices heard as loudly or as effectively.

From an academic perspective, you wouldn't be able to publish radical ideas because someone else had the power to publish them or not. But now you can completely circumvent the power structures so that you can make your voice heard and connect with other people. The fact that you're connecting with other people who think the same way you do actually makes you feel more optimistic—because you're not alone. You can then build a coalition and get things accomplished.

It makes sense that social media is so popular if a common denominator of so much of our behavior is connection.

Yes! If it wasn't for Facebook, e-mail, and Twitter, I would never have moved to Australia. I would have felt too isolated. But because I'm able to connect with my family, it's doable. And in fact, I like knowing what my sister had for breakfast this morning.

Some people think that this use of technology is superficial.

Yes. Well, it's generational. For example, I've rarely talked to people on the telephone, and in fact, I probably have really bad telephone etiquette. But I'm constantly connected through my BlackBerry. I tell people to send me an e-mail, and then I'll respond within ten to fifteen minutes. Generationally, I am much more comfortable in connecting this way.

I have a running dialogue with my sister on Facebook. It would take us a one-hour conversation to catch up in as much detail. So when we do speak, we're actually able to talk at a deeper level because we no longer have to provide the newspaper report of "On Tuesday, I did this and this and that." She already knows that. This gives us a deeper level of engagement and allows us to have deeper conversations because she doesn't have to know all about what I ate for breakfast.

And so, again, design is really important. It sets up the interfaces that allow people to connect. It is not just the technology. Technology just provides the mechanics. But the values inherent in connecting are clarity and transparency. This goes back to worship. People forget that the telephone wasn't invented to connect with people—it was to connect with the spirit world. People thought they could use it to call the dead.

Really?

Yes! Back then, electricity was magic—so was running water!

It's so interesting to see how much we take for granted and how much we assume things will always be available to us. What we're finding out now is that we can't make these assumptions anymore.

Think about the 2003 blackout in New York, when all of the subway lines stopped running, and everyone had to walk across the bridges to get home. People realized that they could no longer rely on all the things they took for granted. It's time to change our behavior. We can no longer assume we won't run out of the things that we need to happily and safely live our lives.

Brian Collins

Chairman and Chief Creative Officer,
COLLINS:

When I first met Brian Collins, I found him brusque
and impatient. Brian has a willingness to push
buttons and is provocative in a way that doesn't
necessarily earn him instant admirers—but it's
precisely those qualities that make him so brilliant.

At Ogilvy & Mather's Brand Integration
Group, Brian did genre-defining work for Dove,
Motorola, Hershey's, and American Express, among
others. At COLLINS:, a New York–based branding
consultancy he launched in 2008, he's continued to
craft groundbreaking projects for clients such as
Microsoft, CNN, and NBC. In everything he does,
Brian brings a comprehensive understanding of how
design makes brands come alive.

His grasp of the power of the brand is
unparalleled, as is his insight into the dynamics
that make brands, and their narratives, irresistible.
He knows how brands tap into archetypes and
essential human yearnings. Through his work, he's
demonstrated how to do this, and he's become a
master of crafting these dynamics himself.

Brian has an utterly unique point of view on
the topics we discussed. No one else I spoke with
had his level of insight about what makes Apple tick.
His explanation of the company's main archetype is
revelatory, as are his reflections on how brands relate
to a particular theme or social purpose.

Brian has a relentless drive for creative invention, and it's clear how much this feeds the passion for his work, and how that in turn fuels his thirst for innovation. He's created many defining moments in branding, and I'm sure he will shepherd many more.

You have a long history in the branding arena—why do
you like working on brands?

Brands are a ubiquitous part of our culture.
Everyone interacts with them, every day. And these
brands often need a great deal of help with their
communications. There's nothing more rewarding
than bringing clarity or beauty to something with
the scale and influence of a large brand.

What about that do you like?

I like the ability to influence. Large brands
have a disproportionate influence over cultural
dialogues and ideas. If you find a client who sees an
opportunity to use the brand to build a business by
doing good, then you can have a dramatic effect—
not only on the success of the company and the
brand, but also on people's lives.

Dove's Campaign for Real Beauty is a
fine example of this. We were presented with
a very specific business challenge: to introduce
a new line of products that would move the
brand beyond soap into the beauty business—by
including items like skin care products and
moisturizers. But when a brand starts expanding
into other categories, it needs a proposition
people will pay attention to. Because Dove is part
of a very big company, and because it has such an
extensive bandwidth, a lot of people were able to
hear and see the message.

In our research for Dove, we found that other
companies in this arena were telling the same old
story. We realized that no brand of Dove's size
had challenged the damaging effects of the very
narrow view of feminine beauty. No brand had ever
presented this view. We saw this both as a business
opportunity and as a way to open up a bigger
cultural dialogue. I think that dialogue—or that
tension—is what gives brands their energy.

What I'm really interested in understanding about Brian Collins is, Why brands? Why do you choose to surround yourself with brands? In your office where I'm sitting, there are images of brands everywhere I look. Beautiful brands. Big brands. What is it about brands that you find so fascinating?

They have great potential to unify. As the world becomes more and more divided, the more we need to see that we have things in common—that we share things. If my fourteen-year-old nephew sees a photo of a kid in Afghanistan drinking a Coca-Cola, then that's a connection. It's evidence of commonality. So on their best day, brands can make a person feel more connected to other people, which can make them feel better about themselves.

Several years ago, I worked on the brand identity system and the ad campaign for Motorola. We created work for Motologic, Motospin, and Mototurn. I remember being in Moscow, in Revolution Square, where there's an impressive sculpture of Karl Marx. The figure of Marx emerges out of a big slab of granite, and he is looking toward the future. When I was there, he happened to be looking toward a giant billboard that my team in New York had designed for Motorola. In Revolution Square! Now the fact that some kid in Moscow, or a girl in Framingham, Massachusetts, or a kid in Osaka might have the same cell phone says to me that we have hope for a shared future. We have common touchpoints that unite us where religion and politics may not.

Another reason I like working with established brands is that they have a certain cross-generational power. **It's particularly interesting when brands become multigenerational, because that's when they take on mythic qualities: When it's your grandmother's brand, and your mother's brand, and your brand, it takes on an emotional resonance that becomes mythic.**

In my family, someone in each generation has waited in line at Disneyland. I've been there with my mom, my sister, all of my brother's children. They've all had the same emotional response to seeing Snow White walk down Main Street, or to hearing someone sing "When You Wish Upon a Star." My niece, who's three; my sister, who's forty-two; my mom, who's seventy-six; and me: We all know what this feels like. I think the secret to working with existing brands is to help them find their intrinsic story. And then amplify the stories for new generations to share. Brands have become the best device for perpetuating mythic archetypes.

Tell me what you mean by that. How do they create mythic archetypes?

The best brands embody mythic archetypes. They literally are stories. Nike is a great example. Nike calls on the goddess. She is not the goddess of sport, or sportsmanship, or of fair play, or achievement. Nike is the goddess of victory. The federal government put that name on the first nuclear missiles—they were called Nikes. If you were a Greek warrior, you went to the temple and made a sacrifice to Nike before you went into battle. You asked her for victory. She was a mean motherfucker! You did not mess with her. She was about winning and achievement.

Now, Nike—the brand—has done a remarkable job of bringing that story to life. I remember being downtown in New York's West Village and seeing a bunch of kids playing a game of pickup basketball. The next day, Nike had a basketball clinic in the same location. The day before, the kids were just playing basketball. Then, the swoosh goes up, and the activity is the same, but the story has changed.

How so?

The transformation means that the goddess Nike has been called on. She has declared that the players are now devoted to victory! So the emotional charge of that experience changed at the moment the giant orange banner went up and spanned from one side of the court to the other, with the Nike swoosh in the middle. Now the players and participants have called upon the powers of the goddess.

Do you think the kids realize that?

Absolutely. You know there's something different when you're on a basketball court with a Nike swoosh on it. It's a different experience that goes beyond those particular players on that particular court on that particular day. It becomes part of a larger story about triumph.

Is that a good thing or a bad thing?

Well . . . for who?

For either party.

Well, it was a good thing because there were boys and girls on the court who were excited and engaged, and the fact that professionals were teaching them to shoot hoops is an amazing thing. Second, for Nike to run free clinics for kids so that the brand has a presence in their imagination is terrific. From this point of view, I find it promising. It's a basic truth that human beings crave connection to one another, and to the world. When brands can give us that, as Nike does in this example, it's a positive thing.

Also, Nike is doing remarkable things in the realms of product development and sustainability. I know they are hell-bent on using more sustainable protocols to create everything that they make.

But at the end of the day, isn't the goal to sell more products?

Yes. But that is increasingly not being viewed as the only measure of success.

Yes, but ultimately these things are being done in an effort to—

Build a business. Absolutely. I love what the management consultant Peter Drucker said: "Securities analysts believe that companies make money. Companies make shoes!" They are in the business to make products that people want, and if they're making something that people don't want, then the business won't make money. I think what people are looking for is more than the product. I think they want to know what your company's relationship is to the local economy. They want to know how you're contributing in a larger way to the world. More and more people are making decisions based on what a company gives back, and this has become more important than considerations of the return on shareholder investment.

We create brands—we create beliefs, we create belief systems. We construct frameworks through which we may better understand the world. We do this with religion as well. There are a lot of different religions and a lot of different people who feel very, very strongly that because of their specific religion, they have a direct communication to God. Because there is no empirical evidence of any of this, one could make the argument that we create the constructs around Nike sneakers or Coca-Cola in order to create specific feelings or to satisfy specific human needs.

Why do you think that we do this? Why do we as humans create these constructs?

We say we want information, but we don't experience the world through information—we experience the world through story.

So brands are stories?

Absolutely. Stories are how we give meaning to what happens to us. When we call upon them, they activate archetypes—"archetypes" as defined by Carl Jung. They remind us of eternal truths, and they help us navigate through our lives.

When an archetype is embodied in the narrative, in the visuals, and in the artifacts, it becomes instantly recognizable. If I say to you "warrior," you understand what a warrior is. If I say "king," you understand what a king is. If I say "magician," you immediately understand the mythology of that too. People quickly unpack archetypes. I find them to be a remarkable shorthand to get to the truth of brands. I'm now spending a lot of time with my clients uncovering what archetypes their brands encompass. Once we determine that, we're able to get to the heart of the story. These archetypes exist everywhere. For example, people see Apple as a rebel brand in part because it's constantly pushing up against Microsoft. But if you actually look back, Apple is really Eve. Apple is the seductress.

Oh my god, that is so good. I've never heard Apple described this way.

That is the most powerful Western mythic archetype we live with: Eve seducing Adam with an apple. Steve Jobs is using an apple with a bite taken out of it as his company's logo. The apple already has a bite taken out of it! Eve has eaten the apple and says, "I am conscious." Steve Jobs says, "I will give you the consciousness that Microsoft and IBM will not give you. And in order to do that, I am going to seduce you. My products are seductive . . . they are sexy . . . come and play with me." You can see this manifested most prominently in the iPad, and it's also evident in all the comments people made about it: "It feels like I have to have a cigarette when

I'm finished with it." "It's sexy." "It's beautiful." The iPad is an erotic machine. You're inexplicably attracted to it. You play with it. You caress it. Apple invites you to have sex with it.

Often with brands, there's the obvious archetype, and then there's one right underneath it. And that's the really powerful one. The obvious Apple archetype is evident in the 1984 commercial where the woman throws a sledgehammer at the screen showing Big Brother. That is also Eve. In that case, she's using violence, but she's still sexy. The archetype that lies underneath is the seductress. So it's not simply the rebel—it's the seductress-rebel. But Steve Jobs and Apple can't talk about that because it would be too obvious. You can't talk about being cool, and you can't talk about being sexy. You either *are* sexy or you *are* cool. But you can't talk about it. However, you *can* talk about being a rebel. You can act like a rebel. I think *that* is the power of Apple.

Speaking of rebels, you've become famous for saying that you don't think designers should be problem solvers. You'd rather be a "problem maker" or a "problem seeker." Tell me about that.

I liked the idea of "problem maker" only because I'm often accused of being insouciant. I don't think designers can wait for people to come to us with problems. Our sensibilities, as well as our sensitivities, give us great pattern-recognition skills. **We should go into situations, communities, organizations, industries, companies, and start looking for problems.**

I love the Yogi Berra quote, "You can observe a lot just by watching." And that's true for designers. Our problem-seeking skills are more powerful than our problem-solving skills. We can see the things that other people don't. It's our job to ask and answer questions that people might not even know how to ask.

Do you feel that there are certain responsibilities that
people working on brands need to be cognizant of?
In my experience, I've come to believe that there are
intrinsic choices you make when you're working on
brands. Would you agree with that?

>Yes, you need to be really conscious of the power
>you use. Designers and creative people have great
>power. They have the power to make people focus
>on something, to make them kill for something,
>to make them shop for something. They can put a
>texture on a piece of packaging that is so remarkable
>that you're compelled to pick it up.

Do you feel that's manipulative in any way?

>I think it can be seductive. I think it means you have
>to be conscious of your ability to be seduced.

Your company is called "COLLINS:"—you've branded
your company with your name. What do you think your
brand stands for?

>I think that's for other people to decide. Brands exist
>in the minds of the people who interact with them.
>I'll let those people determine what my brand is.

Virginia Postrel

Author, Cultural Critic, Bloomberg News *columnist*

Virginia Postrel is one hell of a writer with one hell of an editorial pedigree. She's been a columnist for The Wall Street Journal *and* The New York Times. *She's been a contributing editor of* The Atlantic Monthly. *During the more than a decade that she was editor of* Reason, *the libertarian-viewpointed political and cultural affairs magazine, the publication gained numerous kudos for its journalism. Joining an impressive roster of writers and editors, she began writing a regular column for* Bloomberg View, *the buzz-garnering op-ed forum that debuted on* Bloomberg News *in May 2011.*

If you want to learn about the art form of essay-writing, journalism, and cultural criticism, read Virginia Postrel. In her commentaries—whether on the magic of the iPad, "consumer vertigo," the Oscars, the appeal of superheroes, or the high cost of local food—there is not one hackneyed phrase or thought.

In addition to being an intellectual powerhouse and a literary craftswoman, she writes with heart and from personal experience, as she did in pieces for The Atlantic *about drug approval for cancer treatments and the aesthetic design of hospitals (she was undergoing cancer treatment). She is a modern-day essayist with few peers, bringing to her writing an evolved mastery of the craft. Some people look at paintings to get the endorphin rush of experiencing the sublime—I get that from falling under the sway of*

Virginia's compositional abilities and the intelligence of her ideas.

The blog DeepGlamour, *which Virginia launched and edits, examines the role and power of "glamour" in our society, a subject that gains new relevance and richness—i.e., true glamour—in her hands. Her book* The Substance of Style *examines the pervasive influence of design in today's culture; in* The Future and its Enemies, *from 1998, she considers the dynamics of innovation and the cultural resistance we have to it.*

From all this, I've concluded that, in essence, Virginia is like a cultural lepidopterist—she studies the specimens of cultural dynamics, beautifully documenting each one. She can tell you all the qualities of its contemporary incarnation as well as how it has evolved over time. In that vein, she offers her keen perspective on how the relationship between status and fashion has shifted in recent decades. She has similar perspective on the interconnections of fame, style, media, provocation, articulating all the different trappings and tricks we use to position ourselves, to attract interest or love, to achieve popular adulation, to assess where we are on the cultural totem pole—to be a member of a group yet separate from it.

Our conversation covers extensive ground, ranging from the surfeit of clothes in the modern wardrobe to political parties, the natural state of the brain, Lady Gaga, attention, and Sarah Palin. Her discussion about clothes is essentially a discussion about language—and how it has proliferated because of the marketplace. On the subject of brands, Virginia says that she often uses Gold Medal flour to illustrate how brands got their genesis. "A brand is a promise of a certain kind of consistency and continuity over time."

As she acknowledges, brands today convey much more than that, and we discuss the challenges of consciously crafting the brand experience. On that subject, a piece that Virginia wrote in 2006 about superheroes and glamour seems to have poignant relevance:

Glamour isn't beauty or luxury; those are only specific manifestations for specific audiences. Glamour is an imaginative process that creates a specific, emotional response: a sharp mixture of projection, longing, admiration, and aspiration. It evokes an audience's hopes and dreams and makes them seem attainable, all the while maintaining enough distance to sustain the fantasy.

You wrote an article for The Wall Street Journal *titled "Saved by the Closet" in which you observe, "In 2008, Americans owned an average of 92 items of clothing." Following the economic crash of 2009, you explain that "the average wardrobe had shrunk—to a still-abundant 88 items." You then compare this to what people owned during the Great Depression, when an average person's wardrobe contained fewer than fifteen items. What created this staggering increase in the amount of stuff that we own?*

At the most fundamental level, the change is a result of our increasing prosperity, which contains two components. First, because of increasing economic productivity and an increase in people's earning power, the real amount of money that consumers had to spend increased quite dramatically, especially when you're looking at that long of a time period. Second, when we think specifically about clothing over a much shorter period of time—from the 1980s to today, for instance—the real price of clothing relative to other goods has gone down quite a lot.

Really? How come?

In short, because of China. It's more complicated than *just* that, but the development of the worldwide sourcing and manufacturing of clothing has reduced the price of the typical garment quite significantly. Also, because of improvements in fabrics and laundry technologies, the quality of clothing has also improved, and clothes today have greater longevity. So that's the "how is this possible" answer. But I think the bigger question that you're asking is why we spend our money on so many clothes.

Correct.

The "why is it possible" question is very important. The people in the 1930s would have liked more clothes too, but for various reasons they couldn't afford them. Clothing, in particular, is very important in expressing who we are, because it's carried—it's worn—on the body.

So, people value their clothes, and they enjoy having options. They'll express this by saying things like, "Oh, I'm feeling *this way* today, so I can wear *this*." Or, "I'm going to this type of encounter—be it a job interview or a first date—and I want to wear *that outfit* instead of some other thing I don't feel as confident in." There is a value to having alternatives. When you go back to the era of very limited wardrobes, you realize that people didn't have the option of changing the signals their clothes sent.

Over the last twenty years, we've not only gotten more well-to-do, but clothing has become a lot less expensive to manufacture. There have also been changes in distribution that have allowed more people greater access to different varieties of clothing, whether that's on the very inexpensive end with stores like Wal-Mart, Target, and other discount stores, or through the more high-tech channels of distribution involving the various ways that people market over the Internet. So even if you live in a small town, you can now have access to all sorts of goods.

You mentioned that people have the ability to change the signals that their clothes send. Can you ever remember a time in our history where clothes didn't send some kind of a message?

No. Clothes have always sent signals. The difference today—in contrast to what's been true for most of our history—is that there's more of a cacophony of signals than there used to be. This isn't just because of economic factors that make it possible for us to have more clothing, it's also because of cultural changes that have broken apart the rules about the signals that clothing sends. The rules for what's proper and stylish are different now. So, if you went back to the 19th century and analyzed the very well-to-do, you would see that there were extremely elaborate codes delineating what could be worn for what occasion and even for what time of day. A Victorian woman was changing her clothes all the time. Also, there were a lot of signals being sent by those clothes that telegraphed her notions of propriety as well as her sense of personal identity.

The way that someone dresses today is still dictated by a personal sense of identity as well as one's own sense of style, pleasure, and comfort. It is dictated far less by social norms.

This is not to say that there are no social norms—there are. As a woman, you probably don't want to walk down the streets in Manhattan topless.

Are you kidding? I don't walk around my apartment topless!

And I'm not talking about the law, by the way! I'm talking about social norms. I write in my book *The Substance of Style* about the idea that visual appearance, whether we're talking about a person or a logo, sends two kinds of signals. The first signal states, "I'm like this as an individual, and this is the group that I fit in, so I share qualities with the members of that group. And I like that." The second is, "This is what gives me pleasure as an individual." So, when you have more clothes to choose from, you get more flexibility and you have the ability to make fine distinctions among the people you see—not only between individuals, but also between groups.

Why do you think we feel compelled to communicate who we are through the way we look?

I would say it's because human beings are both social and visual creatures. Our brains are highly developed to take in visual information and also highly developed to take in social cues. And we don't operate in isolation. These choices help us navigate our relationships with other people. There's also a certain amount of pleasure in experiencing them— even if no one sees you, even if it's just for yourself. But I would say the fundamental reasons have to do with navigating social relations.

You mentioned that a lot of these rules have "broken apart." Certainly, we're not changing clothes as much as we did during Victorian times. That being said, several years ago I went on a vacation with a friend who traveled with her teenage daughter. The daughter brought along twice as much luggage as the adults did and insisted on changing outfits several times a day. She found it thrilling to use her choices as costumes to transform herself for an event as benign as dinnertime. I don't know if that's a specifically teenage phenomenon, or if it describes someone who simply loves fashion.

I think it's a little of both. When I was a teenager in the 1970s, people didn't have enough clothes to be changing outfits like this all the time. But it does seem as if this generation has grown up with tremendous abundance and really enjoys taking advantage of it. I knew a teenager—this is going back a few years—who made a pact with her friends that they wouldn't wear the same outfit to school over the course of a whole year. They defined the "same outfit" as the same ensemble. They were allowed to use the same garments, but could reorganize or layer individual pieces to make a new outfit. They were taking advantage of the ability to combine different styles. I find it interesting to consider whether teens who grow up with this kind of behavior will still be thinking this way when they're forty.

There's an interesting riff on this that's gotten popularity online. A woman decided to wear the same black dress for a year but challenged herself to make it look unique every day. So she modifies the outfit by wearing different accessories, jewelry, and so on.

Sheena Matheiken's Uniform Project.

Exactly. What was interesting about the project was that it was also an exercise in creativity. "How can this basic look be different every single day?"

I find it incredibly fascinating. When I first saw the project, it reminded me of the way kids who wear school uniforms are able to individualize their outfits with kneesocks, jewelry, or hairstyles. They all look so unique, even in uniform! And it takes me back to the interesting tension between wanting to telegraph that you belong to a specific group while simultaneously communicating that "this is what gives me pleasure and makes me feel unique."

If you look at cultural subgroups, there is often a great deal of pleasure evidenced in "defined distinction"—the way that groups display their individuality. You can even have a fragmentation of the subgroup. A lot of subgroup communities are created based on creating clever plays with individual distinction.

But if you deconstruct it, and look at the various Goth, yuppie, or Harley-Davidson biker subgroups, there is still a behavior that I don't yet fully understand. I understand that we want to be able to telegraph who we are and what our affiliations are and what we believe in. But I'm still fascinated by the tremendous need that we seem to have in regard to developing kinship with others. I remember being very young and desperately wanting a pair of Levi's because I felt I would be able to project something about myself that I actually didn't feel. The Levi's would magically make me "cool."

So I wonder if we use these self-decreed amulets—a Harley-Davidson motorcycle, the latest Nike sneakers,

or the shiniest iPad—to telegraph some aspect of how
we want to be seen or recognized. Given how common
this tendency is, I wonder if it has something to do with
the very nature of being human.

There is certainly an aspirational quality to it, which can be about status, which we haven't talked about yet. Status is so often used as the one and only explanation for everything, which is why I tend to avoid it. But that doesn't mean it's not an influence on what's happening.

Status is definitely present as one of the determinants that shape what people are trying to communicate. The trick is not to confuse status with money, especially today, because there are different kinds of status hierarchies. And it's not as simple as perhaps it once was. In 1955, if you were concerned with status and fashion, you would have focused on showing that you were well-to-do, and standing out in that way. Whereas today, while that aspect of it might still be present, status is more about showing off your creativity and your cleverness, your eye and your discernment. Now the outward signs of status are often a combination of high art and low art. People are mixing clothes and accessories from the high status world of fashion and the perfect thrift store finds in extremely interesting ways.

The act of putting clothing on to become who you would like to be—as opposed to representing who you are—could be about status and signaling, but it can also be similar to the way a performer puts on a costume to become a character.

Your outside self projects something to the world and also reflects back into you. The image of you in specific attire helps you imagine yourself as the person you would like to be.

I think these projections allow you to imagine yourself transformed in some way. You are projecting outward and using what an economist would call "signaling"—the process of telling the world something about yourself. And this can be beneficial. Why do doctors wear white coats and why do soldiers wear uniforms? One reason is to allow that person to take on that identity, which includes their own sense of who they are, in a very fundamental way.

I was recently researching the history of flags and how we started using flags to signify where we came from. Originally, it was based on warfare. Flags on the battlefield signaled what side you were on.

Right. Literally, "Shoot here—don't shoot there."

This was before the mass manufacture of clothing when uniforms were not yet used on the battlefield. We needed uniforms to discern one human from another in order to determine who the enemy was.

Think about sports fans dressing up to go to a sporting event.

Or the fans who attend a sports event with their team's colors painted all over their faces. Why do people do this? Is it simply to signal team loyalty or does it have a deeper meaning behind it?

I think it's a combination of signaling which side you're on, like a flag would, and, in this particular case, the communal aspect of watching the game in person, with a group—versus on the television in your living room. You're not trying to lose yourself and become anonymous in a group; rather, you're seeking to become part of a larger group of fans on a particular side. The same thing happens when people go to concerts and either dress a particular way to emulate the band, or wear the band's merchandise.

As our rules are shifting, there seems to be a trajectory toward more risqué behavior as well. I never thought I would hear myself say that a popular female performer

could make Madonna look tame, but that is exactly
what Lady Gaga has done. For a long time, Madonna
was the epitome of edgy, bad behavior, which flew in
the face of what was acceptable "etiquette" for a female
rock star. And then Lady Gaga comes along and sets
a new benchmark for what is cutting-edge in popular
music. Before Madonna, we had Cher. Before Cher, we
had Josephine Baker and Mae West. In this case, why
does it seem that more and more exaggerated sexualized
female behavior continues to influence popular culture?

Well, this isn't exactly an answer, but there's an interesting contrast between Madonna and Lady Gaga. Lady Gaga does this all with a wink, and Madonna has always been deadly earnest about it. Madonna had a cultural agenda to break down rules and get everybody to talk about sex all the time. Whereas for Lady Gaga, it's more about spectacle and commedia dell'arte. She's playing a theatrical character as opposed to providing social commentary. There are times when she tried to provide social commentary—her efforts with the "don't ask, don't tell" repeal, for example, but it seems to me that even when she does this, it has a bit of a wink to it.

We live in a society where there is so much media, but what's scarce now is attention. The fundamental economic fact of contemporary society is that attention is scarce. So, how do you get attention? One way is to be outrageous. The problem is that over time, this becomes more and more difficult to maintain. We become habituated to the latest version of outrageousness.

Why is that? How did that happen?

Well, attention is necessarily limited. There are only twenty-four hours in a day, and your brain can only process so much information. You can pay attention to only so many things at any one time and throughout the day. And so, in some fundamental way, attention has always been limited. But now our attention is being further constrained, because there are so many things competing for it. Because of the explosion of media—which is largely an Internet-driven phenomenon—things, people, and voices continuously compete for your attention. There are an astounding number of avenues in which you can direct your attention, and there are so many vehicles of communication.

You have cell phone calls, texts, e-mails, and web links coming at you constantly. It's as if everybody lives in a high-speed, souped-up version of Times Square all the time, with words and colors and people flying around everywhere.

It's very hard to prioritize your activities and goals unless you're very disciplined.

But we also seem to enjoy the overstimulation quite a bit.

Many of the things we are engaging with online are interesting, and one link often leads to another. In some way, this behavior mimics daydreaming.

Really?

Not exactly in the way we use the word colloquially. The natural state of the brain is an associative state where one thing leads to another. Often these different meanderings are salient and need attention. Think about it: We could be talking about something, and I'll start out listening to you, and then you say something that reminds me that I need to go to the grocery store, and I start thinking about being in the grocery store, and then that reminds me of the last time I was in the grocery store and I ran into Susan, and so on and so forth.

This is the natural state of the brain. And it takes effort to pay attention to one thing and focus. So what we now have is a media environment that is like the natural state of the brain. It encourages that process of bouncing from one thing to another.

So the natural state of our mind is to be multitasking.

Well, it's not necessarily doing different things *simultaneously*. Perhaps "hyperlinked" might be a better way to describe it, because the mind goes from one thing to another. And this behavior tends to be driven by the things that do need our attention. So, how does anyone stand out in this environment, and what can you do to attract attention to what you think is important—whether that's to yourself as an individual, or to a cause, or a brand? It's much more difficult today than it was in a less-media-rich environment.

Do you think that the drive that humans have for fame or to get attention has changed over the last century?

What it means to be famous has changed. The idea that someone might become famous regardless of who they are is certainly new. On the one hand, literally a billion people or more could know you. There are not a lot of people who fall into that category, but there are some figures who are actually known worldwide. And there are more people in that group than just the pope and world leaders—they're not necessarily in categories that existed one hundred years ago.

But at the same time, the idea of being famous by becoming well-known to people who have never met you has become more and more accessible and simultaneously more deluded. It's one thing to be Yao Ming, but it's another thing to be Virginia Postrel.

What do you mean?

Some years ago, my niece asked her mother, "Is Aunt Virginia famous?" When I spoke with her, I told her, "No, not really." But, on the other hand, there are a lot of people who have never met me who know who I am, and this group probably numbers in the tens of thousands on a good day. That's the kind of fame that didn't exist until fairly recently in human history. The idea that a person who is not born into some royal family could be known by tens of thousands of people was very unlikely. Now, there are many, many people who are known by tens of thousands of people they've never met.

It seems that the quest for fame has become as much of an obsession as the fame itself.

Right. That this has happened only in the last ten years is very much a function of reality television shows. It used to be that you did something that made you famous, and then you could parlay that fame into being on television, and that would get you more money. Now, if you can get well-known enough—even if it's just well-known for being a nut—this becomes a financial asset. "Being known" is something that you can use to generate a significant amount of income in the future.

Do you think the desire to be famous today is more about financial gain than it is about being acknowledged for doing something culturally significant?

I think there is an underlying desire to be known and acknowledged. And there are actually some things happening on reality shows that go beyond the appeal of watching a train wreck. The shows also evoke a type of glamour for a certain portion of the audience that imagines being known and acknowledged. They promote the idea that your ordinary, everyday life could somehow be interesting to other people. But it's also true that you can parlay being known into a considerable income-generating asset—if you handle the process correctly.

But I don't think everybody who strives to be on a reality show is doing it because they want to be famous in the way that we might have thought of fame in the past, or even the way the audience thinks of fame. I think a lot of people believe, "I'll get my show, then I'll start my line of purses, and I'll do my personal appearances. I'll have a company, a company of me." This is literally what Paris Hilton did. She didn't even need to work, and now she has a business being Paris Hilton.

So, it's not about being famous for "nothing"—it's about being famous for being who you are.

Exactly. At the moment, one of the great puzzles in contemporary politics is Sarah Palin. Is she a celebrity or is she a politician? She is somebody who has taken this brand—the "Sarah Palin brand"—and she's been playing it both ways. If she runs for president, she'll have to be a politician and not so much a celebrity. But she's got celebrity traction that I don't think she wants to give up. Which is very different from Arnold Schwarzenegger or Ronald Reagan, who were celebrities first, and then became politicians later.

When Reagan and Schwarzenegger became politicians, they actually seemed to rein in their "personal" brands.

Exactly. I think if Palin really runs for president in a serious way, she would have to be less of a celebrity and more of a conventional politician. But right now, she's able to do both, which is fascinating, and unique to our moment.

But what are political parties? Maybe what's different in our time is how our perspective on parties has changed. The parties were once the brands, and these identities were fixed: "You're the Democrat." "You're the Republican." People voted straight-party tickets. In one sense, the politician is the brand more than the party is today. It's similar to the way that a journalist is the brand more than the newspaper.

A brand is a promise of a certain kind of consistency and continuity over time. But that's very different if you're talking about a long-standing brand like Gold Medal flour or a newer brand like Nike or Apple. What is the promise of Gold Medal flour? The promise is that it's consistent, it's reliable, but it's still flour. Whenever I talk about brands, I always start by talking about Gold Medal flour. It's important to remember that mass consumer brands began as a way of assuring basic quality. But it's no longer valuable to think about brands in that way, because we have so much quality in the choices available to us now in the United States.

Today, value is less about brand attributes, and more about brand meaning.

Brands like Nike or Apple associate themselves with a lot of cultural benefits in addition to promising consumers certain brand attributes. And that's where conscious branding comes in: How do you make these cultural benefits cool at a given moment?

It seems like the whole notion of consciously making something cool would immediately disqualify it from being cool.

Exactly. It's the art that conceals the art. I think there's an element of magic to it, and it's very hard to do consciously. It tends to be more organic when it truly happens. So, for example, what makes Apple products cool? Ultimately, it originates from the taste and the aesthetics of Steve Jobs and the organization that expresses his sensibilities. But this is a very tenuous situation, because he can't live forever, and there are a lot of people who are worried about that. The people at Apple will have to figure out how to embed his DNA into the company. Over time, organizations can take on the founder's DNA. It doesn't happen often, but it can happen.

Quality and brand attributes are still important particularly in places like China or Brazil.

Last spring, I went to Shanghai, and while I was there, I got my nails done. I brought along my own bottle of OPI nail polish, and the woman in the nail salon wanted to compare her bottle of OPI to mine so she could see if she was getting the real thing, and to make sure that her bottle wasn't counterfeit. And in fact she did have the real thing.

The notion of a counterfeit brand is fascinating. People want so badly to project the image associated with a certain brand, so it doesn't matter that the product they're using to project that image is actually a "lie." So a fraudulent projection is being perpetuated through a counterfeit totem.

Right. A counterfeit item is about projecting status, and status is equated with income. However, imagine a style created by a famous designer. Then imagine a knockoff of that style that has no tags or labels of identification. The items simply have the same form. The unidentified item would still project something about who you are, what you're drawn to, and what you associate with "your eye," even if nobody thought it was the "original." But, the interesting thing is, it does still conjure those same associations. It really does.

Bruce Duckworth

Partner, Turner Duckworth

Along with his partner David Turner, Bruce Duckworth runs Turner Duckworth, a design and branding firm that has worked on an intriguing array of projects—from a CD for the band Metallica to a brand redesign for Coca-Cola graphics, the firm has crafted seminal work in a diverse range of arenas.

Duckworth is one of those rare people who is sharply inventive in impromptu conversation. I loved his explanation of the difference between advertising and branding, which he improvised on the spot during our discussion. He also has an intuitive feel for the palpable aspect of brands—"the part you pick up, the bit you touch, the bit you wear"—and his enthusiasm for this is infectious. He enjoys the associations and hidden meanings that people find in his designs, both intended and imagined. His fluency with visual language is beautifully complemented by his penchant for creating compelling metaphors, as he does when he draws parallels between design and method acting.

There were some surprises in this interview— one of the biggest that Turner Duckworth makes a point of listening to clients, to the extent of enlisting them to have a significant influence on the final design. This might run counter to a more single-minded approach to design, but Duckworth defers to the ultimate goal: "Our objective is not to get an award-winning design into the market," he says. "Our objective is to sell more stuff for our clients. That's why we're in business."

In this interview, Duckworth talks about the extraordinary pleasure of working on that rarest but most coveted of projects—the redesign of the Coca-Cola graphics. His firm's approach to that project seems emblematic. The graphics had become too frilly, so Duckworth et al. stripped them down to their essentials, expressing the Coke brand with the visual elements that were solely unique to it.

Duckworth brings both acumen and joy to his design work. He clearly takes great pleasure in the work that he does, and he searches to find the joy in the projects he's working on and in the design he experiences. His reflections on the role of wit in design speak to that affinity, and it's evident that his attunement to this has made him a connoisseur of it. For Duckworth, wit is a way of creating layers of discovery and meaning that engage consumers. They might not get it the first time they see the design, but as they come to know the product and its visual language better, the wit becomes more evident, and through that process, consumers develop a deeper connection with the brand. Duckworth's philosophy is a testament to his sensitivity as a designer and his own restraint in design—he knows when not to try too hard and how to make the design subtle enough to be appreciated but not so brash as to be obvious.

There is something very British in Duckworth's enthusiasm for understatement, and, indeed, I found similarities between him and fellow Brit Wally Olins. Both have a wonderful sense of humor and play. Both convey exuberance and a hearty enjoyment of conversation. In his assessment of branding and its machinations, Duckworth echoes Olins's critique, acknowledging the value of market research but emphasizing that it shouldn't be used to evaluate design revisions.

In reflecting on the role of wit and design, Duckworth says, "Every time I see a logo, a piece of packaging, or any piece of brand design with wit, it makes me think, 'I like these people.'" That statement is equally relevant in describing his own work. Duckworth's design oeuvre and reflections have that same quality of wit. Both he and his work are hard not to like.

Bruce, why have you spent most of your career working in the world of branding?

Actually, I think I always wanted to do advertising.

Really?

Yes. When I was in college, advertising was definitely my passion—I thought it was sexy and brilliant.

How on earth did you go from advertising to package design?

When I left college, I couldn't see how I could run my own advertising agency, but I *could* envision how to run a design company. Honestly, what was going on in the world of package design at that time was not great, and I thought there was a lot of room for improvement.

A lot of people get confused between advertising and branding. How would you describe the difference?

Branding is an experience, and advertising is a temptation.
How about that?

Did you just make that up on the spot?

I did. I just made it up.

That's really good.

Branding leads to an ownership, one that has a touchy-feely aspect to it. Advertising is more distant.

How is it more distant?

It offers a promise, but it doesn't actually give you the product. Whereas design is the part you pick up, the bit you touch, the bit you wear. People have a more intimate relationship with brands than they do with advertising.

Have you always had a special affinity for brands?

I think that we all have a relationship with brands. However much you try, you can't really avoid it. Brands are in everybody's world. That's what makes the work exciting. If you design an iconic global brand, billions of people will have that experience.

And I'm a real sucker. I believe what my clients tell me. If they tell me this spread is going to reduce my cholesterol, then I believe it, and I go and eat it. I'm a complete convert. It's like the school of method acting, where you live the part. It's a good thing I don't work for car companies, or else I'd own lots of cars.

So you drink a lot of Coca-Cola.

Well—unfortunately, no. I drink Diet Coca-Cola. It's much better for you. But, yes, I do. Absolutely, I do. I love it.

While we're on the topic, can you talk about the redesign of Coca-Cola? What was it like to redesign one of the world's most well-known icons?

I couldn't stop smiling. The first time you get that Spencerian script logo on your desk, you cannot quite believe it. You think, "Hang on—this is the most famous logo in the world." It was an honor, an absolute privilege.

How do you even start working on a brand like that? How do you know what to do?

The brief was all about simplification. The existing design was appropriate for the time it was designed, but it needed to be refreshed.

Too many bubbles?

Too many bubbles and too much effervescence and too many colors and drop shadows. It came from a world of design embellishment.

Why was simplicity the goal?

Coca-Cola is the real thing—it's authentic. It was the first, and it is the best. Everything else on the package was a generic element that other brands could use in their designs. So it seemed that the way to convey Coca-Cola as the authentic, original beverage was to remove all of the generic elements that anyone else could borrow. Why did Coke need bubbles on the can? Who in the world doesn't know Coca-Cola is a bubbly drink?

Was it difficult to persuade Coca-Cola management to approve a design that was much more simple?

There were some very, very strong client advocates who were in favor of simplifying the design. And I would say that 70 percent of the work we showed in our first presentation made it through to the design that is now on the shelf.

That's remarkable. How do you avoid having your clients interfere in the quality of the work as you're finishing it or as you're taking it to market?

My partner, David, and I often talk about this. We strongly believe that a lot of the reason our work looks like it does is because clients have a big hand in the design decision making. We're not the type of firm that stands on a windowsill and threatens to jump if a client doesn't buy our concept. We actually prefer to have a very inclusive process. A lot of the work that you see out there has been influenced significantly by our clients. Their influence is what makes the work more believable, better, and more real.

Really? You really let clients have that much influence—and don't mind it?

Yes. Honestly, that is true. And the work is actually better for it. The clients know their business so well—why wouldn't you listen to them? Our objective is not to get an award-winning design into the market. Our objective is to sell more stuff for our clients. That's why we're in business.

But we also want to do great work. We're like little tenacious terriers. We keep badgering our clients and trying to make sure that the design is absolutely correct. However much they influence it, we make sure it's correct. I think it's due to the influence Mary Lewis had on me when I worked at Lewis Moberly. Mary Lewis is a brilliant designer, without question. She is a fantastic art director—she is intelligent and fastidious—and she had a huge impact on the way that we design. She always said to never let a piece of work go out that you're not proud of. You might have a favorite, but if none of it is "bad work," you'll be proud of anything that goes to market.

I've always maintained that if you come into our studio, you should be able to open any of the drawers or look at any of the work that we've done, and I would be proud of every single piece of work. The quality would always be there.

You said your objective is to sell more stuff for your clients. Do you ever worry about that—about the endeavor to sell more stuff?

No, it doesn't worry me at all. People don't buy stuff they don't want. I imagine they stop buying the stuff that isn't very good.

When I look at your portfolio, whether the work is for brands such as Waitrose or Coca-Cola, I see a certain element that I could describe as cleverness. But I really feel like it's something more. Or maybe I'm just looking into it too deeply.

Actually, I love people like you. I feel like one of those artists who've written a song, and then people find their own meaning in it.

Some people look at Joy Division covers—I look at boxes of cookies.

Wit is absolutely key to what we do. Wit provides depth and soul. It gives evidence of humanity.

Every time I see a logo, a piece of packaging, or any piece of brand design with wit, it makes me think, "I like these people." It looks like the brand's smiling at you. It's welcoming you in.

Why do you think humans respond so well to that? We're talking about a product, after all. It's not a person.

In this age of mass production, it's the closest you're going to get to meeting the people who made the product.

And why do you think that's important? Do you think that really matters?

I think it has something to do with the sociability of our species. We love wit, and we love the interaction it inspires in people. I recently did a talk in Brussels. I was talking about wit, and a man approached me afterward. He told me that considering all the Europeans there who spoke different languages, at least half of the people in the audience didn't have a word for "wit" in their vocabulary.

I discovered that they have "funny" and "humor," but they don't have "wit," which is halfway between "serious" and "funny." And I thought about how interesting that distinction is, because people don't want to buy funny stuff. Rarely is there an appropriate time to use a joke on a piece of design, or in a piece of branding. But wit is a very acceptable way of including a little touch of warmth and emotion.

Over time, we want people to get all the ideas that we put into our work. But this process of understanding is like a slightly slow-burning fuse. As the immediate reaction from any piece of branding design that we do, we want people to understand what the point of the purchase is—what the brand message is. And then after that, we want them to discover a little bit more, and a little bit more, and a little bit more. Now, wit is very much in that second or third level, and I think all cleverness, or whatever you want to call it, isn't immediate—because who wants to buy a clever piece of design? No one really wants to buy that. They want to buy a product that's going to work. But the engagement and the wit come in that second, tertiary level of the experience.

The wit isn't going to stop a person from buying something. On the other hand, maybe there's a lot of packaging design out there that tries just a little bit too hard. And if you don't get it, if you don't get the idea, or the "joke"—if it doesn't whack you in the chops—then the company doesn't make the sale. And I think that's a shame, because you really don't need to work that hard to make this kind of strategy effective. The process of discovery is such a great way of engaging your audience, and your customers will figure out the different layers as they get to know the brand better.

What about market research? Is that something you feel is worthwhile when redesigning a brand?

We like research, but we believe it should be done correctly. Research is inevitable, but it's often used in the wrong way. When it's used at the end of a project, and consumers are asked to choose a design as if they were judging a beauty contest, it's a disaster. The focus-group scenarios that people are put in are often so inappropriate and so alien to the way people normally make decisions about what they're going to buy. Furthermore, it's not really up to consumers to make those kind of design choices, because they tend to evaluate things based on what they've known in the past, and they don't look at the design in light of what your goal is.

Do you think that design really matters to consumers?

Yes. Yes, definitely. It definitely matters to consumers, without question. Design gets into your psyche. People buy the Nike products because of the Nike swoosh, and the design of the logo, and the design of the overall brand. Yes, it matters hugely to people. For some consumers, it almost becomes a replacement for religion.

Why do you think that happens?

I think it has to do with the process of self-discovery and finding other people or brands that believe in the same things you do. It almost becomes a moral code that you've got to follow.

Moral codes and religion—that gives us a good segue:
What was it like working with Metallica on the design
of the band's album and the identity work that went
along with it?

It was brilliant fun.

Can you talk about the process and how it happened?
How did they come to you—how did they reach you?

The band is based in San Francisco, and when David took his children to a new school, there was a "buddy parent" assigned to show him the ropes at the school. David's buddy parent was the drummer of Metallica.

Nice!

David knew of Metallica, but he didn't know Lars Ulrich, the drummer, at all. Over time, they built up a good friendship, and after about four or five years, the band started working on a new album. Lars loves design and art, and he was very interested in our business and our studio. He asked us to design the cover, and David was initially reticent about it. He was concerned about mixing business with pleasure. But Lars was very keen. The process we went through was actually the same process most of our clients go through. We got a brief, and then we answered the brief, conducted some presentations, and made amendments and developments—we worked in a very similar way that we do with all of our clients.

And of course it was very liberating to do design work that focused on an emotional area—"death"—we hadn't gone into before. Normally, we just do nice things.

Death?

Yes, the album title was *Death Magnetic*. We had to investigate a world we had never investigated before, but we still managed to get wit and cleverness into it.

And you also won a Grammy Award.

Yes, that was a real surprise. We got a phone call one day saying, "You are nominated for a Grammy." That was hilarious.

Maybe it's just my perception—and I might be revealing something about myself when I ask you this question—but is there something a bit sexual about the image on the cover?

I think you're revealing an awful lot about yourself. It has been mentioned, but it certainly wasn't the intention. But if that is what you construe, then let your mind run wild. We told the band at some point that the cover might be seen to have a slightly sexual nature, and they said, "Great!" So I don't think they were worried about that in the slightest.

Please tell me that you didn't do any market research with this.

No, we didn't. I think we asked the band if they liked it, and they said "Yes," and then it was printed.

Every now and then I get a chain e-mail about
hidden meanings in logos, and I usually receive it from
somebody who's not in the design business. One of these
messages referenced the Amazon logo, which Turner
Duckworth redesigned. Apparently someone thought
that the arrow pointing from the a to the z in the logo
was a hidden message, instead of being a visual device
that was intended.

> Yes, it was intended. Brilliant, isn't it? To have *a* to *z*
> in the middle of the word, as part of the design—
> it's fantastic.

Yes, it is. But I guess people mostly see it as an arrow
and as a smile.

> A smile that goes from *a* to *z*.

Was that element on the original Amazon packaging
from the beginning?

> No. The original mark was a similar piece of
> typography, but it contained a yellow underline in
> the shape of a frown. There wasn't a huge amount
> of publicity around the redesign—it was actually
> a very quiet relaunch. A lot of people didn't even
> realize the logo had been redesigned.
>   But that's exactly the function of wit, isn't it,
> when we find ourselves reading things into logos? It
> would've been nice if people discovered this earlier
> than eight years after the redesign. It's such a shame
> that that goes on.

I wish designers would be optimists about change. Unfortunately, most aren't.

Why is that?

> I think it's because about 98 percent of all the work
> we do is rejected. It's a very wasteful process. If you
> think about all the concepts that don't get through,
> you think we would be used to rejection. Also, as a

designer, the first thing you tend to look for is the problem.

Given the fact that designers are subjected to so much rejection, is it ironic that a designer's knee-jerk reaction is to reject any new design?

Yes. But I think that's what we're always looking for as designers. We're always looking for the problem. Once we see the problem, we feel compelled to correct it. But I wish we could see the good side. Because when change occurs, we may as well celebrate it.

David Butler

Vice President of Design,
Coca-Cola Company

As the vice president of design at Coca-Cola, Butler
has an influence on culture that is unparalleled. He
is the design ambassador to an audience of billions.
Imagining the present and future of the Coca-Cola
brand, he is both a brand guardian and a brand
visionary: He ensures the continuity of Coke's design
legacy and simultaneously conjures the brand's future.
He shapes the experiences that consumers will have
when they interact with Coca-Cola and its family
of brands.

Butler is an advocate for the importance of
design strategy and has been working to make design
integral to the company culture and infrastructure—
which it wasn't when he arrived at the company in
1994. Butler's experience searching Coca-Cola's archive
is itself revelatory in that regard. When he asked Coke's
archivist about the company's design history, the
archivist responded, "What do you mean by 'design'?"

As part of his responsibilities, Butler has
become intimately familiar with key milestones of
Coca-Cola's design history. He's become well-versed
in the interplay between business, brand, and design.
He's seen the original brief that led to the creation of
the iconic contour bottle. He's pored through Coke's
history, looking at everything from vintage point-
of-sale materials to a clothing brand Coke started.
All of this helps him to consider the way that design
influenced and defined the brand's success.

In seeking to maintain Coke's visual integrity, Butler noticed that the design of the Coke can had become too frilly—too frivolous. He led to the initiative to simplify its design. He's also led the effort to transform and modernize Coca-Cola's vending machines so that they become 21st-century multimedia experiences of their own. The new machines, equipped with screens, provide Coke with yet another platform to connect with consumers. They are a model for the way that brands must seek to engage customers at every touchpoint possible.

Coca-Cola, as Butler observes, plays a very significant role in people's lives. It is an icon present at key moments and transitions in the life narratives of millions of people. It is an avatar of democracy, freedom, optimism, and economic growth. All those associations are essential to Coke's success, which means that the brand legacy must be carefully shepherded into the future. Yet if it's not carefully tended, the brand could easily become stale, or—in a worst-case scenario—shunned. Butler is very conscious that the challenge for Coca-Cola is to be simultaneously familiar yet surprising. He balances on the razor-edge between innovation and brand continuity. Butler's vision is to create a brand that allows Coca-Cola to "design the future that we want to have."

Why did you decide to become a graphic designer?

I have three daughters—nine, six, and four—and the other day, one of them asked me what I recall wanting to be when I was their age, and I told them exactly what I remembered. I wanted to be a dentist. Now, to go from dentistry to design may be a stretch, but in looking back, I realized that what fascinated me about the world of medicine was its system of interrelationships. You can't work on one tooth without considering the whole mouth, its history, its hygiene, and so forth. I've always been fascinated with systems involving people, organizations, and environments.

So in the beginning, it was all about teeth.

I can't really explain that one. Now that I'm thinking about it, I remember being ten or twelve years old, and there was a poster competition in my school in which we had to promote dental health. We needed to communicate that the path to happiness involved brushing and flossing your teeth. I designed a poster for the contest, and it won. From that time on, I thought, "Wow, I can do this!"

Years later, I went to college in Tampa and spent a lot of time studying Marshall McLuhan. After graduating, I worked at a small design firm. During the mid-'90s, this thing called the "World Wide Web" captivated me. The typical assessment at the time was that this new form of media was simply a fad, and it would pass. But being the brash person who I was, I decided to start my own design firm with a few friends so we could find out. We designed the first streaming radio and video player on CNN.com. Our little firm started growing. I had big aspirations, but my partners didn't. I decided to sell them my share of the business and joined Studio Archetype to work on building digital brands with Clement Mok. It was an incredibly exciting time to be alive and to be a designer.

You worked in the strategic planning role when you were at Studio Archetype. Did you start first as a strategist and then work as a designer, or were you always a bit of both?

Debbie, I was always a brilliant thinker! I'll tell you how it happened. My time at Studio Archetype was during the rise and fall of the dot-com bubble. I became fascinated with the opportunity to rethink business models and rethink how people interact with companies and brands. My fascination developed to the point where I didn't want to do design anymore. I lost interest in winning design awards and looking cool. I hated that small way of thinking about design. So I went to Clement and asked him if I could start a consulting group inside the company. He gave me the opportunity to do that, and I formally moved out of the design function. But what I realized was that the thinking remained the same. You can call it "design," or you can call it "design thinking," but to me, it's the same.

What would you say is the most important thing you learned from Clement?

Clement Mok has the most intuitive—almost religious—understanding of user-centered design. That's why I wanted to work there. What he taught me still influences everything I work on now.

Tell me a little more about user-centered design. How would you explain that to someone who'd never heard the term before?

User-centered design is about creating systems that are intuitive, inevitable, and quite natural. This is very hard to do. It has to be something intentional—something you do through an act of creativity yet that feels completely inevitable when it's finished.

*Can you give me some examples of how you're trying to
use more intentional, user-centered design in the work
you're doing at Coca-Cola?*

One example is our vending machines. A vending
machine is a pretty benign object, right? For as long
as I can remember, vending machines have been
pretty innocuous—they've been in the background
of most people's lives. So we took that as a challenge
and looked at how we could actually use those
vending machines to create a whole new experience.

At Coca-Cola, our vending business is
primarily in two markets: North America and
Japan. About 60–70 percent of our sales in Japan
are done through vending machines. Japan is one of
our top ten markets, so it's quite significant for our
business. Yet, as I said, the vending machine itself is
a pretty benign experience.

So we wondered, how could we redesign
that in a very cost-effective way? And rather than
redesign the whole machine, we asked ourselves if
we could redesign a piece of it to create a modular
element that could snap on to what we already had.
So, essentially, we decided to redesign the door. We
redesigned the door and the interface to include a
forty-four-inch touch screen monitor that can display
any kind of digital content that we create. As you can
imagine, we create a lot of digital content in the form
of advertising and other things, so these monitors
created a whole new media channel for us. Not only
does it vend products—you still put money in and
get a Coke out of it—but it actually created a whole
new communication channel for us. We completely
redesigned the whole interface of the machine, which
includes the way you do the transactions, where you
put your money, and how you get the product—as
well as how you make your selection and how you
interface with the machine in general.

So when we put that vending machine in a
mall or similar venue, it creates a dramatic new

experience and has led to double-digit increases in sales volumes. And it's created a whole new connection platform for teenagers who we're always trying to encourage to fall in love with our brand.

Coke has certainly been much adored by consumers even before these new interfaces debuted. That leads to my next question: Why do you think people fall in love with brands?

I think people love brands that play a critical role in their lives or that help them form their identity. This is the case with Coke everywhere around the world. From Africa to India, people describe Coke as their favorite "national brand." But Coke is international; it's global. It's no single country's brand, but people everywhere consider it their favorite national brand. This is utterly fascinating to me.

Why do you think this is the case? There has to be more to it than the fact that people think it tastes good.

I think it's because the brand plays a role in their culture.

How so?

In India, everything is growing at a hyper speed. We play a role in the lives of our customers in India that is completely different from the role we play in North America. That's by design, but it is very difficult to do.

Can you be more specific about the role that the brand plays for customers in India?

We refer to it as "freedom within a framework." We come up with an idea we can scale, and then we tailor and customize that idea for a local market. In a macro sense, Coke stands for optimism. We intend for it to be the most optimistic brand on the planet. Everything we do in relation to Coke is intended to bring optimism to whatever the company touches—people, our portfolio, and our customers. But the way that's experienced is different in each market. It means different things in different countries and markets.

How did you arrive at "optimism"? Was it something you planned, and wanted the brand to achieve? Or do you feel that you discovered this expression of the brand while analyzing your consumer?

That's a great question, and it has a complicated answer. In terms of the way you've framed it, our process involves elements of both. Coke has been around for 125 years, and we're constantly working to maintain the connective equities of the brand. People connect over a Coke, and with a Coke, in numerous ways. Connections and optimism are two equities that Coke owns and has owned for many, many years. So the challenge is to continue to maintain our equity but to create a sense of surprise around it as well.

We actually have a design principle that helps us to achieve this. We want to be utterly familiar— we want people to know that everything we create is Coke, and to expect the same high quality that they've gotten for years. But we know if we do this in a repetitive way, we become as invisible as wallpaper: where we're everywhere but nowhere at once. The challenge in developed markets is to be continually surprising. So we have to consider, how do we do that? How do we say that? How do we allow you to experience the brand in a new way?

Our vending machine redesign is a great example of this. It's just a vending machine—a technology that, by now, has been around forever—but by creating the touch screen display and pumping digital content through it, it becomes surprising. That's where our design principle comes to bear.

How is it that after 125 years, Coke is still one of the
biggest brands on the planet?

One reason is quality. We go to great pains to maintain the same taste, the same flavor profile—which is our secret formula—around the world. When you drink Coke in Thailand, it tastes the same as it does in North America or Mexico.

You must go to great lengths to achieve this, because
water is one of the ingredients in Coke, and water
tastes differently everywhere.

Exactly. We have incredibly high standards for everything, whether we're talking about the temperature of our products, the design of our packaging, or the recipe of the product inside. This is how we've been able to maintain our brand status for so long.

Do you ever personally worry about being unable to
fulfill the promise of the brand in any of the creative
work that you do?

Every day. It's a huge responsibility to carry the weight of the brand's equity. A lot of people ask me, "What's your favorite thing about working at Coke? And what's the thing you like the least about working at Coke?" I have the same answer for both questions: scale. When you take advantage of our scale, we can sell a lot more Coke. But this can work in reverse as well. The scale that we operate in is like no other, so a misstep in our design can have a big impact on us. We hear a lot of talk now about brands that are design-driven, like Apple and Nike, but even those companies don't approach our size. We operate locally in 206 countries. A quarter of the Earth's population drinks something from our company every day.

Are you bothered by people who criticize the brand for being unhealthy?

Actually, quite the opposite. Think about our scale— we have a brand portfolio of five hundred brands. That's not products, that's brands. We have three thousand products and five hundred brands. **To be honest, the thing that keeps me up at night is how to build Minute Maid, Dasani, or Sprite into icons like Coke.** That's actually a much bigger challenge.

You mentioned before that you consider yourself to be a brash person. Do you bring that brashness to your work?

I'm not really brash. I've found that brashness doesn't work inside of a large environment like this. Collaboration is essential. Design is a team sport. It's not about one person. You have to work with people, with teams. Nothing brash or personality-driven works well inside this environment. We focus on building a design-driven capability, not personal reputations.

I certainly didn't bring this notion to the organization. When I was first invited to join Coke, the company was in the midst of turmoil. It was 2004, the stock price was very low, and the company had a very complicated portfolio as well as a very complicated operational model. It was at that time that the senior leadership wanted to try to regain the competitive edge the organization had historically had because of design, and they created a "vice president of design" position. When I arrived, I was given a tremendous amount of support, but I quickly realized that there was no infrastructure or culture around design. So, for the last six years, I've been a consultant, a practitioner, and a teacher of design. I've used every metaphor, every illustration, and many, many examples to continually articulate the value of design.

*What was the first thing you did to try to ignite a
culture of design?*

I went to the archives. The archives here are
quite vast.

I can only imagine!

Ah, but you'd be surprised what the material is
and how it's organized. In this company, we sell
brands; we don't sell design. This company is
focused on driving shareholder value, not winning
design awards. As a designer living in a very small
community—in the sense that design was not a major
focus at Coca-Cola before I came here—entering this
very large system is daunting. You can get lost in the
culture that is the Coca-Cola Company. So I went to
the archives and I asked our archivist, Phil Mooney,
"If I were to learn about design, where would I
start?" And he responded, "Well, what do you mean
by 'design'?" So I changed my approach and asked
about packaging, the role of the contour bottle, the
point-of-sale materials, and the posters. I asked him
to tell me about the clothing line Coca-Cola started
in the '80s. Through this process of learning about
the business, I began to see how design affected
and impacted the organization. Applying what I
know about design to the context of business—as
opposed to the other way around—has been the most
challenging aspect of this job.

*Is it true that the original Coca-Cola bottle was
designed so that if you opened up an icebox in the
middle of the night, you could find it by feeling the
unique contour shape of the bottle? Or is that an
urban myth?*

It's true! There was actually a design brief—and
it included two objectives: One, they wanted a
package that was so unique and so differentiated
that you could find it in the dark. The second was
even more surprising.

They wanted glass that was so distinctive that even when it was shattered on the ground, you could still tell that it was once a Coke bottle.

This design emerged in 1916, when a packaged beverage was a relatively new thing and Coke was trying to expand a small regional Southern brand into a national brand. At the time, there were two ways that the product was sold—through fountain sales and through individual prepackaged purchases. Considering those two options in the marketplace, the decision was made to create a truly differentiated package. That was the design thinking back then! All of these decisions were intended to drive the business, to create a national brand and a national business.

During that same decade, Coca-Cola also designed the first franchise system. No one had ever designed a franchise system or a chain store before. We take all of this for granted now, but it didn't exist before Coca-Cola created it.

As I perused through the archives, I found this incredible, magical decade from 1910–1920. So I started telling that original story, and people got incredibly excited and inspired by it.

When you were in the process of the redesign, was it hard to convince the marketers within your organization to take the images of bubbles off the pack? The bubbles had been a consistent feature on the packaging for a long time.

That was definitely a challenge.

How did you persuade them to do it?

I kept reiterating our goal: to design a 21st-century version of our beloved icon. The need for simplicity was implicit. We went deeper and deeper into the archives and kept proving the historical leadership, and significance, in the use of red, the Spencerian script, and the bottle.

*This is a brand that has endured for 125 years. I read
that the top three brands on Facebook are Starbucks,
Coca-Cola, and Skittles. After 125 years, Coke is a
leader in a brand-new medium! What makes this brand
such a beloved part of our culture?*

I'll share my personal view on this. I'm about to
move to Mexico City on a six-month assignment,
and I've been spending a lot of time learning
Spanish and studying Mexican culture. Mexico is
one of Coca-Cola's top ten markets. On a per capita
basis, every person in Mexico drinks three Coca-
Colas per day. And after all these years, the brand is
still growing volumetrically. You can't help but step
back and say, "Gosh, how does that happen? Every
person in Mexico?" Again, I think it has to do with
maintaining high standards of quality, but also with
playing a significant role in people's lives. There are
certain aspects of the company that we don't talk
much about but that help to explain this.

Historically, we've been there for people
when they've needed us most. Again, we don't talk
about this a lot, but whenever there is a national
disaster—whether it be a hurricane or a tsunami—
we immediately stop production of everything
except water, and we distribute it all for free. We
have the biggest distribution network in the world.
We have more trucks on the road than FedEx, DHL,
and UPS combined. So whenever we help people,
we can do that in a way that no other company can.

*But do you really think that's why the people in Mexico
are drinking three Cokes a day? Why are they drinking
three Cokes a day as opposed to three Pepsis or three
Dr Peppers? Why do people love Coke? Back in the 1980s,
when New Coke was about to be launched, my father
became so worried about losing "his brand" that he went
and stockpiled as many bottles of Coca-Cola as he could
find. I remember driving around with him going from
store to store and collecting cases of Coca-Cola to keep in*

*our basement. What is it about this brand that reaches so
deep into somebody's heart and takes hold of it?*

On a completely practical level, it tastes better. And
on an emotional level, people associate Coke with
the special moments in their lives that they want to
share with other people. As I said earlier, it represents
optimism. It's hard to explain, but we have all these
established facts that I could share with you—such
as the fact that people associate the contoured bottle
with democracy, with higher ideals of freedom and
optimism, and with economic growth. My challenge
is to help maintain that by, and with, design.

*You've said that Coca-Cola is one of the world's largest
design companies. That statement reminded me of
something I heard from a very senior executive at
McDonald's during a conference many years ago. He
said that he didn't consider McDonald's to be a fast-
food company—he considered it to be an entertainment
company because people go to McDonald's to be happy
and to experience good feelings. Is there something
specific about Coca-Cola that brings you to consider it
one of the world's largest design companies?*

It depends on how you define the word "design."
If you look at all of the problems in front of us, and
you consider the power and the opportunities that
corporations, companies, and brands like Coke have,
it isn't hard to realize that we have the resources,
we have the reach, we have the distribution, the
networks, the people, and the wherewithal to design
the future that we want to have. As a designer and
as a person who thinks about design in this more
ambitious way, my hope is that we can leverage the
opportunities we have to not only build our business,
but also to change the world.

Stanley Hainsworth

*Chief Creative Officer, Tether;
Former Vice President Global
Creative, Starbucks; Former
Creative Director, Nike*

*Stanley Hainsworth has been a catalyst for the great
brands of modern times. He was creative director
at Nike and then Lego. He was vice president global
creative at Starbucks in an era when the coffee
purveyor was experiencing phenomenal growth.
Starbucks has been hailed, acknowledged, and
praised again and again for its excellence in branding
and marketing, in creating a branded experience that
can satisfy the connoisseur, bring in new converts,
be accessible to all, and irresistible in its appeal.
Stanley defined the very feel of Starbucks in an era
when the brand was becoming a cultural icon.*

*Stanley has a reputation for being extremely
rigorous in his work, comprehensively rethinking
brands when necessary, and helping them to expand
into new areas of endeavor while remaining true to
their original identity. As he had done at Nike, he
helped Lego expand into entertainment properties
that allowed the company to gracefully enter the
brand multiverse. At Starbucks, he created an
innovative criteria of five filters—handcrafted, artistic,
sophisticated, human, and enduring—that defined
the work for the company. Stanley's extraordinarily
thorough approach to design and branding is
complemented by an equally good nature; he has been a
revered colleague and mentor at the companies where
he worked.*

With such an extraordinary range of experience, Stanley has become ever more articulate about how brands work, and he has now devoted himself at Tether to invigorating existing brands and crafting new ones. Having guided brands at companies that have gone through dramatic growth spurts—or needed to move on to a new phase—he has compelling thoughts about how brands stay relevant and authentic as they get older and grow. Many brands have lost their way in the process of evolving from a small company to a much bigger corporation. Finding themselves disoriented, they must reassess. "In order for brands to recapture their spirit, they almost always go back to their core," he says. Authenticity in branding requires a step-by-step, measured methodology that doesn't veer from a brand's key identity. Certain brands have not been able to articulate that, and Stanley's comment about Microsoft never having told its story was wonderfully sharp.

In this interview, Stanley reveals his secrets about the magic that helped to create a brand that conquered the world. The sensation that is Starbucks required elements of wisdom, integrity, showmanship, and intelligence. I got the sense talking with Stanley that each of the points he made—about Starbucks and other topics—could be explained in even greater detail. Each could have its own commentary in which Stanley unfolds, like an accordion, the full three-dimensionality of his experience and insight.

Stanley speaks here about the importance of vision. It is a point that is discussed by other thinkers in this book, and it is a theme that can't be emphasized enough. Nike had vision. Starbucks had vision. Stanley shares an insider's view of the Starbucks's history, and it's interesting to learn that even Starbucks CEO Howard Schultz didn't fully realize his company's potential for growth. But he had a vision, and, like the leaders of Nike, he was relentless in bringing this to fruition and using it to craft the brand experience. Rigor in matching the vision to the brand experience is essential, and that must define every brand touchpoint. As Stanley says, "No one is going to pick up your product and try it if they don't want to buy into the experience." The man has vision.

Stanley, how would you define "brand"?

A brand is an entity that engenders an emotional connection with a consumer.

What do you mean by an "emotional connection"?

Consumers emotionally connect with brands when the brands repeatedly provide something that the consumer wants, desires, or needs.

Let's return to the moment a person first realizes they have to make a choice between coffee brands or soda brands or shampoo brands. How do people really make choices? Do you think people are conscious of the processes they use?

I think the best brands are those that create something for consumers that they don't even know they need yet. A coffee brand like Starbucks created something people didn't know they needed. Same with Nike. Who knew we needed a high-end performance running shoe? I think when people are surprised or delighted by how a brand can change their lives by just making it a little bit better—or a little bit more fun or a little more performance-oriented—that's when they start creating a connection with that brand.

The concept of a person not knowing that they need something is a fascinating one. Clearly, there were millions of coffee shops all over the world before Starbucks launched its particular brand of coffee shop. How do marketers create desire for something that consumers don't know they need?

I think great brands create the "end state" first. When launching a new product, marketers are not very specific about how a product actually works. They express more about the result. They talk about what you will feel or what you will be like if you choose to engage with that brand or that product. The Apple commercial in 1984 was a great example of this. There was very little about the product in the spot. It was all about the aftereffect of the product.

During your tenure at Starbucks, how deliberate were the choices that the Starbucks marketing team was making? Were they very intentionally creating a scenario and an environment that people would want to experience?

I think it was very deliberate from the beginning. When Howard Schultz first came to Starbucks, he wasn't the owner of the company. He joined a couple guys that had started the company. He went over to Milan and saw the coffee culture and espresso bars where people met in the morning. He saw how people caught up on the news while they sat or stood and drank their little cups of espresso. That inspired the vision he crafted from the beginning—to design a social environment where people not only came for great coffee, but also to connect to a certain culture.

Howard was very wise in knowing that Starbucks was not the only company in the world to make great coffee. On the contrary, there are hundreds of other companies that can make great coffee. So what's the great differentiator? The answer is the distinction that most great brands create. There are other companies that make great running shoes or great toys or great detergent or soap, but what is the real differentiator that people keep coming back for? For Starbucks, it was creating a community, a "third place." It was a very conscious attribute of the brand all along and impacted every decision about the experience: who the furniture was chosen for, what artwork would be on the walls, what music was going to be played, and how it would be played.

*Did Howard anticipate that Starbucks would grow as
quickly as it did and become as pervasive? Was his goal
to create a global brand?*

I think the vision was always for Starbucks to
become a global brand. There were big ambitions
from the beginning. I once asked Howard how it felt
to have thousands of people here in our offices, and
thousands of people in thousands of stores all over
the world working for the brand. He just looked at
me and shook his head and said, "I had no idea that
it could become this."

**No one could have predicted
the success of a brand like Starbucks. But on the other
hand, it was the vision. And Howard's always been very
gracious in saying, "I didn't invent this. I didn't invent
great coffee or even the experience." He gives a lot of
credit to the Italian coffee culture.**

*Over the course of your career, you've worked in
three different companies that have an iconic role in
our culture. With two of them, Starbucks and Nike,
the products are sold at a very high premium. Both
organizations have taken commodity products and
turned them into desirable, sexy, coveted products that
incite enormous loyalty and an almost zealotlike
behavior. Do you see a common denominator in the
way these products are marketed? Would you say
that there's something that these companies have in
common that has generated this fervor?*

What I observed working in both companies is the
rigor and unfailing attention to the product, and the
unbelievable energy spent on creating the brand
experience. I describe it as experience first and
product second, because no one is going to pick up
your product and try it if they don't want to buy into
the experience. This experience comes through the
advertising, the retail environment, and the online
experience—every single brand touchpoint. There
is a very intentional effort to inspire people to get

caught up in that experience and say, "I want to try that"—whatever that thing happens to be.

I can understand the allure of coffee. It tastes delicious and helps you get going in the morning. But what baffles me is how an athletic shoe got to be so sexy and alluring to the point that it would have so much social cachet.

I remember being a kid in the '60s and reading an article about how sneakers were bad for your feet. I think this was something that was marketed by leather shoe companies. We weren't allowed to wear sneakers unless we were exercising, because my parents thought they weren't healthy for regular walking. The people at Nike took note of this and created a performance product that people could wear off court. And that shoe became part of their identity, a way of saying, "I play sports." So wearing your basketball shoes or wearing your running shoes telegraphically expressed who you were.

And then people began to wear the running shoes as a fashion statement. It became really popular. It didn't mean that the shoes were any less performance-oriented. It meant these newly designed shoes also looked good with jeans. And then, with everything else. And then, finally, it became a symbol that was acceptable in any situation.

But it's important to remember that a challenge for any authentic brand as it grows—and I observed this with Timberland—is when fans of the brand zealously adopt the products. If a brand moves away from its core essence and starts to pander to consumers with trendy fashion stuff, those fans will quickly abandon the brand.

What is the most important aspect to consider when creating a brand?

For me, it's all about having a story to tell. This is what will enable you to create an experience around the brand.

What do you mean by "a story"?

Every brand has a story, whether it's the founder's story or the brand's reason for being. Some brands have never told their story well, or have lost their story. Microsoft is a good example of a brand that's never told its story well. It's a huge consumer product software platform, a mega conglomerate, and there's no love there. There's no emotional story to rally around. The Bill Gates story is such an incredible story, but it's never really been expressed by the brand.

It's really interesting to watch brands get older, and gain more competitors in the marketplace, and struggle to stay relevant. Look at Levi's or Gap or any of the great American brands that have gone through these struggles. Look at Starbucks! In order for brands to recapture their spirit, they almost always go back to their core. They seem to forget for a while, then remember, "Oh yeah, we're a coffee company!" Then they get rid of the movies and the spinning racks filled with CDs and start focusing on coffee again.

What if the brand manager of Kraft American cheese asked you to develop its story? How do you create a story if something is essentially manufactured?

You go back to the essence of the brand. Why was it made? What need did it fill? Go back to the origins of a brand and identify how it connected to consumers and how it became a relevant, "loved by families" product. What were the origins of this story? Whether we're talking about Tropicana orange juice or Kraft American cheese—these products were all created to fill a niche. Why? That's where you'll find your story.

What would likely be the next step after defining or developing a story?

You develop a story, and then you start to identify who the consumers are. Who are you talking to?

How are you going to talk to them? How are you going to tell your story to them? What are your opportunities or your channels through which you can tell that story? Do we need to design some new products, or do we need to redesign our existing products because they aren't true to our story? Or maybe you determine that your products are fine, but you haven't been talking to your consumers in the right way, so it's a communication issue. Examine every touchpoint and look at how you can tell one clear, consistent story.

People who aren't very experienced with branding, or are new at it, sometimes feel that they can get away with something being off-brand. But I think that genuinely good branding involves an examination of every single way the brand, the product, and the experience is viewed. Everything that you do, everything you release, everything you say—everything is the cumulative expression of your brand.

What made you decide to work with brands in the first place?

As an American, my earliest days were immersed in brands. Brands became my acquaintances and friends as I grew up. When I got old enough to understand what was going on, I couldn't help but wonder about all that power.

What brands did you have emotional connections to when you were younger?

I think boys always remember their first really nice pair of running shoes. Mine were Adidas. I remember them exactly—I remember what they smelled like, what they looked like. I remember every single detail about them.

What made you want those shoes?

I loved the look of them. I even remember going to buy them. I had earned money mowing lawns. I went to the sporting goods store in Benton,

Kentucky, the nearest town that had a sporting goods store—the little town where I grew up didn't have one. I looked at the shelf, and those were the shoes that called out to me. Even now, when I go into sporting goods stores or shoe stores now and see the huge wall of shoes, I see that one style of shoe—Adidas still makes them—and I have a deep connection to them.

How did you feel when you first put on that first pair of shoes?

I felt like I had joined another world. I didn't know it at the time, but I had joined the world of consumers. Suddenly, I liked the feeling of earning money, of buying something, and then enjoying it. That started my dangerous journey of buying footwear and apparel over the years.

Did that experience of wearing the shoes—which you had wanted so badly—make you feel better about yourself?

Yes. Yes. Yes.

Why or how do you think that happens?

If the brand has been advertised widely, then you've just bought your way into a world that you've only seen from the outside. The experience is like when there's a club that you keep walking by, and you finally enter that club, and now you're a part of it.

Do you think that there's any danger in that?

That's what brands play on. It's part of our nature to want to be accepted. Yet, at the same time, we have this desire to feel like we're different from everyone else—which is the complete opposite of that yearning for acceptance but is nonetheless relevant. I found that strategy particularly intriguing—when brands create things that make you feel like you're different from everyone else.

I remember being in London in the 1970s and first seeing punks in Trafalgar Square. They had their hair "Mohawked" up, and they wore jackets covered in safety pins. I couldn't help but imagine them at home, preparing themselves to go out, in order to look very different from anyone in their household or in their neighborhood. But once they were out, they looked exactly like everyone else in Trafalgar Square.

No matter how hard we try to look different, we almost always still look like *someone*. Once a lot of people get access into an exclusive club, the original members get turned off and leave to find another smaller, more exclusive club to join.

I have often wondered if I should feel guilty because of my role in this. On the one hand, it *is* disturbing, but on the other hand, I admire it.

Being a part of Nike or Starbucks is like being part of a religion. You learn all the tenets of the religion. Our job, as brand evangelists, is to gain converts to the religion.

But as much as I believe in this, I also realize that no one *has* to have those products. You can live without them—they're not essential to life. I've probed deep in my soul to see if I felt bad doing this work, but I never have. I have never felt guilty.

Are you somehow disappointed that you don't feel guilty?

No. I've come to the conclusion that it's like entertainment. If I write a book or make a movie, I'm going to promote the hell out of it. It's the same thing in any arena. I make a shoe, and I'm going to promote it and try to get people to buy it. It's all part of making a living. Some people sell coffee, some people sell bread, some people sell shoes, some people sell toys.

I remember leaving work several years ago, when I was still at Starbucks. I felt so good after a whole day of working with everyone and critiquing everything. At the end of the day I suddenly realized, "Wow, I am really good at this." I knew I could make emotional connections between consumers and products and brands and things. I've achieved a level of expertise in the same way that a doctor or an accountant who practices for many years gets really good at what he does. We practice for years and years and years, and we learn all of the techniques. And then we make up new techniques and new ways to do things. And we get really, really good.

Precisely for that reason, you were brought in by Pepsi to resuscitate Gatorade after a failed brand reinvention. What did you do to resuscitate it?

I borrowed a lot of what I learned from my years at Nike. Gatorade needed a culture of innovation. For the last few years, their only innovation was related to introducing new flavors. That's not innovation. They needed to start creating products again that showed that they were the leader in both hydration and in sports drinks. I came in and developed a strategy to help them do that. I worked directly with the CEO to design a new identity for the brand, as well as for the products. Then I created the overall brand guidelines. It was a great experience.

What's it like to start working with a brand when it's in the middle of a disaster?

You only have one place to go, and that's up.

Are they bringing back the Gatorade name?

The *G* logo is being used in the same way as Nike uses its swoosh. Gatorade is the name of the brand and the company, and the *G* is the equivalent of the swoosh. The company had gone a bit overboard when it got rid of the Gatorade moniker, and now it's coming back to help reidentify the brand.

Did you do a lot of market research in the process of working on this project?

Yes, we did a lot of market research. It was interesting coming to this considering my background at Nike, where ideas were validated by gut instinct, not the consumer.

Wow, that's amazing.

Starbucks was pretty much the same way. As Howard Schultz used to say, "If I went to a group of consumers and asked them if I should sell a $4 cup of coffee, what would they have told me?" Both Starbucks and Nike have modified their position on market research now, and do more of it, but they aren't like a P&G-type organization where they do heavy-duty qualitative and quantitative market research. When I left Nike, that type of validation was foreign territory for me. I had to learn it all afterwards.

What do you think of the state of branding right now?

I think branding has become a consumer-friendly word. It's being used in political campaigns, and it's being used in the boardroom. Schools have even started to talk about branding. On the one hand, there's a danger the word will become watered down and less meaningful than it has been in the past. On the other hand, it will be fascinating to see how communicators use this opportunity. We have the ability to lead this cultural shift, and I hope we can do it before the term "branding" becomes just another generic, overused, and misunderstood word.

Cheryl Swanson

President and Founding Principal, Toniq

Cheryl Swanson is the president of Toniq, a brand consultancy based in New York City, and she is a brand culture soothsayer. She can tell you how luxuries relating to spirituality and creativity are influencing culture, or give you the lowdown on the colors that reflect the contemporary mood. Way back in 1998, when the pervasive Internet was still a twinkle in Mark Zuckerberg's eye, she had coined the phrase "survival of the fastest" to describe the influence that technology was having on the human race.

She's advised companies including Kraft, Pepsi, and Nestlé, which means she brings the force of experience and a measured contemplation to everything she says. She helped Gillette conquer the world with its Venus shavers for women. In that success story, there is a key ingredient of the spells modern-day brand strategists cast. Gillette didn't garner sales by claiming that Venus razors would give women the best shave in the world. The company did it by associating the shaver with the aspiration to fulfill one's inner goddess.

With that kind of strategy on her curriculum vitae, it's not difficult to see that Cheryl is one of those brand thinkers who help us tap into myths and archetypes. She is, after all, a former anthropologist, and talking with her led me to an epiphany that tied together ideas from conversations with other brand thinkers. I think her use of the word "totems" set off something in my mind.

I was reminded anew of how essential it is for each of us to connect with a mental state in which myths, archetypes, and symbolism reign; where our identities are given much more potent rendering. The point might initially seem quotidian, but it gained new resonance from our discussion. Even when we're religious, we of the modern world don't have shamans who help us tap into a more primordial world of symbols.

Yet we do have these modern mythmakers— brand shamans—who connect us to a parallel universe of soul aspirations. They pick a constellation from the cosmos of archetypes and invoke it to be associated with a particular brand. Some brand creators and business leaders do this very well, and the brand succeeds. When it doesn't, it's as though the graft—the invocation—didn't take.

Cheryl has the intense, observant attentiveness of a psychologist, and this attribute is combined with a detective's eye for detail and systematic investigation. She is particularly effective in her work because she understands the numerous audiences of contemporary brand culture as though they were members of her own family.

Her portrait of the millennials reflects her attuned sensitivity to who they are and why they are drawn to qualities of authenticity and longevity. She has an appreciation for their optimism and makes trenchant observations on how their relationship with their parents—and the realities of their upbringing—have defined their identities.

If I were somewhat more abstract in describing Ms. Swanson, I would say she's a Jungian psychoanalytical brand composer and historian. She's aware that archetypes and authenticity are essential to the brew that leads to brand success, and that both are revealed through research. For one recent project, she helped the tea maker Lipton attain a more upscale cachet for the brand. She did so by invoking a dimension of the company she uncovered while exploring its structure and history. Coups like these are why clients have reverence for Cheryl. I've been in branding for years, and I can tell you that not all of these grafts and invocations take. Cheryl's do.

How would you define the word "brand"?

A brand is a product with a compelling story—a brand offers "quintessential qualities" for which the consumer believes there is absolutely no substitute. This underscores the importance of what I describe as the "emotional pillar," which is one of three pillars necessary in building a brand.

Three pillars? I've never heard of that—what are the three pillars?

The functional pillar, the sensorial experiential pillar, and the emotional pillar. It's the emotional pillar that actually transforms a product into a true brand with a compelling story. This then creates the bond that convinces consumers there is no substitute for it. That's why Coke and Pepsi—beverages that essentially consist of brown sugar water—each have fanatics. There are Pepsi fanatics and there are Coke fanatics, and the people in one group rarely migrate over to the other side. This is largely because of that emotional bond. There's something compelling to Coke drinkers about Coke. It could be its connection to American heritage or the classic nature of the brand—or it could be Coke's newly emerging future orientation. Whatever it is, the Coca-Cola story has succeeded in winning the heart of the consumer.

What is it about brands that causes people to have such a strong connection to them? We're talking about brown sugar water—brown sugar water that we fall in love with. Why do you think this happens?

The brands are totems. They tell us stories about our place in culture—about where we are and where we've been. They also help us figure out where we're going.

Brands have become time capsules, and in many ways, they're now navigation and identity devices. They've transcended their transactional economic function and now reflect our culture and who we are in a way that no other objects can.

Ancient totems were often extremely artistic. They visually telegraphed the values and visions of a tribe or a group of people. Do you feel that there's a similar level of artistry embedded in brands?

Yes, I do. Think about everything that goes into the formation of a brand. They're not just decorative creations that come in packages. Rather, the entire visual language of a brand is rooted in cultural trends, in what's going on with lifestyles, in what's going on with specific consumer groups. The artwork, the visual language, and the entire visual presence of a brand communicate what is truly important to a particular consumer group. A compelling brand story is wrapped up in design, in advertising, in copy—consequently, these brands have that totemic value.

I'm fascinated by the idea that totems are representative of who we are, particularly because totems also signify religion. The zealous attachment people have to certain brands makes me wonder if Apple could be a religion, not just a consumer brand.

It is a cult. So is Method. Think about it: Method is a household cleaning brand! But it has become a beloved icon since its launch in 2001.

How did that happen?

Brands activate emotions. Method has a very deliberate positioning. The brand connects to a higher order, which is about living a joyful, vibrant life. When I worked on the launch of the Venus brand, the positioning was about revealing your inner beauty and your inner goddess. That was the emotional piece. And that's a way, way, way higher order than just scraping hair off your legs.

Ultimately, we transcended the act of shaving—which is the product attribute—and promised a higher order benefit that was embedded in emotion. In doing so, Venus became a half-billion-dollar brand and the number one women's shaving brand on the planet.

Let's talk more about branding for specific niches—do you find that there's a fundamentally different way of marketing to the generation of millennials than to other groups?

Yes.

In what way?

I did a research study on millennials, which helped me to see the extraordinary scope of their optimism. They have an enormous sense of self and individualism. They're very "me" oriented. It's helpful to look at this in the context of other age groups. The Gen X crew, for instance, is very rebellious and skeptical. They're the sandwich generation between the boomers—who used to get all the media attention—and the millennials, who are now getting all the media attention. Boomers, for their part, are rebellious as well, because they grew up in an era when the counterculture was very vibrant.

Why are millennials more optimistic?

They're optimistic because they're cherished by their parents. Many of them are the "by-products," so to speak, of numerous trips to the fertility clinic. Their parents had them later in life, so these children are really, really wanted—and they are beloved for that reason.

Do you remember the episode of *Mad Men* when January Jones is driving, and the kids are hopping around in the back without car seats or seatbelts, and they're playing "spaceman" with a plastic dry cleaning bag? This is an accurate depiction of what was happening when we were kids. There wasn't that sense of "safety" that we have now. Because these new millennials are so thoroughly wanted and cherished, they have a pervasive sense of safety. Car seats became the norm when they were babies. Nowadays you would never, ever put a kid in a car without a car seat. I think this sense of being wanted has made them very secure and very achievement-oriented.

When we did our study of millennials, we came to see that many of the behaviors evident in teenage Gen Xers or boomers—smoking and drinking, for example—are actually decreasing with this generation. And their SATs have increased!

But there is also much more pressure on the millennial generation to achieve. They don't want to let their parents down. They actually like their parents. They don't rebel against their parents like prior generations did. They're more conventional. They feel very powerful, largely because they've been imbued with a sense of confidence and being so wanted in the world. This has enormous benefits for the psyche, and it's proven to be very powerful.

They also like the structure that's provided by institutions—they're driven by this. These are people who won't rebel against "the man," if you will. They actually like "the man"—they think the "the man" is cool. They have a profound trust in authority.

Boomers have always been fighting against authority, and Gen Xers are really cynical about institutions. What's interesting is how often marketers are boomers, advertising creatives are Gen Xers, and the people they're trying to talk to are millennials. Each group has a very different lens on the world.

Do you think that millennials like brands more than any other generation?

I don't know that they like them more, because boomers grew up with brands. Boomers were the first generation to experience the full onslaught of modern marketing—they really are the branded generation. Boomers feel that they have a right to brands and that everything should be marketed to them first.

Brands were with boomers from day one. Gen Xers are skeptical about brands. But everything millennials use is branded, and they use brands to help them navigate their lives. Brands help to focus identity for them, and help them to focus on where they're going. In the same way that rules help them navigate the world and figure out how they're going to dress themselves and achieve, brands help them figure out their identity.

If you had to make a prediction about how the generation after the millennials will be interacting with brands, what would it be?

I think brands are going to become even more entrenched in our lives. But because there are so many brands and there's so much choice, there's a potential for brands to become part of the wallpaper and devolve back to product status versus "brand story" status. So now more than ever, the strategy of being simple, sensory, and optimistic, and maniacally focused on that mandate—is critical. I would encourage corporations to act like visionaries, and brand stewards to act like a Steve Jobs or an Eric Ryan to ensure that a brand message is really simple, clear, and optimistic. What I'm nervous about is that brands will revert back to telegraphing social status. And I think that to continue to be successful in the future, they need to have an almost-iconic, maniacal sense of focus.

What about truth? Do you think truth is something that people will continue to demand from brands? Or do you think this is something that's temporarily in fashion?

I don't think it's temporary.

Truth has become extraordinarily important. Millennials, in particular, are embracing authenticity and genuineness. There is no way that this can be every brand's mantra—but it is critical that marketers go back and find the inherent truths in their brands instead of trying to hide them.

Ironically, millennials like heritage brands a great deal. This is because they give credence to brands that have stood the test of time. They actually acknowledge longevity as something quite favorable. This is in direct opposition to the Gen Xers, who tend to want the next newest thing and who tend to eschew things that are too old. Boomers do that too.

Millennials love the idea of authenticity. Authenticity, roots, and honesty are fundamentally key to them. They expect brands to tell the truth and to have "honest" ingredients. So the era of high-fructose corn syrup is coming to its end. That's also why "throwback brands" are doing so well. Pepsi has introduced a limited-edition product featuring 1970s packaging, and they're also eliminating the high-fructose corn syrup. They're going back to using pure cane sugar and old-fashioned ingredients. What is interesting is that, in doing this, they're not only going back to the original packaging, but they're also going back to their original formulation.

Millennials love this. Because cane sugar is natural, and the drink doesn't contain any chemical names they can't pronounce, they feel it's truly authentic. It might be sugar, but it's *real* sugar. This is a strong, strong cornerstone to what millennials like and cherish in brands. You also see this in brands like Levi's. Levi's is becoming more popular, and it's because the brand has an authentic past. Millennials also love the Gillette brand. They know that Gillette is rooted in the past, but they feel that the brand has been stewarded forward in a really interesting way. Millennials love brands that have that longevity.

Do you think that we run the risk of having corporations try to get on the authenticity bandwagon and create a false sense of heritage?

Yes. And I think we can't have every brand extolling their authentic virtues, because then we'll be bombarded with a cacophony of authenticity which will then become highly inauthentic.

What advice would you give to those who are interested in branding and are looking to represent something authentic? How would you go about doing that?

You can't buy authentic values—you can only create them from what the brand does and what its history is. Don't look to parrot a popular brand. Go back to a brand's roots and uncover the story that you can believe in and steward forward. You steward the story forward. But steward it in a way that presents it in a modern context. Again, think about Coke. The company has translated the brand, and all its authenticity, into a very modern context.

When I worked with Lipton Tea, we went deep into the brand's archives and analyzed all of their rich, rich history. One of the things I learned is that Lipton has had a master "blender" on staff, who works on all the tea blends—of every tea that they make. Lipton has a master blender!

Really?

Yes. We realized that nobody knew this. Nobody knew this part of their history! Nobody knew that Lipton owns the world's greatest tea plantations all over the planet: in Africa, Sri Lanka, and China. This is authentic, honest, and genuine—an example of a brand story that nobody knew anything about. And Lipton happens to be the biggest tea brand in the world. This level of tea mastery was something that they were not communicating. So rather than simply talk about authenticity, they're now talking about "tea mastery." Lipton is still a mass brand, but it's beginning to inch more upscale, which is very, very hard for brands to do. This is providing them with a plethora of opportunities around a more premium positioning. This is what they're doing with their new Pyramid Teas offering.

So in many ways, what you're doing in this work is taking away decades-old layers of marketing and revealing the true purpose of a product.

Yes. I'm interested in peeling all those layers back and looking at a brand as it truly is.

Joe Duffy

Chairman, Duffy & Partners

Joe Duffy has built his design DNA from a collection of experiences that have added up to an extraordinary proficiency in branding and design. Each piece of his history has provided him with an aesthestic chromosome that informs his design work today. In college, Duffy was a painter, and he still wanted to be a painter when he graduated, so illustration and design seemed like a logical career if not his initial dream. The first company he launched, in 1975, was a design and illustration studio. After a couple of years running that business, he started an advertising agency where he was a partner before eventually launching Duffy Design, a partnership with the ad conglomerate Fallon Worldwide, in 1984.

After breaking off from Fallon, he relaunched Duffy & Partners in 2004. The payoff of the individual experiences is evident in his successes: Duffy had such a long and fruitful partnership with Fallon because he nimbly understood the deep interconnections between design, advertising, and branding. He has been praised again and again for his ability to integrate these into compelling branding stories via design.

Duffy's crafted a slew of classic projects. His studio has redesigned the ubiquitous Diet Coke can; he's created a new design iconography for International Truck and Engine Corporation, and has created packaging and identity work for Wolfgang Puck and Jim Beam. For the Islands of the Bahamas,

Duffy & Partners created an identity system that is nothing less than a design and branding masterpiece. Joe is able to tailor his studio's design vocabulary to fit the client in a way that is überflexible, far beyond the range of most design and branding consultancies. His design work perfectly fits the bill, reflecting an unwillingness to relinquish to design clichés. That commitment to creativity is evident in the fact that Joe Duffy continues painting to this day—no doubt part of what makes his consulting work still vibrant.

The breadth of Duffy's work is another measure of his appeal and insight. He works with big and small clients—from local restaurateurs to multibillion-dollar companies—in an eclectic range of industries. He's not just a food guy, a technology guy, or a car guy—he has a healthy agnosticism about his clients.

But what he is not ambivalent about is his commitment to doing exemplary work. As part of that ethos, he's chosen to work only with clients who will let him do the work that he feels will best serve their interests. Unlike brand and advertising firms that bloat up with benefactors where there's no true synchronicity of sensibility, Duffy isn't content to have anything less than meaningful resonance. This means that Duffy has stayed small and even sized down when necessary—as he did after the downturn of 2008—in order to preserve the integrity of the firm's work. Joe gets to the nuts and bolts of what it takes to be authentic—he gave me a list of criteria that must be considered when considering new clients. "I don't want to work with clients who simply manage design as a necessary evil," he says.

What I like and respect most about Joe Duffy is that he doesn't have to.

Joe, why branding?

I think the real question really is, "Why design?"

Then—why design?

Because I couldn't make any money as a painter.

Ha! We have a lot in common.

Yes. I went to school for fine art and wanted nothing whatsoever to do with any form of commercial art. In fact, the situation back then was more like the "jocks versus geeks" situation now. If you were involved in fine art, you were in one camp, and if you were involved in art direction or design, you were in another. The people in one group would have nothing whatsoever to do with those in the other. Anything that was commercial was seen as selling out. And I didn't want to have anything to do with that. When I found out that I couldn't sell my artwork enough to support myself, I decided it might not be so bad to pursue a career in commercial art.

Did you always know you were creative?

I knew in kindergarten, from the time when the teacher gave us an assignment to draw our favorite saint.

I assume you went to Catholic school.

I did. And I drew a picture of St. Michael the Archangel. The teacher put the students' drawings up on the board, and all the kids gathered around mine and could not believe how good it was. No one could believe I did it. Right then and there, I knew I could do something better than anyone else. I wish I still had that drawing.

That experience had a significant impact on you. Do you think that brands can provoke a similar feeling of fulfillment more powerfully than anything else?

Absolutely. I think that generating that feeling is the desire of anyone who runs a big consumer-branding company. Well, perhaps not everyone. Fortunately, the people who I've worked for over the years have all wanted to be the best. They want their company, their brand, and the products they make to rise above the fray. I think that aspiration is a basic part of human nature. And it really is what branding is all about.

But can brands make someone feel better about himself or herself?

First of all, a company needs to understand that "someone." Understanding the audience of any brand is absolutely critical. A brand needs to be honest about who it's right for, and why. Once that's defined, it becomes much easier to encourage mutuality with an audience. But people choose certain brands for all kinds of reasons. If you believe that something is going to make you feel superior, regardless of whether that belief is right or wrong, it makes you feel better about yourself. Of course, the feeling is false. But that falseness is not the fault of the brand—that's your own personal construct.

Do you think that brands are capable of honesty?

Sure they are. Especially in this day and age, when cynicism is at an all-time high. Everyone has the ability to investigate things online, and to find out where something is made, who's making it, how it's made, what the ingredients are, and so forth.

At the end of the day, successful branding is about making someone feel that they've made the right choice, that they are better for it, and that their life is going to be better as a result. Whether that involves putting on a pair of Levi's or putting on a pair of work boots, if you feel that this choice is absolutely right for you, then you're going to have a better experience as a person.

We all have a portfolio of brands we live with. We have a fine-tuned control over how these brands enter our life, convey their messages to us, and sell to us. If someone sees a brand on a supermarket shelf, and they choose that one over another brand, what they're saying is that this particular brand relates better to them. Perhaps they think it tastes better, but more importantly, they feel that the brand relates to them better.

Every brand becomes a badge. Whether you experience that when you open your refrigerator, your pantry, your closet, or your whatever, the brands we choose to live with become statements about who we are as people. Most people don't talk about brands in the way that I'm talking about them right now. But it *is* the way that we think. Every brand we choose helps express our own personal individuality.

Tell me about your first experiences as a designer.

I learned on the job. I wasn't trained in art direction or design. I was just a kid who wanted to be an artist. In the beginning, I designed everything from window displays to signs for head shops and organic food stores. You name it, I did it. Then I started doing illustrations for advertising agencies. An art director would hire me, and I would do an illustration for an outdoor billboard or a print campaign. Inevitably, it would be incredibly frustrating working with art directors because they would insist that I "change this and do that," and I hated it. I felt like a pawn. So I said, "You know what? I'm going to be an art director." And I got a job as an art director.

How did you make the switch?

I did some ads for my dad's bar. My father was a very successful Irish saloonkeeper in Minneapolis. He owned a bar and nightclub called Duff's. I had been doing some illustrations and ads for his menus and table tents, and I created posters for the bands that played there. I put together a portfolio primarily showcasing this work, and got hired as an art director. I did that for a while, and then broke off to start an ad agency with some of the people I worked with. I was creative director there for four years, but got tired of the compromise and politics required in advertising, and I decided to go back to design. I wanted to get my hands dirty again. I started Duffy Design in 1984. I started out in this business with the philosophy that I am not going to work with anybody who won't allow me to do work that I am proud of. Right now, I have an independent company with my kids and a few other people. Altogether, we're twelve people.

How do you manage to only do work you're proud of?

I have to keep the firm small. I think the only way you can continually do work that you're proud of is to work with a short list of clients. Most clients won't allow you to do what's right. But, fortunately for designers everywhere, there are more and more clients—especially the big ones—who are beginning to understand the power of design. They're realizing the importance of standing out and being different. **The list of clients you can convince to do the right thing is growing. Despite the economy, I think design is in a damn good position right now.**

Do you think there are brands that are capitalizing on design in a way that's inauthentic or disingenuous? Are those the kind of clients that you don't want to work with?

I don't want to work with clients who believe they have all the answers. I don't want to work with clients who are successful in spite of their lack of design or in spite of their bad design. I don't want to work with clients who simply manage design as a necessary evil.

Do you find that there are a lot of clients like that?

Absolutely. Most of them are like that. But, as I said, more and more of them are getting it every day. And they are seeing results from brands like Apple. That's design, period. Yes, it's also technology, but it's more than that: It's design.

Okay, here's a hypothetical question: You start working with a client who you believe you'll be able to do good work for. Halfway through the project, you realize they don't get it. How do you navigate through that situation?

We keep serving up good design. If it gets to a point where it's absolutely fruitless, and they keep saying, "No," or they try to tell us to do something in a prescriptive way, then we part company. But I try to have really honest, intelligent conversations *before* I start a relationship with any client.

What do you mean?

You can't let yourself rationalize that it's okay to work for a bad client because you're getting a big fee. There are always a few telling questions you can ask to find out whether you're going to be able to do really great design for someone. But you have to be honest. I think an awful lot of people working with bad clients start out believing that during the project, they can convince the clients to understand great design. They think great design will convince them. Bullshit. Ask the right questions before designing and listen to the answers, and nine times out of ten, you'll know whether or not you'll be able to do great work that you'll be proud of.

What are some of the questions you ask your prospective clients before you decide to work with them?

Obviously, the questions vary, depending on the prospect and their business situation, not to mention their corporate structure. However, there are some general questions that can help determine what you're in for. In no particular order, they are,

- How would you define success as it relates to this design initiative?
- Who will be involved in the approval process, and what roles will they play in our collaborative effort?
- Will we have regular access to the final decision maker?
- Can you describe previous design projects and the experiences with outside design firms, both good and bad?
- Will your internal design team also be developing design directions? This is an important question, because we've found ourselves in this situation twice recently without our knowledge of it going in.
- Who do you consider your strongest competitor, and how would you rate their brand design?
- What attracted you to our firm?
- Will we have access to and be able to collaborate with your other marketing communications partners—your ad agency, PR firm, web developer?
- What is your position on research? How will qualitative and quantitative research be conducted on this design?
- What's the design fee?

I imagine that you've continued to refine these questions during the twenty-seven years you've been working in branding. But you always seem to work with good clients. When I was looking at your body of work, I was struck by how consistently great it has been. How have you been able to achieve this consistency for so long?

Perseverance is part of it. Don't put money before your standards. Don't put money before your integrity and your knowledge of what's right and what's wrong. What you do as a designer—and what you believe in and stand for—is going to be evident in your work. It's no more complicated than that.

It's also critical to work with people who are actually capable of doing great creative work. In this regard, I've been very fortunate. But I've also been very diligent in maintaining an environment where the best young designers want to work. Think about it from a young designer's point of view. All they want to do is build a portfolio. When applying for a job, they'll apply first at firms that are doing work they admire. It's as simple as that. If I start compromising and start doing shit work, I can't get the best designers to work here.

And I've surrounded myself with absolutely brilliant young designers. They create great work all the time! And if you make sure they're working on projects that they're really proud of—and if you help foster great design—they're going to wake up every morning and look forward to going to work. Most importantly, they're going to have great careers.

Designers often talk about Milton Glaser's essay, "Road to Hell," and his design edict to "do no harm" as well as his philosophy about the designer's obligation to do work that can inspire social change. A question students often ask me reminds me of the dilemma you faced as a young designer—when you realized you couldn't sell enough paintings to pay your rent. There are many designers wondering how to make the right decisions when they're confronted with the necessity of paying their rent. You and I could both look at the portfolios of most brand design firms and point out where they might have chosen money before standards. Over the years, I've felt guilty about taking on a questionable project, but I did so because I was worried about not only paying my rent, but also making payroll. It seems to me that you've been able to figure out how to do both: make money and maintain your standards. How have you done this?

I guess I've always gone about it in a rather naive and simplistic way. If there aren't enough clients out there who want the kind of design work we do, I have to cut back. This is the worst thing about my business. I dread it and I hate it. But if there aren't enough clients to pay the freight, and allow us to do good work, then I have to cut back. It starts with my salary and then—unfortunately—sometimes I have to let people go. This is the main reason we are twelve people right now. Given this economy, I expect we're going to be on a roller coaster for some time. We'll be fine with the overhead that we have now. But if it turns out that the only way to get by with my current overhead is to do bad work, I will cut back. I *will* make less money. I've put my need to be happy and complete in what I do ahead of concerns about money.

Design is really so damn simple. It's so straightforward. Anyone who tries to make it complicated or convoluted does a disservice to designers everywhere. Anyone who buys crap gets what they deserve.

Margaret Youngblood

Principal and Executive Creative Director, Trinity Brand Group; Former Principal and Executive Creative Director, Landor

Someone seems to have scattered design pixie dust on Margaret Youngblood. She has quickly and uncannily gained entrée into the design pantheon, and she has been embraced by design's superstars. She worked for Raymond Loewy—who, she says, taught her how to think like a designer—and studied with Milton Glaser. Early on in her career, she won a competition that allowed her to follow Glaser and fellow design legend Saul Bass for a few days. In later years, she worked with a man who eventually became prime minister of Italy.

All of this amounts to a rather extraordinary pedigree, and there is yet more to the story of Youngblood's charmed life. She went from the Kansas City Art Institute to the University of Arizona and then to the Sorbonne. She was flying to Europe at the age of twenty-six to present branding projects solo to company CEOs. She didn't know brand strategy when working on some early projects, but she winged it, and subsequently gained kudos for her work.

Margaret worked at the branding consultancy Landor for twenty years—initially turning down a job offer from Milton Glaser, no less—at a time when branding was becoming a much more significant influence on our culture and when companies sought to consciously craft their identities. She worked her way up to principal and executive creative director at Landor, overseeing the consultancy's corporate identity work. She worked on seminal projects for clients like FedEx, Xerox, Danone, Pathé, the 2002 Winter Olympics, YWCA, and H&R Block. Walter Landor helped to define the world of branding that we live in now, and Youngblood has had a lasting influence on visual culture—numerous icons of today's visual landscape can be traced back to her.

After two years as Vice President of Marketing and senior creative director of Banana Republic, where she guided the development of the company's brand communications, she returned to the brand consulting work in which she thrives. She is currently principal and executive creative director at Trinity Brand Group.

Margaret is reserved, with a quiet demeanor that conveys her integrity. Despite her accomplishments and connections, she does not draw a great deal of attention to herself. You won't find her written about or extensively profiled in magazines and newspapers. Hers is not a household name, yet she is revered for the consistent quality and intelligence of her worldwide creative legacy.

In our conversation, Margaret talks about the importance of authenticity. She's had close personal experience with these kinds of issues, and her thoughts on the topic are heartfelt. At Landor, she was involved in the rebranding of British Petroleum, when then-CEO John Browne was trying to transform the company, an initiative that became a laughingstock because of the Gulf of Mexico oil spill.

She argues that there has been a cultural shift relating to branding and consumer sentiment. Consumers are much more skeptical of both companies and the government, and they want their values to be reflected not only in their purchases but in their day-to-day jobs as well. "They want to work for an organization they respect and which has the same values they do," she says. "I'm not sure how or why that happened. But consumers do not want to be marketed to or lied to now. They are demanding the facts and the truth."

Margaret doesn't paint a pretty picture when it's not warranted, and she acknowledges that there are quite a few crises in the United States at the moment. She makes a fascinating connection between the importance of brands and the brevity of our attention spans. Having worked for clients stateside and abroad, Youngblood came to appreciate the European view of graphic design. In Europe, it is viewed and respected more like a fine art, and "design is rarely researched." To work for clients like that is a dream—where did Margaret get that pixie dust?

How did you get started in the branding business?

It was very purposeful. After I graduated from college, I was in France to study medieval illuminated manuscripts. I knew that the only way I could stay in France was if I worked. I had my degree in graphic design, and I was able to get a job with Raymond Loewy.

How did you get a job with Raymond Loewy?

I was studying with Milton Glaser and won an illustration contest. The prize was a scholarship to the Aspen Design Conference, and it also allowed me to go wherever Milton and Saul Bass went. I went to every event that they did, and joined them for dinner and lunch. The two of them put me in touch with an agent in Paris, and she put me in touch with a group of Americans working in Paris. Someone from that group put me in touch with a fellow who was the executive creative director at Raymond Loewy. It was all very serendipitous.

What were the most important things Raymond Loewy taught you?

He taught me how to think. I knew how to see and how to draw, but I wasn't thinking like a designer. He taught me how to think.

I also did not learn, until I came back to the United States, that Europe is far more respectful of the creative process. Europeans are much more creative in their thinking, and are much more courageous.

Why do you think that is?

I think Europeans see graphic design as an extension of art, and it's appreciated as much as architecture or fine arts. It is also much more respected. When I was in Europe, clients received nearly every design project I worked on very differently. European clients accept your design recommendation because they see you as the expert. They're also much more willing to take chances. Design is rarely researched.

When you came back to the United States, where did
you work?

I went to Landor. I had originally accepted a position
with Milton Glaser, and then I got an offer with Landor
in San Francisco. After talking it over with Milton,
I took the position at Landor. And I stayed there for
twenty years. I would have had a totally different life
had I not made that choice. It wasn't until I went to
Landor that I started to work on big identity projects.

Were you interested in pursuing a career in identity
work and corporate communications?

Yes. Initially, I was very interested in doing packaging
as well, but Landor wasn't structured to allow that.
Each group was specialized. But I did love working
for my first boss at Landor. He was an amazing man,
and he gave me many great opportunities. He trusted
me. At the age of twenty-six, I was flying to Europe by
myself to present to CEOs.

Twenty-six and presenting to CEOs! He really put you
out there, didn't he? What was that like?

It was great! At first, I was scared shitless, but I got
used to it. Then, once you're presenting so continually,
you start to sound like you know what you're talking
about. It was a great turning point in my life. I was
working with Romano Prodi, the chairman of the
Istituto per la Ricostruzione Industriale, who later
ended up becoming prime minister of Italy.

We were working together on a very large
project for an industrial company. It was a post–
World War II organization that had been started
by the government to stimulate the economy in
Europe. I was working with Romano to develop the
strategy. I never studied brand strategy in school,
and we made it up as we went. Realizing the power
that we had made the work very appealing. We
recognized that we could impact a large number of
people in a truly positive way.

How did you learn to talk strategy with your clients?

I learned a great deal from the people I worked with at Landor. And a lot of I learned from my experiences on projects.

Our work for General Electric was also a big turning point for many of us at Landor, and it ended up defining the bible for what branding could do for mergers and acquisitions strategy in the 1980s. We were a group of fifteen people sitting in a room figuring out the advantages and disadvantages of a product-dominant strategy versus a corporate-dominant strategy. It was amazing.

Why do you think consumers have such strong opinions now about the way corporations are branding themselves or their products? Why do you think consumers revolted to the redesign of Tropicana's packaging and Gap's logo?

Actually, you need to include BP as well. I think there are different reasons why consumers revolt. A key reason consumers are so opinionated now is that they want to be able to trust what they're being told. If the visual language of a company is not trustworthy, consumers now push back and say, "You're lying." Initially, I think the intent of BP's repositioning was very noble. It was authentic and honest. After chief executive John Browne left, the vision became something else, and that was a problem. Now the logo has become a metaphor, or an emblem for people's lack of trust.
Regarding Gap, the question for me is, "Why would you change something that's not broken?" I actually think the product is a lot better than it's been in a long time. So, why did the logo have to change? They weren't having problems implementing the design. It was reproducible. Is it a little bit dated? Maybe. But consumers are questioning intent.

Consumers want to know what the company's intent is. I think they want to know that now more than they ever have before.

Why?

Because they're smarter. In the past, consumers were okay with their job meaning one thing, and representing a different set of values than the values that they lived at home. But now consumers, and people generally, and kids who come out of school, don't want to go to work for just anybody—they don't want to just get "a job." They want to work for an organization they respect and that has the same values they do. I'm not sure how or why that happened. But consumers do not want to be marketed to or lied to now. They are demanding the facts and the truth.

Let's face it: There is a lot of bad stuff out there. Think about all the advertising that's focused on kids. It's bad stuff—there's a lot of bad shit going on in our country. We're contending with obesity and major environmental issues. From a health standpoint, there are many things that aren't being regulated. Ultimately, I think people now feel that companies aren't being honest with them, and that their government isn't being honest with them.

And yet it seems that brands are more important now than ever before, as a way that people can declare or telegraph who they are.

Yes. I think a branding sensibility is required now in order to compete. It makes it easier for people to either like you or not, and the brands end up helping people determine who they want to align with.

Do you feel that this is more prevalent now than it has ever been, or do you think this behavior is hardwired into our DNA?

It's wired into who we are as humans.

It really is quite astonishing how we can construct who we are with the brands that we buy.

It's become shorthand for who you are, what you're like, and what you value. This is becoming more and more important as people's attention spans become shorter and as the world becomes more cluttered. Certainly the Internet and electronic media now have a huge part in this transformation. Brands can help us clearly communicate who we are.

You've helped many different corporations create their identities and their brands. As the vice president of marketing and senior creative director at Banana Republic, you helped to create the visual world of Banana Republic, which has its own persona. I'm curious to hear your thoughts about these constructed personas as they relate to companies and individuals. In The Social Network, *Mark Zuckerberg is shown wearing what one character describes as "'fuck you' flip-flops." It seemed as if everything Zuckerberg was wearing—whether a ratty T-shirt, a hoodie, or a pair of shoes—fit the mold of what a brilliant tech geek would wear. The wardrobe choices suggest that it's easier to understand someone's persona if they fit within a previously established archetype. Do you think there's more skepticism with corporate symbols than with the symbols of an archetype like the tech geek?*

Yes, and I think this is because the intent of a corporation is to make money. You can see those symbols and wonder why these businesses want to make money and what they're doing with their profits. And you wonder how they treat their employees and their partners, and if they're making a product that's safe—something that's good for you and good for the world. I think that's the difference.

There seems to be as much effort on the part of individuals to present themselves in a certain way, whether with makeup, hair color, boob jobs, hair implants, or any number of things people use to make themselves more "attractive." But when a company changes its logo for a vision or values clarification, there seems to be a lot more uproar than there used to be.

I think that's true. That generates a lot of eye rolling and distrust. Ah, the irony.

Seth Godin

Author, Entrepreneur, Marketing Guru

Seth Godin is not going to let you off the hook. He relentlessly writes, consults, blogs, and speaks. Whatever the medium is, Godin is consistently pushing individuals and companies to find their voice—to synch up with current and future cultural realities in order to get their message, product, or idea across to as many people as possible. He is a tireless entrepreneur. He has launched several start-ups, among them the vanguard e-marketing firm Yoyodyne and the peer-to-peer website Squidoo, which has soared in popularity since its 2006 debut and allows users to create web pages showcasing their expertise. He launched his own MBA program. He worked for Yahoo!

*Godin is an authorial powerhouse, putting out book after book—*Purple Cow, Meatball Sundae, Tribes, Linchpin, Free Prize Inside, *among others—about branding, marketing, the future, and about maintaining one's relevance as a business, a leader, or a creator of ideas. He has exemplified the work ethic and self-promotional wherewithal that is necessary to be successful in the modern media day, when countless avenues of content seek to waylay the attention of readers and consumers. The man has also done an extraordinary job marketing and branding himself.*

Ideas are at the core of what Seth Godin does: Creating them. Implementing them. Figuring out the best way to share them. He is consistently pioneering new frameworks for working and inventive models for sharing ideas. He has developed novel strategies for both individuals and companies to share information, viewpoints, and products—to share creativity and innovation. He introduced the concept of permission marketing. He strives to ensure that ideas have the ability to permeate culture without any obstacles whatsoever. And he refuses to kowtow to existing orthodoxies or business models. His latest book, Poke the Box, is a prime example. Instead of selling the book through traditional publishers, Godin formed the Domino Project, a collaboration with Amazon that is an entirely new model of book distribution, to reach his audience.

In his experience contemplating and exploring the way that companies connect with individuals, Godin has come to be a perceptive commentator on the deep-seated connections we have with brands, and the different ways that brands tap into our own individual histories. He explains that point by referencing Starbucks and the Catholic Church, each of them a brand in their own right.

In our discussion, he considers the way that each design we experience references a complex mosaic of ideas that tells us we're about to enjoy something—or not. A good designer is able to craft all those associations, bringing in "the right mix of history and the future" to create a resonant narrative for consumers. Brands must build on past associations but go beyond nostalgia to novelty.

Godin has helped companies to refine their marketing techniques, but one can sense that he seeks to undermine the system. He acknowledges the downsides of consumer brainwashing and critiques the negative effects of advertising. Brands provide us a sense of joy and connection, and he yearns for a world in which we find something other than purchases to achieve that satisfaction. "I'm hoping that over time people find other things," he observes. If Godin has anything to say or do about it—and he most definitely does—they will.

What does the concept of "brand" mean to you?

I believe that "brand" is a stand-in, a euphemism, a shortcut for a whole bunch of expectations, worldview connections, experiences, and promises that a product or service makes, and these allow us to work our way through a world that has thirty thousand brands that we have to make decisions about every day. One of the cues and clues that we use for identifying a brand is, "What does the packaging look like?" But the packaging is *definitely* not the brand.

So what do you think the brand actually is?

I wrote a post about this on my blog in relation to TCHO chocolate, and it made my friends who run the brand really angry with me, because they didn't understand what I was trying to say. I was writing the post about an article I read about the brand, which was filled with designer, marketing, and branding doublespeak that meant, as far as I was concerned, absolutely nothing. When the brand's package is described as "a modern form of currency . . . for a new generation of chocolate enthusiasts," that's not the brand. That might be good design talk, but to appeal to real people in the real world, the brand will have to be able to connect to a series of feelings we have that go back to the time we were four years old, and then— maybe—reconnect that experience to a chocolate bar that people can buy for $4.

How do you think those feelings begin at four years old, and why do they begin in the first place?

Well, it's *really* complicated. If you get taken out to Starbucks for a Frappuccino as a treat after a baseball game when you're a young kid, twenty years from now the brand is going to mean something to you that's different from someone who grows up in a place where there isn't a

Starbucks and encounters it for the first time much later in life. Or, maybe the person who experiences it for the first time is at their new job in New York City, and in their excitement they go and celebrate their yuppiedom by buying a $5 espresso—it's going to mean something different to that person because of that association. Or, if someone meets their friends after work and it's usually in a place like Starbucks, then the brand comes to have an entirely different connotation for that person. The design of Starbucks may have contributed to the experience, and the design may have helped them establish a feeling in a certain zone in the brain, but design and brand are two different things.

Let's talk about that "zone." Many people seem to be able to recall a moment from their childhood when they experienced a sense of euphoria or self-realization caused by an experience with a brand. You talked about how that might be generated by having a Frappuccino as a treat after a baseball game. Do you have a sense of why that happens?

That's the definition of "brand."

One of the things that I'm so fascinated by in this experience is the role that memory plays in our expectations. Brands often make people feel good about themselves based on some earlier experience. Do you think that's something inherent to a brand?

I'd like to answer a different question, which is, "What's the designer's role in helping brands leverage memories or create experiences that people are seeking out?" If I were to ask, "What kind of brand does the Catholic Church have?" there would be all sorts of design answers to that, but, in fact, for someone who has never encountered the Catholic Church, there is very little brand awareness of it. For someone who has been involved in it since they were a week old, it fundamentally has a very different meaning.

It also depends on whether you're a devout Catholic or not. If you're a devout Catholic, you may not even think it's a brand.

People who are honest about branding understand that the Catholic Church is, by definition, a brand. Designers can use iconography [small pun intended], type, smell, and light to capture specific feelings and then associate them with a charity or a perfume or a politician. When they do that, what they're really doing is creating a visual or other sensory cue to trigger feelings that human brains will recognize when they encounter this specific input. Great designers leverage all these elements. So when Chip Kidd designs a new book cover, he's using a set of highly leveraged icons, colors, type, and other cues to remind us of something else we read one day that we were glad we read. It's the potency of this process of reminding that makes it a good book cover.

Do you think he's doing it intentionally?

Yes, I'm sure he is, and if I consider on one hand the clueless person who thinks that being a designer is knowing how to use Photoshop or Illustrator, and, on the other hand, the insightful person who uses a pencil and paper but brings in the right mix of history and the future—only the latter is worth paying for. But I don't call that person a "brand designer." I call that person a designer who's helping create the future foundation for a brand.

Talk to me about this mix of history and future.

If, as a marketer, all I do is remind you of the past, then it's going to be very hard for me to grow. In that scenario, there isn't any promise, it's only an ambiance built on nostalgia. For example, let's consider *Reader's Digest*. *Reader's Digest* reminds me of being at my grandparents' house twenty years ago. The magazine is likely not going to attract new readers who didn't have that previous experience, and they're not going to get old readers to pick up every single issue because most of us are subject to the human drive to continually seek out novelty. The reason we keep refreshing the way so many things look is because of our ceaseless race to leverage the feelings of safety and nostalgia this old thing imparts, while simultaneously injecting a sense of newness to seduce us into reengaging in the experience. The film *Toy Story 3* is a good example. The producers successfully added a few new characters to the movie. This was critical. If the movie simply featured more adventures of the same old characters, there wouldn't be any excitement about what was going to happen next.

So in many ways, Toy Story 3 *is a successful brand extension.*

"Brand extension" is another term that makes me a little nervous.

Why?

If a brand is what I'm defining it as—a collection of expectations, etc.—then all brands are constantly extending themselves to the extent that they want to have more people embrace them. A line extension means that you are adding more products to the line so that you can get more shelf space or so that people will buy a second or third thing from you. It's more accurate to call *Toy Story 3* an extension of their line, as opposed to an extension of their brand, because the brand is constantly being extended every time you interact with it.

A lot of people think that brands are the reason civilization is doomed, and that they are part of a consumerist society that is inherently evil. Do you have any thoughts on this?

If you amplify anything too much, it backfires.

Brands have been around since before there were factories. Louis XIV had a brand, and years later, so did Marie Antoinette.

I don't think that the problem is brands; going back to what we're talking about, brands are just a description of expectations. I do believe that the shortsighted, selfish, and somewhat mindless attempt by factory owners to get people to buy more stuff regardless of the consequences is already coming back to haunt us. The U.S. marketplace for self-storage was $6 billion last year. This is to store stuff that we shouldn't have in the first place.

So why do we need these things? Why do we think we need these things?

Ever since humans began collecting rocks and twigs, we've wanted to trade one thing for another. Sometimes, the reason we make these trades is to feed ourselves, but after we've done that, the primary reason for such exchanges is to generate joy or connection. The trade we have in contemporary society is this: You go to work all day at a job you don't like and then trade some of the money you earn for something that you think will make you happy. The reason you think it will make you happy is that advertising and the like brainwashes you into believing it will. Some people live happily doing this for fifty or one hundred years, and die with no regrets. It is possible that this is a way to entertain and keep yourself happy. I'm hoping that over time people find other things.

So marketers and advertisers brainwash us? Why do we let ourselves get brainwashed? Isn't this something the government should be regulating?

What is brainwashing? I would say brainwashing is someone persuading you to do something that's not in your long-term interests. The hundreds of thousands of obese New Yorkers getting diabetes is proof that this is happening—and it's happening because Pepsi and Coke figured out a shortcut to a part of their brain. A while back, the managers at Pepsi were faced with a problem: The Coca-Cola bottle was so iconic that Pepsi was always going to be in second place. As long as the battle is on to see who can sell more bottles of sugar-water, Coke was going to win. But [former Pepsi executive] John Sculley commissioned a study and discovered that if you gave people an unlimited amount of soda, they would drink it. And when the bottle's bigger, people consume larger quantities. So Pepsi caught up because they started selling two-liter bottles of Pepsi—and Coke wasn't able to put that quantity into the fancy-shaped Coke bottles. Pepsi did something that was really clever. By putting more Pepsi into people's hands, the company got more people to drink Pepsi.

There's something in the way that human beings metabolize sugar that makes us want to keep drinking these concoctions. It's in our nature. We're hardwired like this. There are plenty of ways you can show this by hooking people up to an MRI to see which parts of their brains light up and what they'll do under the influence of sugar. We can do the same with rats and cocaine in a scientific experiment: They'll keep ingesting the drug until they die—they'll ignore food. I would argue that this is a classic example of what brainwashing would look like: If people could rationally look at their choices and develop enough wherewithal to think hard about it, they wouldn't keep drinking Pepsi until they died, which is what's happening.

So why do we let ourselves do it? It's not about "letting ourselves." It's about the fact that different people have different weaknesses and different amounts of willpower. And this is a classic example of how enough advertising and enough emotion will get people to do something that they probably shouldn't do. To answer the second half of your question, the reason the government doesn't stop this is because, over the past two hundred years, governments around the world work for the factories and corporations that employ us all. So as a brand marketer, the essential questions are, What kind of work do you want to do? How do you scale it? What is the thing you're trying to deliver? I think that a Hershey's bar a month might give someone joy—a Hershey's bar every three hours might make someone sick. If the only way that you're going to succeed as a brand is to make your best customers sick, then I think you need to wonder about whether that's a good long-term strategy.

So do you feel that companies like Pepsi or Coca-Cola are doing a disservice, or is it that people who buy Pepsi or Coca Cola have no control?

This is the real interesting question about free will. At what point does society say, "You're an adult. If you want to screw yourself over, go ahead." When I see a one-and-a-half-year-old in a baby stroller drinking a Pepsi out of a baby bottle, I have to question whether or not this is okay. At what point does this stop being an individual choice and start becoming something that society wants to or should do something about? It's a great question. I'm not sure I'm the person to speak to that. But it's pretty clear that when we're marketing things like tobacco and other products that clearly cross the line and become dangerous, we as a society take a deep breath and say, "No, this decision should not be left up to the individual." The question isn't whether there is a line—it's, "Where do you draw it?"

Let's shift gears a little: I listened to an interview with you where you talked about being insecure and a workaholic in remission. Is that true?

I've never been a workaholic. I know people who are workaholics. Workaholics are driven by fear, and I have not found myself in a position where I need to spend six or eight more hours at work because I'm trying to make everything okay.

What are they fearful of?

There is a part of the brain—that old prehistoric part—that controls the voice in our head, and it wants to be safe, to get through the day, and to make sure we reproduce. All of this is to ensure that it can continue. One of the ways you give in to that reptilian brain is when you constantly check your BlackBerry. Because if there's an incoming message on your BlackBerry, it just might be from your boss, saying, "You got caught; you're a fraud. You're fired!" So go ahead and check it, because if you didn't get that message this time, then your reptilian mind will be pacified until your BlackBerry vibrates again.

If you're in this frame of mind and need control, being a workaholic is a socially acceptable way to try to achieve that. Your boss thinks it's great, and you can get a raise for doing it. In the short run, it works really well because you can—at some level—control what you're doing and keep pushing the ball forward. You get into trouble when you get better at your work, and there's an increase in the number of people who want to interact with you and have you do more. So this kind of working method doesn't scale—you end up exploding.

The people who are doing great art and having an impact on the world aren't approaching their work in this way. I recently did an interview with the architect Michael Graves. Michael Graves works a lot. He's been in a wheelchair for more than seven years. He would be excused if he decided to scale back now after what's been an amazing career. But, instead, he's working on a multibillion-dollar development in Singapore, etc., etc. If you look at the way Michael works, he brings a good heart and the right attitudes to his projects at all times. He *is* doing important work—work that changes things. But he's not a workaholic because he's not doing it defensively. He's doing it productively.

So that's the difference: defensive versus productive. When you say "good heart and right attitude," I'm wondering how that is expressed. Can you talk more about that defensiveness and the need to be safe and reproduce and get through the day? Do you think that these drives have something to do with our addiction to brands, soda, and other things that we think are going to make us feel good—when in fact they might just be a temporary fix?

That's a good question. Here's the distinction: the reptilian brain only has one tone of voice. There are lots of voices in our head when we're picking out wallpaper or imagining the senior prom or talking to a friend. There are lots of different emotions that we can seek out and enjoy. But the fear the reptilian brain produces always sounds the same. It's just as nervous when we hit turbulence as it is when we see the boss's name on our caller ID or when the teacher calls on us and we're not prepared. It always has the same feeling and tone of voice. That is the key distinction between the different mental postures. If we're running around in this defensive mode, trying to make everything okay, it's very one-dimensional. There are certain products that are sold to us to soothe or placate the lizard brain. There are certain products that are sold to us with the expectation that if you don't buy it, people are going to make fun of you.

What are some brands that do that?

The TSA tries to make you feel this way in airports when they get you to surrender a snow globe and then feel as though you're being a good citizen for doing so. I would argue that the cosmetics industry does this by trying to sell hope in a bottle—and selling fear as its counterpoint. They tell you that if you don't wear this concealer, or if you have stinky underarms, everything is going to fall apart, because you won't be popular or attractive anymore.

Do you think that brands like Levi's, Nike, or Apple have capitalized on some of that fear?

When Apple is doing its best work, it's doing exactly the opposite. If you go to an Apple store on the day a new product is released, you can see nerds walking out holding boxes lifted over their heads, and they're being applauded by the very employees who have sold them the product. The sense of belonging, the experience of overcoming loneliness, and the thrill of reaching the pinnacle of geekhood can be yours for a few hundred or a few thousand dollars. The brand experience gives these people a joy that they don't have in many other areas of their lives. So I don't think Apple at its best is selling you with a strategy that's about avoiding fear. Something like Axe antiperspirant is, however, an example where half the time they're selling to you by appealing to horny avarice, and half the time they're selling to you by tapping into the insecurity that only a fifteen-year-old can feel.

Axe is owned by Unilever, which also owns Dove, and Dove has leveraged "real beauty" as its point of difference. Its ads feature women who are imperfect, chubby, and wrinkly, and Dove lauds the idea that it's okay to have physical imperfections. The company has even created viral videos of a young woman facing an onslaught of advertising images that portray women as surgically enhanced and übersexualized beings. Yet it seems as if the Axe brand is using the very image that the Dove brand so willfully protests. Is it possible to reconcile both messages?

I think that's a fair question. It comes down to worldview. Different people have different worldviews that change the way they see the world. The question I'd ask before your question is whether Unilever has an obligation to change the worldview of fifteen-year-old boys. If the answer is, "No," then selling a product to fifteen-year-old boys that matches their expectations of the universe is exactly what Unilever's shareholders need the company to do. If the answer is, "Yes, they do have an obligation to reconcile those messages," then I think there's a long list of brands that we could talk about, regardless of whether the company that owns them also markets Dove or a brand like it.

Do you think this kind of dissonance makes one brand less authentic than another?

I don't think I've ever said branding is authentic. Hanes panty hose didn't have a woman running the brand for fifty years. Every once in a while, a man would go home wearing panty hose under his jeans so he could find out what it felt like.

Branding is rarely presented to the world with a message of "authentically made by people who believe exactly what you believe."

I think there are people who would like to believe branding has always been authentic. But there have been popes who have had multiple children of their own running around the Vatican. Now there's a long, long history of marketing not being authentic.

Dan Formosa

Cofounder, Smart Design

Dan Formosa and his colleagues at Smart Design have revolutionized the world of objects and interactivity. In the process, they've transformed branding and the field of design. With their innovative approach of designing for people at the "edges"—both the connoisseurs and those with physical limitations—they've brought both a democraticization and refinement to the design world. The objects they craft—kitchen tools and accessories as well as digital devices—can be used by left-handers and right-handers, tall and short, longtime experts and first-time novices. That philosophy of accessibility is what continues to drive Formosa, and he feels it is an important tenet for any brand. "Everyone should have access to whatever technology or product your brand offers," he says.

When Formosa cofounded Smart in the early '80s, companies were designing products without devoting much thought to the question of whether or not they were usable. Usability tests were a rare exception in that era, and, as Formosa recalls, marketing divisions looked at designers with antipathy. The marketing teams were the power players when it came to deciding what consumers wanted, and the nascent design firm's desire to talk to consumers "freaked our clients out."

Of course, the Smart Design posse changed all that, and their story is indicative of the way in which branding and design is continually evolving. Once upon a time, human-centered design was unheard-of, which suggests that there is now some emerging or as-yet-undreamed-of discipline that may one day have a similarly dramatic impact on the field of design.

Formosa has been ahead of the curve for decades, and, as such, he has keen insight into the way we adopt—or resist—new technologies and innovations. This topic became a consistent theme that threads throughout our discussion. At the time when Formosa started, using computers to design was looked on as "evil," and usability was not considered to be a designer's responsibility. Formosa ignored such knee-jerk claptrap and experimented with computer-based design in school, when he could only create a rudimentary wire-frame schematic. He later used his expertise to help design one of the first laptop computers. He also devoted himself to creating work that was suited to the biomechanics of the human body, an ethos that went iconic with the groundbreaking OXO kitchen products.

Formosa applies his foresight to managing the rate of innovation—while he might clearly envision the technology and design of the future, he acknowledges that change must be introduced in a step-by-step process that allows innovations to be digested and integrated into our everyday lives, ensuring a positive feedback loop for both brand and public. And more important than this is the necessity that brands have vision. With Formosa at the helm, there is no doubt they will.

Smart Design recently received a National Design Award for "Product Design," and you were also recognized for "Corporate and Institutional Achievement," since OXO was nominated in that category. You had a very major role in creating OXO as a brand. Tell me about that process.

My partners and I began Smart Design in 1980 and 1981, just a few years out of college. Back in the '70s, the state of design was not great, and generally, the design firms were doing very superficial work. At that time, design was considered to be primarily about aesthetics, and was mainly associated with designer jeans, fashion, and the superficial appearance and presentation of a product. Designers did not have a lot of understanding or interest in terms like "usability" or "quality of life." Design and advertising were very much controlled by marketing groups within organizations who assigned projects to designers. Very often, the design projects were not based on any actual understanding of consumers or needs. They were based on marketing opportunities.

So it was reactive.

It was very reactive, and design usually happened at the very end of the project. It would be done when the engineering was already completed. It was very superficial.

We had a different point of view about design. It wasn't unprecedented—there were some great examples of design through the '30s, '40s, '50s, and '60s, but it wasn't the norm.

When we were asked to work with a company on a project, we would always request to talk to their consumers. The reaction from the people at the company was always, "*What*? You can't do that. We're the marketing group. We own the consumer. You have no business talking to consumers."

There were no usability tests? There was no way to understand how people were actually going to physically interact with a product?

It was rare.

If you went into a store and bought something and tried to use it—a coffeemaker, for example—you could immediately tell that there hadn't been any usability tests conducted, given how hard it was for people to get it to work. In fact, if you saw something that looked "designed," you'd be a little suspicious.

We came out of college in the 1960s and '70s, and we wanted to change the world. We wanted to do work that had some sort of social relevance.

Was that the actual, specific intention? Did the three of you think, "Okay, there's a real need for testing product usability with consumers, and no one else is fulfilling that. We can change the world by doing this"?

Yes. You have to understand that marketing had a bad reputation then too. It wasn't unusual to think marketing is evil, and we all did. And actually, many things *were* evil back then: big business, government—everything was evil. We wanted to change the world. I think it was in the DNA of that whole generation to question authority, and with good reason. The idea of working in a system that we didn't align with philosophically wasn't acceptable. So, it seemed possible to try living our ideals when we started the studio—we had nothing to lose. It was a lot better than getting a job in one of the companies we didn't trust.

When we opened the office, it was all about design and about people. I'm not sure we sat there and yelled that out from our seats, but that was our intention. We knew we needed to get out into people's homes and witness how they actually behaved. We knew our vision wasn't about the perfect people being portrayed in television commercials. From our own observations, we knew that these were idealized images that companies were feeding the public—but they didn't exist in the real world. So we purposefully took a more reality-based approach.

How did you end up working with the designer Eliot Noyes at IBM? Did he simply call and say, "Hey, Dan, we're trying to change the world. Want to help?"

It was completely by chance. When I got out of college, rather than get a job just anywhere, I decided to freelance for a while. I figured that this would allow me to meet a lot of people, and see how different people work. The trick to doing this sort of work is being able to respond when people call you at the last minute or at odd hours or when they need help with a difficult problem. And the project in this case was making the first IBM PC. At the time, IBM knew that there were some guys out in California who had started building a computer in their garage—that was Steve Jobs and Steve Wozniak. IBM was a huge, behemoth organization, and the secrecy around their PC project was tremendous. So the work wasn't positioned as, "Hey, we're introducing the first IBM PC." At that point, it was about helping to build a home computer.

What motivated Eliot to call you?

I was recommended to him through a personal connection. I was a young, junior designer just out of college, and I imagine that I seemed like a reasonable person who would show up to the job. I had also taken a lot of computer courses when I was in school, and there weren't too many of us around.

Why was that?

You have to remember that back in the 1970s, computers were seen as evil. It's hard to even imagine that now. Radical student movements were against computer companies, and put them in the same category as Big Brother. Computers were as evil as marketing was. It's hard to relate to this now because everyone has a computer on their desk or has cute little friendly devices that beep at them and that they can keep in their pockets.

But to give you an idea of the difference, I remember that back then, I was able to create a very crude wire-frame shape. After I drew a line and rotated that line 360 degrees, twelve or twenty-four times, I was able to define the shape of a bowl. And so I decided that I was going to design a bowl by creating an outline. Of course, now that process seems very simple. But I was able to spin the line around, and what I got was a very crude wire frame—and I was able to produce a very crude print of that. I brought it into my college design studio, and I was ostracized for designing something on a computer. The students thought I was evil.

That was the last time I ever showed to my colleagues something that I made on a computer. They thought I was selling out. They couldn't understand how I could mechanize an artistic creation. The next thing I know, I'm out of college and I get a call for a project to design a home computer. I was one of a handful of people with experience using a computer to design something, and I was one of the few who knew what "CPU" meant. When the engineers came in and did their wiring diagram, I understood it.

So my background was very helpful, and then working together, it was very interesting imagining what a home computer would be. Initially, IBM envisioned it as a vehicle for entertainment that would sit in your living room. It was a cross between a computer and a high-end audio/stereo unit. But no one knew what people would do with a computer in their living room. It was just an idea. We assumed that the way into people's hearts was through entertainment. But the computers had keyboards, and the question was, "How are we going to get a keyboard to be appropriate in a living room?" That was unheard-of. So it was very interesting. The action monitor would have been someone's TV screen, but we didn't actually design a monitor.

This is all amazingly early in the timeline of modern technology. We were trying to envision what a home computer could be! I have a collection of memorabilia from the project, including the original wiring diagram proposed by the engineers that I then drew to their specifications.

Did you have any idea of the impact that this piece of technology was going to have?

No, but I remember two things very specifically. The person who was running this program at IBM made a comparison between Betamax and VHS. He told me they didn't want something like Betamax, where Sony owned the system and they wouldn't license it out to anyone. Instead, very early on, they envisioned developing an operating system that other computer companies could use. That eventually turned into Windows. The Microsoft Windows system is available on hundreds of different computers by hundreds of different manufacturers. Apple went the Betamax route.

IBM very specifically didn't want to do that. They also had a particular plan about development. They said, "We're not going to develop the operating system ourselves. We have this group on the West Coast that is going to develop the operating system."

Who was that?

I'm assuming it was Microsoft, but I was so young and it was so long ago, I don't remember. But I remember thinking, "Wow. That's odd. IBM has one hundred thousand employees—why would they possibly need to go to an outside group to develop an operating system?" If I had had my wits about me, I would have gone to the West Coast and become employee number four in that company. But I wasn't thinking that far ahead about what was happening.

I was interested in usability issues and in how a keyboard would work if it was folded—and so forth. In my work as a designer through the late '70s, I was equally interested in design and in the basic physical biomechanics of humans, such as, "How does your hand fit this?" Or, "If you're going to press something, maybe it should be a shape that you can press down on," or, "If you're going to pick something up, make it easy to pick up. Figure out where the center of gravity is. Figure out where the balance is." I was very practical.

As we started Smart Design in the '80s, we had the idea that design could be for everybody. At the time, design was primarily applied to things that were expensive. But we thought typical household items could be designed with intelligence and that expense wasn't necessary.

We actually felt that if you design things well, it could be less expensive, because we understood how things could be manufactured more efficiently. We knew how to get the most out of nothing. Very early on, we made sure that when we designed a product, it was as usable by left-handed people as it was by right-handed people.

We felt that design should not be elite, and design should not exclude people. And as we worked with clients, we had a lot of projects where we proposed that we needed to go out and talk to people. This freaked our clients out.

Designers didn't do market research. Marketing researchers were supposed to do market research. Then we tried calling it "consumer research," thinking that it might go over better if we didn't use the word "marketing." But that wasn't received well either, because the market researchers were the ones "in charge" of consumers. Then we realized that if we write a project plan and call it "design research," they might not feel so threatened, given that the term starts with the word "design."

Back then, if you went to a design meeting and started talking about ergonomics, mechanics, or psychology, you actually got a lot of resistance from designers who felt that design wasn't about these things. It was a very odd time for design.

I've heard a lot of stories about designers being reluctant to accept new technologies or new methodologies. I wonder why that is. I remember back when compact discs first came out, I remember people saying they'd never last. Back in 1987, when Sinéad O'Connor's album The Lion and the Cobra *came out, I bought the album because CDs were a new technology, and I still had so much allegiance to vinyl. And that was the last album I ever bought. Do you think there's something specifically human about resisting new things.*

Yes. We see it all the time. Sometimes when we're trying to innovate, we may think of the first step as a baby step. We need to consider how we're going to wean people over to the new system. Often, there's an in-between product that will begin to change the way people perceive things. But if you take too far of a leap all at once, people may not be ready for it.

Do you have to manage change as much as you manage innovation?

Sometimes. Sometimes that's a good strategy, but it isn't a universal rule. But I do agree that designers in general can be a very conservative group. And it seems like a contradiction in terms that designers are conservative, but they tend to be.

I understand that you have several different degrees outside of your degree in design.

Yes. By the mid-'80s, I decided to get a master's degree in biomechanics and ergonomics. I became very interested in biomechanics and the physical aspects of design, as well as in psychology. So I decided to get a master's degree in biomechanics that I could apply to design, usability, and understanding how people use things. Then, in 1990, we were approached to think about kitchen tools that would accommodate a wide range of people's needs—that project is what developed into OXO. The collaboration turned out to be a very good match. The intent behind OXO was literally to design for everybody.

How do you do that? How do you design for everybody?

The way to think about "everybody" is not to think about the average person in the middle, but to think about the extremes. Think about people at the edges of your potential buying public and think about people who are most challenged. Also, you have to look at people who are experts. In the case of OXO, we looked at chefs and cooks. We wanted to understand both ends of the spectrum—those who are challenged and those who are experts.

We also needed to recognize that someone with arthritis was not also an expert cook. Yet we couldn't assume that we have to consider people with arthritis and people who are experts at cooking as separate categories. They could be the same person. And you could also have a healthy person who knows nothing about cooking. Our research needed to be reality-based. We could not stereotype.

What's most interesting about the OXO work is that we never conducted any marketing studies.

The founder of the company, Sam Farber, shared his vision with us, and we expanded and enhanced his vision. But it was never subjected to marketing studies, and we never sought the permission of consumers. We simply conducted usability studies to ensure that people could use the products and to make sure that the products we were designing were usable.

But it was a very radical idea. It was never based on asking permission, and twenty years later, it's rare for OXO to veer from this approach.

Do you think that truly innovative companies do less market research in general?

A common element to a really good brand is a vision. We work with a lot of different companies, and that vision is not always solid or established. Sometimes there is no vision. And we've also seen companies who have brilliant vision. But vision is not a solution or even a design. The vision is where you see yourself going. The vision is essentially a goal.

But we also see companies who turn to research with an expectation that the consumer is going to give them that vision. That usually doesn't happen.

Is there a particular mind-set that companies need to embrace to be truly innovative? It seems that so much of what marketing is doing now is managing fear, not innovating new paradigms.

Yes. What happens in the typical design process is very linear. Phase 1 is research, and phase 2 involves creating concepts. Phase 3 focuses on refinement and development and eventually the team finalizes the design. This is a model that's being used by virtually all design and product development groups. But there's probably a much better model where you actually begin by putting together a really good team with a vision. And if you don't have a vision, don't go on.

*In the case of OXO, you said that you were designing
for the edges and not the mainstream. But if you try
to design for everybody, is there a risk of designing for
the lowest common denominator? How are you able to
innovate if you're trying to please everybody?*

Thinking about designing for everybody does not mean that one product has to suit everybody.

For instance, if we're designing a T-shirt,
it's not like one T-shirt fits all. I'm not politically
outraged if I see that people wear different shoes
and they're all different sizes because you can't
wear the size that I wear. But if there's a cell phone
that's not usable by a certain segment of the
population, that turns into a form of discrimination
or segregation. If there are people who can't use
that technology even though they want to, but it's
not designed for them, you're alienating or isolating
those people because of the fact that they have
certain limitations. What you should realize is that
this provides you with an opportunity, through
design, to accommodate a wide range of people. But
this approach doesn't start first with design. It starts
with the vision that everyone should have access to
whatever technology or product your brand offers.

In designing a building, which is a public space,
or a bus or a taxicab, of course, you need to make those
accessible by everyone. You can't have individual
buildings with completely separate entrances for
people with different limitations. In architecture, it's
pretty normal to think about accessibility.

*Accessibility is a topic that comes up in relation to
the Internet—and though it's somewhat different
from what you're discussing, it's still also relevant
to branding. In that sense, given the accessibility of
the Internet, do you think that it's changed the way
brands are perceived?*

I think the Internet has given us the ability to communicate rapidly, globally, and instantly. People are now enabled by technology to do things that they wouldn't have otherwise conceived—it's not as if technology was there and people aspired to achieve what we're able to do now. You can find like-minded people, and you can trade ideas, tips, secrets, and techniques. And it's fascinating, which is probably why so many people are glued to their electronic devices. But I don't think they're in love with the technology or the devices! I think that what they love is that they've found a personal connection to someone, either across the room or across the world, with whom they share a common bond. And I think they're in love with the effect that they can have by connecting with people.

Do you think that people are now addicted to this effect? People talk about being addicted to e-mail, Facebook, Twitter, or any number of technological hubs where they're connecting with people.

Yes, that's true. I do think maybe you can get out of your computer chair once in a while. But I think that connecting with people is not a bad thing, and the devices have enabled this. People want this—companies are not forcing it down their throats. Back in the 1980s and '90s, the products were about the technology. People were willing to follow technology and decide that they wanted a new camera because it had better resolution, or they wanted a new computer because it was faster. But now, those kinds of concerns are less important. People are not as focused on technology as they used to be. What they want now is to experience personal meaning through their phone, their computer, their Facebook account—or their camera. They're not interested in following technology; they want to understand how technology will be a benefit to them. People were a lot more enamored with brands and technology throughout the '80s and '90s. They became less so in the 2000s, and will continue to become less so in the 2010s.

Why do so many people think that spending time on Facebook or Twitter somehow means that we are burying ourselves in technology or that society is doomed?

It's a little bit funny to say that we're burying ourselves in technology when people are using technology to communicate. There's probably a human on the other end of that string.

Considering all the predictions about the future of technology, I wonder why no one was able to predict how popular text messaging was going to become.

When the French first upgraded their phone system, they created a system called Minitel, which gave users access to basic information and interactivity. The designers of the system found, to their complete surprise, that people were using it the most for quick messaging. This speaks to the singular appeal of this kind of expression: Text messages are a completely unique communication form. You can get away with expressing things that are not necessarily full thoughts. It's a method of communication that is casual, instant, and immediate.

Do you think it's going to change the way we spell? If you look back four hundred years ago to the writing of Shakespeare, the language and the spelling he used is very different from the language and spelling we use now.

Absolutely! If you read the Declaration of Independence, there are strange spellings all over the place.

How do you think our language is going to evolve? Do
you think that we're going to end up spelling the word
"you" with ...

        ... the letter *U?*

... instead of Y-O-U?

        And the question "Are you okay?" will be
        spelled "ruok?"

Yes!

        Sure. Why not? Language has always evolved.
        The dictionary gets updated every year because
        language evolves—new words come into play, and
        words change meaning.

It will be interesting to see what our language is like in
one hundred years.

        One hundred? Let's see how different it will be in
        ten years. It won't take one hundred. LOL.

Bill Moggridge

Cofounder, IDEO; Director, Cooper-Hewitt, National Design Museum

---

Bill Moggridge is a design legend. He helped to create some of the milestones of modern design: the first laptop among them. As one of the cofounders of the design firm IDEO, he's helped to craft and shepherd other key projects. Throughout its history, IDEO has had a dramatic influence on design and continues as one of the seminal forces shaping the way our world is designed.

Through the cutting-edge work he did at IDEO, Moggridge in effect educated the general public, through example, about the extraordinary value of design. It could inform the way we work, the way we interact with machines, could define the very nature of many of our day-to-day activities themselves.

Education may not have been Moggridge's initial goal when he started designing, but as his work progressed, he became more interested in "telling stories about design." So he began writing design criticism as well as teaching at London's Royal College of Art and Stanford University. He's now written two books, Designing Interactions *and* Designing Media, *in which he explores the aesthetics, revolutions, and key design principles of the modern multimedia phantasmagoria.*

Moggridge has recently become the director of Cooper-Hewitt, National Design Museum. One of his mandates in this role is to educate as wide a public as possible about design. As part of this effort, Moggridge has identified four audiences that would benefit from some design schooling: young children, business professionals, the general public, and business and government leaders. Moggridge is developing strategies so that each of these audiences will have access to design and understand the benefits of it. "It doesn't occur to most people that everything is designed," he says.

Through education and exposure, Moggridge aims to enrich the vocabulary and possibility of design. He would like high schoolers to study design in school and business leaders to understand that seemingly intractable conundrums can be solved by interdisciplinary design teams. Beyond this, he wants to build Cooper-Hewitt into a "national design resource" and an "international design authority." Moggridge has been a tireless advocate of design, and thanks to his work, Cooper-Hewitt is evolving to fulfill that much more expansive mandate.

How does branding fit into all this? Moggridge's central concern throughout his career, as he notes at the beginning of our conversation, has been his interest in people and their relationship to things. Brands are at the crux of how people define their relationships to objects—providing a way of navigating the complexity of modern life while creating the lasting satisfaction we derive from brand affiliations.

The importance of human-centered design is a mantra for Moggridge. Having contributed to the creation of the first laptop, Moggridge is well versed in the foibles relating to the adoption of new technologies. A fascinating part of our discussion focused on this, and Moggridge makes an interesting point about technologies that have premiered and then floundered. Years later, similar technology is reintroduced—and flourishes.

Moggridge emphasizes that the success of design also hinges on designers' empathy for a public that may not be as well versed in design as they are: "We're guilty of designing for ourselves too often." Yet if design literacy improves through Moggridge's efforts, then designers will be able to employ a more complex, a much more nuanced language.

You're currently director of the Cooper-Hewitt,
National Design Museum, and you've said that your
career had three phases before you took on this latest
role. First, you were a designer, then a manager of
design, and then a communicator, when you worked
as a writer, graphic designer, and video maker. And
you began by studying industrial design at the Central
Saint Martins College of Art and Design in London.
Why industrial design?

> Well, I think it was probably because my older
> brother was studying architecture, and I wanted to
> be like him. But then I discovered you could design
> things on a more intimate scale, in the sense of
> creating the objects that are around us. That led me
> to industrial design.

I read that you're fascinated with what people want
from everyday things. Is that true?

> Absolutely. If there is a simple, easy principle that
> binds together everything I've done, it's my interest
> in people and their relationship to things.

Are you fascinated equally by people and things, or are
you interested in one more than the other?

> Well, it's definitely people first—the relationship
> people have with things, places, and our
> environment. I'm interested in why people like
> things, and what gives them a feeling of long-term
> reward, what gives them pleasure, and what excites
> them. Ultimately, my interest centers on the effect
> that design has on someone.

Why do you think people like certain brands or certain
things? What is the primary reason someone will
choose one thing over another?

> I think you build a relationship with something that
> you know and use. At the moment you buy it, you
> may not be quite certain about it. But as you get to
> know it better, if your relationship gets better, then

you enjoy it more. You may not notice the change, but after a time, a sort of satisfactory relationship between you and that thing emerges. That is the foundation for a brand relationship.

I recently read that the average supermarket has about thirty-five thousand different products in it, and that—believe it or not—there are over one hundred brands of nationally advertised water.

I think this is another symptom of the information overload that we face in every walk of life. When you do a Google search, it's very tempting to go for the "I'm feeling lucky" option, so you get the single page that comes up. Similarly, the brand is the thing that allows you to recognize that particular kind of water that you had before, and that you probably don't mind having again.

So it simplifies your relationship to this confusing morass of possibilities. And although I wish that water wasn't bottled, the fact that there's a choice of brand helps us get through that confusion.

You were involved in designing the first laptop. Do you think that the laptop is going to continue to exist, given the advent and introduction of devices such as the iPod, the iPad, and the Kindle? Do you think the laptop is still going to be around in ten years?

Ten years, no question. The laptop is an input and output structure. The output is display. And that display is pretty much the equivalent of an iPad, only bigger and better. So it could easily be replaced by another form of information display, perhaps one that would involve projection, for example. And then there's the input. It's very surprising how good the mouse still is. Until we find something a lot better than the mouse, the mouse still remains pretty good. The trackpad is pretty good, the stylus is pretty good, but the mouse is better. So in terms of things that will allow us to input, perhaps the future will entail voice recognition or handwriting recognition, sketching, mousing, all those methods and input devices. But they would probably still be resident in laptops.

But in the spectrum that ranges from the little thing in your hand, like a smartphone, to the in-between size like the iPad, and to the large-scale workstation, the laptop is still a very good in-between place to be. It's something that gives you maximum work capability and is, at the same time, easy to carry in your backpack or your briefcase. That's still a pretty good formula.

Several years ago, you wrote a book called Designing Interactions. *It was named one of the ten best innovation and design books that year by* BusinessWeek *magazine. In the book, you talk at length about the creation of the laptop. And one of your colleagues at the time—a man named Alan Kay—is quoted considerably in the chapter about developing the GRiD Compass, the first laptop, which you designed in 1979. You described him as saying, "In the 1990s, there will be millions of personal computers. They will be the size of notebooks today, have high-resolution flat-screen reflexive displays, weigh less than ten pounds, and have ten to twenty times the computing and storage capacity of an Alto [one of the earliest personal computers, developed in 1973]. Let's call them 'Dynabooks.'"*

He said this in 1971, and nearly everything he predicted has come true! How did he have this ability to see the future so clearly?

Alan is a genius of invention. If you look at so many things that came out of PARC—the Xerox Palo Alto Research Center—during the '60s, '70s, and '80s, Alan was a key figure in many of them. He had the unique ability to both visualize the future and to invent it.

While you were working on the laptop, did you
have any sense of how significant a contribution to
technology and culture it was going to be?

I think there are very few opportunities that a designer has in a career to do something that is truly precedent-setting. And it was clear to me that everything we were doing in that project was precedent-setting. In fact, I signed part of the patent that detailed forty-three different items of innovation on the GRiD. My part was only one of those. I realized there were so many things happening on that project that were different from anything that had come before, and it was very exciting to think these things could really make a big difference. But I don't think I could have predicted it was going to spread in the way it did.

When did you first start working with David Kelley,
who later became your partner at IDEO?

David and I started collaborating in the '80s. We got very used to working together—we called it "eight years dating." Eventually we got "married" and created IDEO together.

Why do you think you were so successful together?

The thing that was really powerful in our initial success was the combination of our expertise in technical and human-centered design. We were both good at both, and we were able to put the two together in a very unique way for our clients.

What do you mean by "human-centered design"?

If you think of innovation as being depicted by a Venn diagram, human-centered design is the overlap between technology, business, and people. If you look at people who are going to business schools, they tend to start with a business proposition, but in order to innovate successfully, they have to find the right technology and the right customers. If you look at people in science and technology, they tend to start with a new technology, which is true of many Silicon Valley companies. Then they go to a venture capitalist and try to get some money, and they think about what kind of customer is right for the product. We were interested in the "people first" point of view.

Can you give me an example of a brand where a "people first" point of view was particularly successful?

The Palm computer is a good example of "people first." Palm founder Jeff Hawkins wanted to create a computer that would fit in a person's pocket. He had a goal of making a really simple product and defined his four design criteria as size, price, synchronization, and speed. At that time, Apple had already tried to make something small-size.

The Newton.

Yes, and it was not successful. The Newton was a mixture of being too big and too expensive and having too unique of a user interface. And there were several other devices as well. Jeff was successful because he was able to work with his team to develop a product that delivered on all four attributes, which was truly breakthrough. If you took the same kind of design brief at a different generation in palm computing—say, ten years later—you wouldn't use those four criteria. There would be new criteria based on the maturity of the technology. But it was a breakthrough initially because of those four attributes.

Do you think that the inability to fulfill any of those four attributes is what ultimately made Newton a failure?

Yes. The Newton was too expensive, too big, and too heavy. It wouldn't fit in a pocket, and it wasn't quite clear what it could be used for. But it was incredibly cool and a beautiful piece of user interface design. And it contained a lot of lovely little attributes. For example, when you threw something away, the file went up in a puff, a design trope that still exists on Macs today. But the Newton didn't have the right attributes to succeed in the marketplace. This is often the case with new technologies. They seem as if they're about to work, and somebody creates an experimental version that looks great. But then nothing happens. And then the right time comes along, and the right set of attributes come together, and suddenly the new technology flourishes.

Can you explain how that happens? Why is something unsuccessful at one particular time and then nearly the same thing is incredibly successful years later?

Well, I've worked a little bit with Paul Saffo at Stanford University. He calls himself a forecaster and spends a lot of time thinking about the future. He was the original founder of the research group called Institute for the Future. One of the things that was most interesting in coteaching with him was the way that he talked about innovation. He refers to the acceptance of a new technology as a "twenty-year hockey stick curve," where the curve starts out relatively level and then has an inflection point where it increases exponentially. Paul believes that when you discover a new technology—when it starts to seem possible—it's usually too expensive or too heavy or too wrong in some way. But it looks as if it's going to have great potential. Then there's a lot of interest in it, and people invest a lot in it, and it fails. And then after a period of about twenty years, people have got rather bored with it, and they think it's dead. And just when people lose interest in it, somebody gets the specifications right, and finally it takes off.

What is nearing the inflection point in the twenty-year
hockey stick curve now?

Well, handwriting recognition and voice recognition are probably far along that curve right now. We're now getting to the point where automatic voice recognition on telephones is not too painful. Remember ten years ago, how awful that was? That was the beginning of the curve. I think we're on our way up now.

How hard is it to differentiate between what people
really need and what a designer might want to create
for himself? For example, if you're designing something
for an audience that could include you, how much of
your needs and desires define the prototyping versus
those of the audience?

Well, I think as designers and engineers in general, we're guilty of designing for ourselves too often. One of the things that we have to be careful to remember is the very simple principle that not everybody is like us. For example, if you're designing something like a chair, you're not going to design the height of the seat only for the average person, are you? You're going to design it for an adjustment, so that it can accommodate the smallest person that might sit in it, or the tallest, as well as the heaviest person and the lightest person. So, we're always looking at a range that accommodates extremes, and for that reason, looking at the extremes is usually very useful.

Of course, you look at the middle as well, but you always need to be thinking about the oddest and the most conventional, the fattest and the thinnest, the most clever and the least. You must always look at the edge of the bell curve.

You were appointed the director of the Cooper-Hewitt,
National Design Museum, in March 2010. I found that
news surprising, because I recalled reading an article

in which you said that your main goal in life was to
design things. What changed?

> At the very beginning of our conversation, you spoke about three phases of my life. The first involved designing things. And although I helped create IDEO, after the foundation of the firm was solid, I began working with interdisciplinary teams that designed things together. And I got interested in telling stories about design, so I began doing my writing and teaching. When I heard about the Cooper-Hewitt vacancy, it occurred to me that it might be possible to do these things on a national scale. I looked into the requirements and the position description, and there it was, in black and white. They were looking for a person who would help the museum both physically and virtually, but they were also looking for someone to help develop a national design resource and an international design authority. I thought this was a perfect opportunity for storytelling. So I applied for the job.

What are your plans for the museum?

> I've identified four broad audiences to communicate with: kids, professionals, the public, and leadership. We'd like every kid in America to have an experience of design by the time they are twelve, and have the opportunity to study it in high school if they want.

When you say "design," do you mean any and all
aspects of design? What kind of experience do you
imagine that young students could have?

> The important characteristic of design is that it creates a bridge between the sciences and the arts. People understand the necessity of education for the sciences, and there is a renewed movement to bring that back into education. They understand something about the arts. But I don't think many people understand the power of design to join these two things together.

Why do you think that there is such a barrier to the public's understanding of design?

I don't think that anyone has really told them what design is. It doesn't occur to most people that everything is designed—that every building and everything they touch in the world is designed. Even foods are designed now.

Even water is designed.

Exactly. So in the process of helping people understand this, making them more aware of the fact that the world around us is something that somebody has control of, perhaps they can feel some sense of control too. That's a nice ambition.

The fourth category you talked about was leadership. What do you mean by that?

I think it would be great if every business leader in America knew how to use design in order to create more successful innovations and solutions. There is a strong movement at the moment for that to happen. Most business schools have design programs, although if you think about the number of students who go through a business school, only a small proportion of them will actually take design classes. But the fact that there are now design programs in the business schools is a huge step in the right direction.

But we could do a lot more to help business leaders understand how to use the design process or "design thinking"—in order to be more successful. I'd like everyone to have the mind-set that whenever you have a challenging, seemingly intractable problem, then you need to solve that problem with an interdisciplinary team. No individual can succeed alone. In order to help business leaders succeed, we need to put together those interdisciplinary teams, and they need to use design processes. We can help explain that and help make leadership aware of it.

*How do you feel about new technologies that are
connecting people, such as Facebook and Twitter?*

Social media? Actually, for my latest book,
Designing Media, I interviewed many of the people
who founded these new companies and created
these new technologies, including Facebook,
Twitter, YouTube, and so on. My interview with
Mark Zuckerberg was quite interesting. He
seemed really enthusiastic and genuine. It could
have been that the interview was a calculated
performance on his part, but that was not the way
he came across to me. I thought he really did have
an ambition to make things that could work for
people. Of course, he's also incredibly young. I
interviewed him in 2009, so he was twenty-four
at the time. It was a really interesting experience.
I went to the interview accompanied only by my
cinematographer, and we were waiting in the lobby
of the Facebook offices. Then we walked through
the beautiful building they have, where several
hundred people work. And you could see in this
open space all these people around the office space.
I realized that anywhere I looked, there probably
wasn't a single person who was more than half my
age. So there was a little bit of a generation gap.

*I'm sure he was quite respectful of the contribution
you've made that has allowed him to get where he is
now—I'm sure he understands the continuity of one
innovation leading to another.*

The one thing that's interesting about social media
is that it has fulfilled its promise at last. Look at the
way the Internet has developed: When it started to
become popularized, people thought of it as being a
place for community. Of course, it wasn't initially—
it was a place where you looked through various
pages. So you browsed one page after another in
a rather tedious way. In that sense, it was really
an information provider. With e-mail, it became a
communication platform.

But it wasn't a place where people developed community. And what's happened in the era of Web 2.0 is that social media are, at last, fulfilling the promise that technology has for people to build communities and to be friendly with each other.

In Designing Interactions, *you quoted Palm's Jeff Hawkins as saying, "What makes humans special first and foremost is that we can model the world, and we can predict the future. Then we can imagine the future." You've done a great deal of visionary work—the laptop, the Apple mouse, and different iterations of the Palm. What do you imagine for the future?*

I have to go back to the principle we talked about before: I'm hoping design will still be created with people in mind. As designers, we can create solutions and synthesize results to improve people's lives and make things better. I think the context of design is changing and expanding. And you can think of that in three concentric circles.

Think of the inside circle as the individual. The second circle is the built environment, and the one around that is the overall, holistic environment. Each concentric circle is changing and moving in a design context that is itself expanding.

In the past, we thought about designing things for the circle at the center. So your PDA, for example, is something that you use as an individual.

The slightly more expansive context is to think about the health and well-being of the individual, rather than the specific things the individual uses. This more comprehensive view requires broader thinking about people. Rather than thinking about the things in isolation, we're thinking about the whole person.

Similarly, when you think about the built environment, we historically have thought about architecture. But as we move towards an expanding context for design, we find that we're thinking more about social interactions and innovations as well as buildings. It's not that one is replacing the other—it's that the context is simply expanding. Now we're thinking about social connections as well as the built environment we're living in.

And then when we think about the larger circle, sustainability is the big issue. In the past, we thought of sustainability as being about materials: choosing the best material and designing for disassembly. But now it's absolutely clear that a sustainable planet is one that's completely connected.

Globalization has shown us that the effect of industrialization on the world is of planetary concern. We can't just think about designing materials, we have to include a consideration of the entire planet. And that, again, is an expansion of context.

This seems to fulfill some of your original goals at IDEO—to form interdisciplinary teams to work together and create innovative human-centered solutions. Except that now you have your sights set on solving the world's problems.

I hope so. It's interesting that as so many things change around us, the evolution of technologies, social relationships, and so on seem to similarly change very fast. But that basic principle of human-centered design—"start with people"—you can rely on it.

Sean Adams

Cofounder, AdamsMorioka

Sean Adams is tired of the idea that there's something intrinsically wrong with consumerism. He's tired of people who have that particular anticonsumerist sentiment that leads them to think that if you're selling something—or helping someone to sell something—you must be doing something wrong. He's had it with design students who overintellectualize and unnecessarily complicate design. He's tired of peers who think that the only way to do good through design is to create posters for social causes. Adams feels the same way about so-called altruistic design as the so-called altruistic designers feel about branding work. Dismissive. Did anyone actually change their point of view from seeing a poster? It's preaching to the choir, he would say.

Sean's frustration with hackneyed, airily altruistic, historically nihilistic thinking was palpable during our conversation. I could hear it in his voice.

In 1993, Sean and his partner, Noreen Morioka, launched AdamsMorioka. They've branded Sundance and the University of Southern California; they've developed visual architectures for the Academy of Motion Picture Arts and Sciences, Mohawk Fine Papers, Nickelodeon. Clients go to them for clever, thoughtfully orchestrated and visually rich designs. AdamsMorioka is based on the notion that ideas should be communicated clearly without any

unnecessary embellishments or complications.
"We want to do work that my grandmother could
understand," says Sean. "Something as simple as
legibility is important to us." He and Noreen strove
to be the Beach Boys of the design world: "We wanted
to be great at what we do but at the same time appear
effortless and accessible," he explains. Certainly, there
is something "Sourthern Californian" about their
work. Brian Wilson would be proud.

Sean's view of accessible means that brands
must have resonance with consumers; like good pop
music, they must bring delight and joy into people's lives.
To create such visual compositions, AdamsMorioka
developed a process of working with clients in which the
design team identifies "defining characteristics, defining
values, and defining promises" that they use to guide
the branding sensibility and product offerings of the
company. These are the gauntlet through which all ideas
must pass.

Sean also gives his clients the straight talk. He
educates them on what design is as well as what it
can or can't do. He helps to illuminate those clients
who feel that the logo is the sum total of the brand. If
he feels that they are making a promise to consumers
that they can't keep, he will tell them. He does this
because he is aware, as are other brand thinkers
in this book, that in the era of "power to the peer"
reviews, authenticity is of the utmost importance.
Inauthenticity will get sniffed out and exposed
quicker than you can update your Facebook status.

His dialogue with clients involves reminding
them that identities, like empires, are not built in
a day. Consumers will not instantly recognize the
meaning and brand values of a newly introduced
brand icon, however obvious it might seem to the
people on the inside. There is a lot of hard work
invested into making great brands and their
symbols—Nike and Apple among them—part of our
culture's lingua franca.

Sean has meaningful thoughts on the relationship between branding and the power structures that be, and the way in which that has been expressed in everything from advertising to kitchen appliance color palettes. He's got an interesting POV on the dynamic of subversion throughout different phases in our history, and the way in which antiestablishment sentiment has been used for the benefit of the establishment. This isn't to say that Sean doesn't feel that design can make the world a better place. It can. It's just that Sean has a different take on what that involves. If his design helps a business do better, then someone at that company can keep her job, and afford to send her child to college. Voila. Design has contributed to the improvement of the world. Sean might ask, can those social-cause poster designers say the same?

*You wrote an article titled "Confused Consumerism"
in which you criticize the unnecessary complications
of some design, argue for a "message of clarity, purity,
and resonance," and discuss the relationship between
design and corporate culture. What was the genesis
of this article, and why do you think consumerism
is "confused"?*

The idea for the article originated when I kept finding myself in situations where I would be invited to lecture and there would be a distinct anticonsumerist reaction to what I was presenting. There seemed to be a prevailing sensibility that somehow consumerism was wrong, that it was damaging to the earth, and that it was a sin.

Obviously, I think being completely materialistic is not a good idea. But the fact is that as designers we're in the business of selling things. We sell things and ideas. Sometimes, we "sell" people. Whatever it is, we're selling something.

That's the basis of consumerism: Collectively, we make something work, we make something look better, we make something more attractive or seductive, and someone wants to acquire it. Or there's a political party or movement that someone wants you to believe in or join. The part that bothered me about all this was the idea that it was all negative. I wanted to start talking about the fact that consumerism is not necessarily a bad thing.

*Why do so many designers respond to consumerism
with such dismay and despair or chagrin and hostility?*

I think that in the design community, it's somehow fashionable to say, "Oh, I'm in this for the ideas. I'm not in it for the hard, cold, practical facts of it." Some designers believe that design is somehow a more lofty profession if you're just coming up with big ideas and big thinking that will make the world a better place. In my mind, when I think about what designers or thinkers do, I know that, yes, we can make the world a better place. I really, strongly believe that if I do a good job on a project—for instance, if I redesign an identity for a corporation and the business does well and the new materials increase sales—someone keeps their job. That person is able to afford braces for their kids. They send their daughter to college. The world keeps moving in a good way. It's like every grain of rice tips the scale that much more.

These little changes can contribute to better lives for people. It's just too easy to say, "You're damaging the world unless you only make posters for social causes."

Do you think that posters for social causes actually help social causes?

No. I think they're irrelevant. I think they make people feel good, but 90 percent of the time, you're preaching to the choir. People don't change their minds like that—they don't look at a poster and say, "Oh my god. I was so 100 percent wrong about gay marriage. Jesus Christ, why did I not realize that?"

In the "Confused Consumerism" essay, you write, "The anti-commercialism and mistrust of the corporate and governmental structure in the 1970s manifested itself with—not a retreat from mass production—but an attitude of disguise. If the products and messages could be disguised as 'non-materialistic, non-corporate, non-establishment,' perhaps they would sell. As this idea is in contradiction to the stated purpose of mass-production and consumer activity, the messages and visual manifestations of the message became schizophrenic."

I think a couple things happened in the 1970s when marketers realized that no one was going to buy a product in the same way they did in the 1950s, when products were connected to the political and social structures in a vastly different way. For example, in

1950, buying a Chevrolet was an act of helping the American economy, of making us a better nation, and proving that America was number one in the world. You couldn't say that in the 1970s. All of a sudden, corporations were somehow tinged with the idea that they were corrupt—as was government.

But marketers still had to sell products. In order to get around these new obstacles, they had to change their stance. So they converted it to an antiestablishment posture. But it was just a veneer of antiestablishment.

If you think about Coca-Cola in the "I'd Like to Teach the World to Sing" era, you see it clearly. Those commercials paint America as a great nation, and Coca-Cola is a part of it in a very touchy-feely, friendly, "We Are the World" type of a way. You can also see it in something as mundane as color palettes. In the '70s, the color palette became very natural. You could buy an avocado-colored refrigerator and harvest gold counters. It all became a fairly consistent, eco-friendly, earthy approach.

Then, of course, an entire generation of people experienced a radical countercultural movement. And these same people were later in positions of making marketing decisions. Look at a brand like the Gap. The company's initial premise was based on an entirely antiestablishment concept.

"Fall into the Gap."

Yes. "The Gap" referred to the generation gap. That's what they were talking about. There was an intuitive sense that rejecting the mass market and behaving in a more subversive manner was somehow more appealing to the mass market. And it worked! People felt great thinking that they were not supporting the military-industrial complex and believed that they were making the world a better place. Now, we see that, obviously, they were mistaken. That was the equivalent of the current "greenwashing." At the end of the day, people were still trying to sell products. That's what their goal was. They weren't trying to stop pollution—they were trying to sell more jeans.

What are your thoughts on what "brand" means right now?

I think the biggest misconception is that people typically think their logo is their brand, and they believe that if they redesign their logo, they've somehow managed their brand. The logo is irrelevant. The logo is a nice foundation, and it's an identifier. But it's not the brand.

A brand is not necessarily visual. It's a promise of an experience. One of the things that we're running into with clients now is that they want to make brand promises that they can't keep—promises that are clearly not true.

Things get difficult when we have to tell someone, "You just can't say that."

Do you really do that?

We do. We have to. We tell them that they are going to lose all credibility when even one consumer realizes that the company is lying. Which, inevitably, someone will. Marketers may *think* their brand is delivering on a specific promise, when in fact it's really not. You can't promise something that you're not going to be able to deliver. You just come off as being inauthentic. People nowadays are completely mistrustful, and even the slightest appearance of dishonesty can destroy a brand.

I think "quality" is an attribute that almost all of our clients think they're bringing to the table. But there are times when I have to point out, "No, quality is actually job two here." Furthermore, shouldn't quality be a given? Would anyone ever declare, "We're not about quality—we're crap"? A company can't get away with saying, "We're all about quality" unless they're really willing to invest in their product and deliver a much higher standard. If not, focus on something else.

Do you think brands now contribute to how we declare
who we are?

I think it's code. I think there's always been some sort of code, and the only difference now is that we operate in a world that's much more oriented toward conveying messages in a consumer context than it might have been in, say, the 18th century. Now people can attach themselves to a code that signifies to others, "I'm in this group. This is my tribe. This is what I believe in." You can then feel some kind of identification with that person or not. They're making a telegraphic statement. But I think that's always been the case—it's just been done in different ways over the course of human history.

For example, in the 18th century, your name literally identified your standing. When you met someone, your name conveyed the message that "I'm part of this tribe. This is my group." Someone would know that if I have Washington in my name, then I'm part of a certain group. Names were used as signifiers to let people know where you stood in life.

This still occurs, but to a completely different degree. Look at the people who are related to the Kennedys. They may have a totally different last name, but they always include "Kennedy" in there somewhere.

What does that association do for us psychologically?
What does it do for us as a species, as humans?

I think we're tribal beings. I think that we have a natural tendency to separate into tribes and to feel comfortable in tribes. And I think that those identifiers help tribalize us—they make it clear that "I'm part of this group." And if I meet you and you have the same signs, then it's clear to me that you're part of that group too. This allows me to feel comfortable with you, now that I can understand we're in the same world. If I were to meet you for the first time, I'd be like, "Yeah, Debbie's part of my tribe." I can see that. You've got the right glasses—you've got the right haircut, the right clothes. Conversely, if I went to a party and met someone who was wearing a Christmas sweater and polyester pants, I'd think, "They're not part of my tribe." I wouldn't dislike them, but I probably wouldn't have much in common with them. This all relates to how we set up meaning.

Do you think that certain clothes or haircuts declare to others, "I should be believed"?

I think the answer to that question falls back to individual authenticity and brand authenticity. Are you delivering on your promises? If you are, then there's probably some authenticity there. But there's an old saying that goes, "You don't dress where you are, you dress where you want to be." I think this is true for a lot of people. But every now and then, you see an individual who is completely confident and goes out in the world with no regard whatsoever for what they're wearing, what car they drive, and what products they buy.

I admire people like that. We both admire that. Why?

I think life would be much easier, for one thing. My dad was a bit like that. He had a real clunker of a car, and I didn't even want him to take me to school in it— it was that beat-up. But he just was in his own world— he was a math geek—and that was how he operated.

It's interesting that antibrand stances can be measured through the construct of "brand," and can communicate what a person stands for—or is against.

I remember sitting in a conference watching a presentation by the folks at Adbusters when they proposed a "Buy Nothing Day"—a day where people choose not to buy anything. But if you

go to the organization's website, you can buy
T-shirts and *Adbusters* subscriptions. That
doesn't sound right to me.

*They're branding themselves using the very tenets of
branding that they disdain. "Buy Nothing Day" is a
brand. But it's interesting to realize that, somehow, we
as humans are hardwired to create these constructs
with which to understand things.*

It's a way to decode the world and understand your
place in it.

*This might be somewhat of a non sequitur, but do you
think this has anything to do with why people enjoy
shopping so much?*

I think that has to do with our hunter-gatherer
instinct. We're hardwired to be hunter-gatherers:
You shop, you find something pretty and shiny, and
you bring it home.

Maybe that's why there's that old stereotype
that women love shopping more than men. Women
were typically the ones who were out hunting and
gathering for the nuts and berries, and the men
were out killing animals.

Why do you think people talk about the
importance of visuals? Why should it matter if
something looks good? Why should it matter if
it's appealing? Well, obviously it matters, because
otherwise you're living in the world of Soviet
Russia, where everything is gray. You're going to
have better-selling toothpaste if the toothpaste
tube is more attractive and has colors that people
respond to. We actually see color because, from
an evolutionary perspective, it was necessary. You
needed to know which berries were the poisonous
ones and which ones you could eat. An appreciation
of beauty is hardwired into us as well. We need it to
perpetuate the species.

But our ideas of beauty are learned. Attractiveness
is a human construct. Things that are beautiful in
one culture may be considered repulsive in another.
Judging what is or isn't attractive is based on a
construct, yet we seem to have a tendency to make
judgments without acknowledging that. And our
tolerance level of what's acceptable is mutable. Until
1920, women didn't have the right to vote. Until
1967, interracial marriages were against the law.
Looking back now, it seems we were ridiculous and
small-minded. Do you have any idea, biologically or
philosophically, why we behave this way?

I may be beating a dead horse, but I think it has to do with our tribal tendencies. You want to make clear that "I belong to this group, and in my group, these are the rules: This is what we accept and what we don't accept."

The other day, I was reading about colonial Virginia, and there was a description of what people wore. If you were part of the gentry, your clothes were fairly restrictive physically. You really couldn't move around in them, especially if you were a woman. You were bound in—the hoop skirts were made so big that you had to turn to get through a door. You were literally unable to do physical labor, and that communicated to the rest of the world that you were of a certain class and didn't work. The way one dressed signified what was acceptable and even possible behavior.

At that time, having pale, light-toned skin was
considered more attractive than having a tan. If you
had pale skin, that meant that you didn't spend time
outside, working in the sun. Now people sit in tanning
beds because being tan is more sexually alluring.

Right. Theoretically, a tan now also signifies that you don't have to work—you can be outside and on vacation all the time.

In India, you can buy a whitening cream to bleach your
skin in order to appear more "attractive."

I find that really interesting. I was talking to one of
my students about the values we have as a culture.
I think a lot of it comes from introspection. We ask
ourselves if we're happy or if we're unhappy. We ask
ourselves if we're satisfied, or if we should be part
of one group or another. This self-analysis is very
modern, and I think it stems from reading. If you
look back at preliterate times, people really didn't
think this way. Introspection wasn't part of life. And
it occurred to me that reading is an introspective
activity. When you read, you're forced to sit still,
construct something in your head, and think about it.

I wonder if even cave paintings are related to that, to
the urge to document an experience so we can reflect on
it or share it.

Absolutely. Typography, pictures, and words
are all intricately related. Obviously, brands also
are a way of communicating with symbols and
iconography. That's one of the big issues that comes
up when you're dealing with an identity project.
Oftentimes, you'll have a client who is insistent
that the company needs some kind of wacky icon.
And that icon is meaningless unless we're going to
repeatedly beat the audience over the head with its
image and its significance. Initially, that icon has no
meaning. And it shouldn't. In reality, an icon should
be neutral enough to be able to withstand all kinds
of cultural or generational shifts. But someone at
the company says, "Everyone will know us because
of this." I'm like, "No, they won't." It takes years for
people to build up recognition.

Many times we're really adamant that we
need to connect an icon to a word mark. I tell them,
"We need a word mark here. I need a word. I need
your name here." No one is going to automatically
think of the company "Apple" when they see the
Apple logo unless they've been beaten over the

head with marketing for twenty years. I realize that sounds counterintuitive, but it's true—it's just hard to recognize because we're so immersed in brand culture.

Apple and its creative team—like Nike and its agency, Wieden+Kennedy—have made it look so effortless. Their cleverness and clarity has made it seem easy, when in fact it's quite difficult. They've made it so alluring to do it this way.

It's quite difficult, and very expensive. It takes enormous amounts of work to get those brands and their icons so widely recognized throughout our culture. It takes a very single-minded vision. Noreen and I first started AdamsMorioka in 1993, a time of extreme excess and a lot of oblique messaging in design. Complicated was better, and "more is more" seemed to be the flavor of the day. That wasn't working for us.

But the reality is that being clear with your messages allows you to communicate more successfully with a wide audience. Designers often like to make messages that are intentionally oblique, difficult to understand, and illegible, something that will only appeal to five people who go to a specific gallery downtown.

That is not what I'm interested in. That's still going to exist, and if someone else wants to do it, good for them. But I don't want to do work like that. I think there's something inherently elitist and condescending in working that way.

Why is it elitist and condescending?

That just doesn't work for us at AdamsMorioka. We want to create work that my grandmother could understand. Something as simple as legibility is important to us. We want to create type that is legible, and we want to design messages that are readable. We don't want to create work that looks as if it was run through a Xerox machine thirty-seven times and then cut apart and pieced back together again to the extent that it becomes a challenge to understand. Clarity has always been really critical to us, and it still is.

I actually see this type of convoluted work from a lot of design students. They don't want to create work that's clear because they feel that it's "just so ordinary." They think they're so much smarter than that, and they're going to prove it by creating work that's incredibly complicated and difficult to understand. Their intent is that only the most "design savvy" viewers are ever going to get it, and they exemplify a faux intellectualization of design—which is hogwash. What they're actually doing is making something oblique for the sake of making it oblique.

When we're working with a client, we'll try to come up with defining characteristics, defining values, and defining promises that allow us to figure out not only what the visual language should be, but also what kind of products the client should make and what kind of activities the company should engage in. Everything needs to be measured against this belief system. But I am never tempted to design something that's totally illegible and difficult to read.

Unfortunately, there seems to be a stigma against accessibility. There's a belief that if the work is accessible, it can't be good.

I agree. Anything that's mass-marketed and has a mass appeal is seen as not "cool." Why is that? You see this attitude in music as well. When someone new breaks through, there's a small group of early adopters who rally around the artist and support them. The minute one of their songs hit the Top 40, those same fans abandon the music. The music hasn't changed—the only thing different is the number of people who like it. I wonder why bleeding-edge, early adopters can't continue to enjoy something once it's embraced by the mainstream.

Somehow, it isn't good anymore. This was one of the things Noreen and I tried to decipher when we were positioning our own brand. We asked ourselves what musicians we would aspire to be like, and I felt we were like the Beach Boys. We're not John Cage, we're the Beach Boys. And the reason I feel proud of that is because I think the Beach Boys are remarkable musicians. Brian Wilson is a genius. But at the same time, he makes his craft look effortless. The music has extraordinary appeal, and it speaks to a broader audience. We felt this is what we could aspire to. We didn't want to be an obscure composer making discordant pieces. We wanted to be great at what we do, and at the same time appear effortless and accessible in our work.

The other two attributes we want our work to embody are "purity" and "resonance." For us, purity means that if a design element doesn't need to be there, it shouldn't be. We strip away everything that doesn't have to be there. This doesn't mean everything we create is minimalist, but it means that if something is not contributing to the communication of a message, it shouldn't be there. There should be nothing extraneous—everything should have a purpose. We won't add anything to a design just because it would be "fun" to do so.

And, finally, when we talk about "resonance," we mean emotional resonance. A brand must make every effort to connect with people. When people ask about what makes a brand successful, my standard response is, "What is it communicating?" Brands are successful when they bring delight and joy into people's lives. You should feel good when you see and experience a brand, not repulsion. I'll let other people make work that leads to repulsion. I'm more interested in doing something that's seductive and life-affirming.

Daniel Pink

Cultural Critic, Author

I first came across the work of Daniel Pink when I was cochairing the FUSE Conference. His lecture presented a revelatory understanding of modern times and the shifts that have taken place in business and culture during the past twenty years. While other business leaders and cultural commentators are stuck in old-thinking paradigms, Daniel Pink gets it.

In his books Drive, A Whole New Mind, *and* Johnny Bunko, *Daniel consistently showcases his savvy about what we're doing, where we're heading, and where we're missing the paradigm shift entirely. His insight on brands is especially sharp, and when I interviewed him, he and I spoke about the subtleties of brand relationships in ways that I've never thought about before. A brand, says Daniel, is a promise exchanged, and brands derive their appeal from two key factors: their utility—whether or not they fulfill their function or purpose—and their significance—the range of affiliations that a brand generates between a person and an object, whether it be a computer, a pair of jeans, or a television. By making a significant leap forward in utility or significance—Apple's iPhone might be a good example—companies are able to corner the market in a particular category, at least until the next advance forward.*

In our conversation, Daniel created an informal system of assessing a successful brand: It creates products that make its consumers feel good, gives them a sense of affiliation, and has a compelling backstory. With that in mind, a brand promise can prove to be a boon or an albatross. As a boon, brands act as an insurance that we'll be getting something of quality. When assessing the broken promises of companies like BP, Daniel incisively notes that while the brand itself may recover its sales and even recoup some trust, a lingering problem will remain: Because of the business's damaged reputation, talented people in the field may no longer want to work for it. That resistance can lead to long-term stagnation in a business's integrity and innovation, both of which are essential in developing vibrant relationships between consumers and brands.

In addition to his eloquence about brands and innovation, Daniel speaks quite compellingly on the dangers of the "hedonic treadmill," in which we relentlessly pursue the next branded object that will finally bring us lasting happiness—but inevitably doesn't. To counter this attitude, he urges a "buyer beware" mindfulness so we can nurture our self-worth without relying on external supports. He suggests that social media outlets like Twitter and Facebook have allowed us to subvert some of these brand mechanics, allowing us to state and affirm our self-worth without relying on the vocabulary of brands. He reflects, "Now we're going to be left with trying to assess who we are, as we are."

*To begin, I want to ask you, how would you
define "brand"?*

I would define it two ways: from the sender's point
of view and from the receiver's point of view. I don't
want to make it overly complicated, but from the
perspective of P&G or Dell or any other company, a
brand *might* be a promise: a promise of what awaits
the customer if they buy that particular product,
service, or experience. From the receiver's point of
view, I think a brand *is* a promise.

What do you think it's a promise for?

It depends. It differs from company to company.
But it's a promise of what you can expect if you
use the product or service, or if you engage in the
experience. When it comes to the Disney brand,
Disney is making a promise that if you go to this
theme park or see this movie, you're going to get
fun, family entertainment. When you see the Nike
swoosh, or you see the word "Nike," or you walk by
a Nike store, you're communicated a promise that
you're going to get a product that's going to enhance
and enliven the athletic part of your life. If you see
one of Procter & Gamble's brands, whether it's
Tide or Pampers, there's a promise made that this
is going to be a wholesome and valuable product for
your family.

*Do you feel that people really choose products and
experiences in that way?*

I don't think anyone thinks that explicitly. I do
think that transactions between companies and
individuals—or between brands and individuals—
are in their own ways conversations. A promise
can be one element of a conversation. It's what
draws people in. I think that's why the dynamic is
different when you look at this conversation after
someone has bought the product or the service.

I think the brand can operate in a somewhat different way then. When the brand is something that an individual takes home, the brand becomes something different. The brand becomes a form of affiliation, or a form of identification—a form of status. I tend to look at it as a form of affiliation. If I open up my laptop and it has the Apple logo on it, that might make me feel marginally more associated with a group of cool, interesting people than if the computer had another logo on it.

Why is that?

It's deeply tribal. Yet, in this regard, there are other brands that are irrelevant. If you asked me about my desk phone, I'd have no idea what brand it was until I actually looked at it.

Did you choose it?

Yes, I did.

What made you decide to buy that particular phone?

It's an AT&T brand phone. I think what made me choose it was a combination of its price and functionality. The fact that it had the AT&T imprimatur on it probably made me marginally more certain that it would work than if it had "Al's Phone Supplies" on it.

That goes back to the idea that AT&T is making a promise: The company is telling you, "We've been in the phone business a long time—our promise is that this phone isn't going to suck."

So that would be what we could call a category of "low involvement" for you. And the decision to get an Apple?

That would be a little bit more significant. Using your terminology, yes, it would be higher involvement.

*Do you feel like the association is something beneficial
to you and to people generally? Does it benefit them in a
meaningful way?*

I think in small ways. I don't think it's that salient
in people's lives. I think it might have a marginally
potent role as a formal affiliation.

*That's really interesting. Marty Neumeier wrote a
book called* The Brand Gap *that's related to this idea.
When he's discussing Nike, Neumeier writes, "As a
weekend athlete, my two nagging doubts are that I
might be congenitally lazy, and that I might have little
actual ability. I am not really worried about my shoes.
But when the Nike folks say, 'Just do it,' they're peering
into my soul. I begin to feel that, if they understand me
that well, their shoes are probably pretty good. I am
then willing to join the tribe of Nike."*

Very interesting. That's the affiliation side of it.
Again, when he's saying the shoes are probably
pretty good, that's a promise. It's not an explicit
promise in the sense of "I promise you that these
are pretty good shoes." But it's an implicit promise.
This is why broken promises are so devastating to
companies and brands.

*What do you mean by that? Can you elaborate on
that idea?*

Let's use BP as an example. The BP brand used to
stand for a semi-enlightened oil company that was
trying to go beyond petroleum. They even created a
logo that was green, as if to say, "Look how forward-
thinking and cool we are." Now that promise is a
joke—it's a broken promise. "We promised you that
we were going to go beyond petroleum. We promised
you that we were going to be green . . . Oops—sorry
about the millions of gallons of oil in the gulf." That's
a broken promise. Breaking a promise is worse than
not making a promise in the first place.

Do you think BP can recover?

Yes. I think they can. I think the bigger problem for BP is not going to be in its operations. I don't think its oil exploration around the world is going to be stalled at all—perhaps just a little. It will probably get a bit more scrutiny from the governments around the world that have to approve its oil exploration projects. I don't really think there are going to be too many consumers who are going to say, "Oh, I'm going to the Exxon station rather than the BP gas station because I don't like BP." I think the lasting brand problem for BP is that really talented people aren't going to want to work there. *That's* the problem BP will have over the long haul.

I never thought of that.

That's branding of a different order. It's not branding in the realm we're talking about. To me, that's a significant problem. And *that's* a hard egg to unscramble. Think about a talented petroleum engineer coming out of college. This person has a lot of choices. Is she going to say, "Oh, I'm going to be really proud to work at BP?" No. Or think about people who are at BP now and they go to a barbecue on a weekend, and they meet someone new. The conversation will go something like this: "Hi—what do you do?" "I'm an engineer." "Where do you work?" "BP." "Ohhhhh . . ." Not good. I happen to live within walking distance of Fannie Mae in Washington, D.C. There was a time when Fannie Mae hired really great people. That has ended. It has nothing to do with Fannie Mae's capacity to pay salaries. It has everything to do with people not wanting to be affiliated with a brand that is stained.

Brands promise a certain affiliation that we end up benefiting from—the benefits come from the association and the affiliation. Then we can use them to project how we want to be seen in the world.

Yes. We're talking mostly about consumer brands and product-based brands, but there are many different types of brands. This consideration applies to certain decisions you might make in the business world. If you run a company and you need to hire some consultants, the brand Deloitte makes a promise. The brand Accenture makes a promise. Maybe there's a degree of "affiliation" that plays a part in this area as well: A company can proudly show off how advanced it is by hiring an Accenture or a McKinsey.

In these situations, there's an inherent insurance policy that these companies will do a good job for you.

God, yes. I'm convinced that the insurance is a huge part of it. If you're at a large organization, and you have a choice of hiring someone from Harvard and hiring someone from a small, unknown school that no one has heard of, you're most likely going to hire the person from Harvard. Not because that person is necessarily any better. You could meet with them and think that the person from the small, unknown school that no one has heard of can make a great contribution. But if you hire someone with a Harvard degree and they turn out to be an idiot, you have a defense: "How was I supposed to know they were an idiot? They went to Harvard!" But if the person who went to the small, unknown school turns out to be an idiot, your boss can say, "What the hell were you doing hiring someone from a small, unknown school that no one has heard of?"

Do you ever listen to the comedian Chris Rock?

Yes—I like him.

He does a whole thing on insurance and says that at the end of the day, insurance is really "'in case' shit."

Well said! That's a very interesting concept. That goes back to the notion that brand is a promise—insurance itself is a promise. Insurance promises that if something bad happens, the company insuring you will pay. In some ways, the kind of insurance we've been talking about—"brand insurance"—is saying, "If something bad happens, you won't get blamed."

In your book A Whole New Mind, *you wrote extensively about the candle business. You explained that, despite the fact that we have plenty of cheap lightbulbs, the candle business is a $2.4-billion industry. Why do we still need to buy candles? How do they enhance our lives? Electricity is cheap and ubiquitous, yet we're still spending over $2 billion on a product that, for all intents and purposes, lights our rooms much less effectively than bulbs. Why?*

I think the candle example is one where the candle itself is more important than the brand. I can only think of one candle brand, which is Yankee Candle. I imagine that they're making the promise that candles will enhance your life. They probably even use language like this: "Candles might help illuminate a room, but, more importantly, they will light up your soul." What is most interesting about the candle scenario is that it suggests people are looking for something beyond utility. Anything available in a marketplace offers a combination of utility and significance. The item has to work, and it has to provide another benefit: It has to make you feel good, give you a sense of affiliation, and it has to give you a compelling backstory. It has to touch you in an emotional way.

In a world full of stuff, you have two options: The first is that you can make a huge advance in utility—you can come up with something demonstrably better. For instance, my family was recently on a trip, and my thirteen-year-old daughter brought along a Flip camera. Now that's a huge leap in utility. I remember the day when camcorders were huge, heavy, and cost thousands of dollars. And my daughter has a little purse where she keeps her Flip, and it cost maybe $100. It's amazing. That's a huge leap in utility.

The other option is to get your margins out of significance. Brands are a source of significance, and significance has a number of dimensions relating to security, safety, affiliation, or status. If a brand is making a promise, it's a promise about utility and significance. Let's go back to the overused example of Apple. If I see an Apple laptop, I know it's going to work well, but I also know it's not going to work monumentally better than a PC. But it has more significance: It's going to look good and feel good, and it's going to give me a sense of affiliation.

In a TED talk you gave in 2009, you spoke about "contingent motivators": rewards, commissions, or bonuses that are used to motivate people to achieve. I recently attended an executive education program, where a Harvard professor spoke about our need for achievement. She compared and contrasted it to hunger: You're hungry, you eat something, and then you stop being hungry for a while. You're thirsty, you drink something, and then you stop being thirsty for a while. But with high achievers, when they achieve something, they continue to need more. Do you think that brands are contingent motivators? For example, let's say a person wants a big-screen TV. It becomes a goal, something they're motivated by. They save up—then they go and buy it. Chances are, after they get the big-screen TV, then they want some big speakers to capture the big-screen TV sound. Is it ever enough? Can we ever be sated by brands, or do they act only as contingent motivators?

This is the dark side of brands. Let's go back to the analogy of food and hunger. Whether it's a big-screen TV or a car, the evidence is overwhelmingly clear that human beings metabolize these things very quickly. I'm specifically using the word "metabolize" because we're talking about hunger and thirst. If a big-screen

TV is your source of stature and significance, it's a fool's game. These kinds of external objects do not provide enduring satisfaction.

If a brand is making a promise that you're going to feel better about yourself if you buy it, they're making a false promise. Human beings metabolize their purchases very quickly.

What about fashion or technology brands that have a built-in expiration date? Do you think planned obsolescence is the underlying cause of that metabolism, or the result of it?

This is an element of what social psychologists call "the hedonic treadmill": If you're always looking to validate yourself and get satisfaction from buying stuff or having a bigger house, then you're on an endless, addictive treadmill. There's no enduring satisfaction to this. If a brand's only purpose is to get you on that hedonic treadmill, it might be good for business in the short run, but in the long run, you're doomed. If you look at the components of long-term well-being, it has nothing to do with material goods. Once you're past a certain level of material well-being, people's long-term happiness and well-being is about having deep personal relationships, believing in something larger than themselves, and doing something meaningful that they enjoy.

This reminds me of being in Japan a few years ago. When I was there, I saw a lot of young women with Gucci handbags. Gucci might not say it's making this promise, but it *could* make the promise that if you buy a Gucci handbag, then you'll feel good about yourself. That's very much an if-then contingent motivator that has a lot of problems with it. That seems to be a classic kind of "controlling" contingent motivator.

But I think you could argue it either way. If a young woman's whole sense of self-worth and identification comes from fashion and large institutions that ultimately don't care about her one bit, that's the dark side of the way that brands work. There is a contingency here. The promises are contingencies: "If you buy this, then you will feel that."

But I'm also thinking about my own clothing choices. I just bought two new suits. I buy new suits when my old suits literally wear out. So where did I go to buy my suits? I went to Nordstrom. Why did I go to Nordstrom? I went to Nordstrom because I've been there before, and the promise when you go to Nordstrom is that you'll get high-quality clothes, and it won't be a hassle. That seems to be a perfectly acceptable promise. Sure, it's contingent—in the sense of "If you come to Nordstrom, then you'll get high-quality clothes without a hassle"—but that doesn't seem such a nefarious contingency.

What are the cultural ramifications of using brands to camouflage feelings of low self-worth, particularly at a time when our culture uses tangible reward systems and brand markers to gauge a person's place in life?

In some ways, I think individuals can control this. Eleanor Roosevelt famously said, "No one can humiliate you without your consent." If you are using brands as a way to camouflage low self-worth, then shame on you as much as shame on the brand.

So no one can humiliate you without your consent. But what if all you understand is the language of humiliation? Then you don't necessarily know how to discern anything else. We're living in a world where this is how we assess our cultural and social standing. We are born into that—we don't know anything but that. It's like Stockholm syndrome, where a hostage develops loyalty for his captors.

I think in some ways our ability to communicate with each other on platforms like Twitter gives us more power, because we can tear that curtain back a little bit to reveal that there are other ways to feel self-worth and power. We're living in an age now where so much of this psychological support we get through brands is falling away because we can't afford it anymore. Now we're going to be left with trying to assess who we are, as we are. That would be a good and very healthy evolution in general.

Do you think we're in the midst of a self-correction?

In a way, it will be very interesting to see if the economy is going to reset brands. You certainly see it in advertising: When the business cycle goes down, you start seeing ads for dollar meals. And I wonder if there will be a deeper reset in brands. I wonder if the deep underlying promise of enduring brands is going to change because of the economic troubles. I have no idea.

DeeDee Gordon

President of Innovation, Sterling Brands; Founding Partner, Look-Look Youth Marketing and Research Consultancy

DeeDee Gordon is one of my colleagues at Sterling Brands. DeeDee arrived at Sterling in the fall of 2010, and she has taken a lead role in helping companies to innovate new products, create compelling consumer experiences, and reenvision brands entirely. She developed a reputation early on in her career for spotting trends that gave companies precisely the information they needed to tap into existing and emerging consumer inclinations. Her company Look-Look, which she cofounded in 1999, was twenty thousand leagues ahead of the curve in the trendspotting arena. Look-Look developed a whole new model of how to research and forecast trends through a curated network of linked-in trendspotters and correspondents. The consultancy broke ground in using all the trappings of 21st-century digital media to get a live feed of on-the-ground intelligence.

At Sterling Brands, she is devoted to innovation, though she continues to focus on sensing the thoughts, memes, trends, and yearnings relating to the young generation of consumers. The digital tools that are so second nature to this generation—Facebook, texting, Twitter—have become a manifestation of the young person's search for authenticity, and DeeDee notes that this applies not only to their own identities but to their perspective on brands. Teens and tweens are deeply concerned with whether brands are being "authentic," and the vast amount of information available on the Internet helps them evaluate this authenticity. DeeDee's litmus test in this category are Nike, Muji, Patagonia, Apple: exemplars of brands that have stayed true to their mission.

Not only is the young generation vastly more informed about brands than previous generations, but DeeDee notes that today's youngsters have much better taste, since they've grown up in a culture where design was much more valued, and accessible, than in the past. This is an important observation for brand managers, designers, and anthropologists alike. In essence, the evolution of branding has brought about a revolution of design that further accelerates the evolution of branding and visual culture.

DeeDee has a visceral sense of the way that brands can make us swoon—how they can seduce us, get under our skin. She has an understanding of the emotions and even pride that arises when we become a member of a brand "club" through our consumer purchases. I think she has a distinctively Generation X insight into the way that irony works in our relationship with brands and the ambivalence we have about joining a group. She gets how we succumb to irony, embrace it, resist it, transcend it.

As is evident in her career history, DeeDee's forte is for identifying and articulating cultural dynamics that other people wouldn't see, and then determining how to transform those into a business strategy. She is able to ferret out the subtle and sometimes more overt dynamics that shape our culture, when other people would see these as solitary instances unrelated to a larger logic. That is a reflection of her rare and remarkable talent for "pattern recognition," which she conveys through a vocabulary—"macro trends," "smug alert," and all the rest—that helps us see these patterns through her eyes.

It might seem an odd admission for a brand strategist to make, but DeeDee acknowledges in this interview that her favorite brands are the "no-brand brands." But that's not to say that those brands don't have identity. They establish their identities precisely through unmistakable visual sensibilities. There were other contradictions that we explored in our conversation, among them the very nature of what brand consultants do. It's meaningful to see how this inner conflict provides an important touchstone for her work, just as an understanding of irony is essential for speaking with authenticity to twenty- and thirtysomethings.

Though others feel that brands do a lot of damage in the world—or are undertaking their social initiatives as a way to assuage their guilty consciences—DeeDee supports the freedom of the marketplace, in which companies make what consumers will buy, without an external authority determining what's "right" or "wrong." She admits that she herself feels drawn to companies that stand for noble causes, and she recognizes that extraordinary power that brands have to do good and to implement ways of doing business that can change the world for the better. "If we can utilize the power of big corporation to make the world a better place, why shouldn't we?"

You recently made a big change in the type of work that you're doing—you were one of the pioneers in trendspotting, but now you're working in new product development and innovation. Why?

> It doesn't really feel like *that* big of a change. I've been working in the arena of consumer insights for over twenty years. I actually began my career in product development. Creating products and coming up with new ideas has always been exciting to me.

How do you come up with new ideas? How do you come up with ideas for products that have never been made before?

> A lot of it comes from closely observing culture, and seeing how consumers are engaging with existing products and brands, and then looking for "white space" and any gaps relating to people's needs.

How do you find these "need gaps"?

> There is no easy answer, but I think that first you have to scour the culture and dive deep into a category or an idea. I need to know everything about the category or idea, and I conduct a lot of secondary desk research, sorting through the research that already exists. This is all a prelude to going on the road, where I immerse myself in various cultures and observe categories—of products or the relevant theme—within different groups and environments, and with different types of people. I talk to consumers about products, concepts, and ideas. From there, I'm able to identify need gaps and find new areas to expand into.

Now what I'm going to ask you will make you roll your eyes, but it has to be asked.

> Oh no.

I know. I'm sorry. But—is it possible for you to define "cool"?

> No.

Okay, then, next question . . .

Are you serious? Define "cool"?

Yes. Can you?

I don't think I can. I've actually never been asked that question.

If you can't define it, can you tell me how people know when something is cool?

I think cool is different for everybody. It's completely subjective, and that's what makes it so wonderful.

But there are certain things that seem to be universally acknowledged as cool by a large group of people. Apple is an example, or a certain brand of sneaker, or a handbag. How does that happen? How does something inanimate become designated as cool?

It triggers an emotional connection. It feels transformative. It feels life-changing.

What do you mean by life-changing?

I don't know about you, but the first time I walked into an Apple store, I felt like I couldn't breathe.

Why?

It felt beautiful. I felt as though I had found a place and a sensibility that understood me. It understood my interests and my aesthetic and my vision. That felt transformative.

What do you think the brand understood about you?

It understood my need to feel engaged, my need for participating, and my need for a clean, minimalist aesthetic. I may not adhere to this sensibility in my everyday life, but it's something that I am drawn to in nearly everything I use for inspiration, especially for my job.

In that sense, do you think that the design of Apple's products is fundamental to the brand's success?

Yes. The fact is that Steve Jobs created a design that is user-friendly—he made it playful, and he made it beautiful and interesting. But I must also confess that my favorite brands are the ones that are the no-brand brands.

But Apple's not a no-brand brand.

It isn't, but you don't really have to see an Apple logo on an iPod to know that it's an iPod. You can put it next to four different MP3 players and instantly recognize the iPod. The brand provides such a strong visual language that you don't ever need to see an Apple logo on any of the products. I can identify an Apple monitor from across the room. This is a testament to the brand's design and visual language, and I think most of the brands that I'm interested in have a similar sensibility. You're able to identify them without ever having to see a badge, logo, color combination, or any type of sign.

There are very few brands that can be identified without any type of label. Cars and candy are two categories in which certain products are instantly recognizable. Apple is another, but this is not true for the entire computer or electronics category.

Nike is another. There are certain products within the Nike family that if you were to see just a silhouette of them, you would know what the brand is. The Nike Dunk and the Air Force 1 are two examples of that.

Aside from the amount of money put into marketing it, do you think that there's anything inherently great about Nike's logo?

It's very simple. I think it's the perfect logo for a performance-oriented company committed to innovation.

Why?

The Nike swoosh encompasses speed, movement, and simplicity. It is both timeless and modern. And it also is the type of mark that can go on any product and not overshadow the product itself. What I don't quite understand is why people tattoo the logo onto their bodies. Apparently, there are people who work at Nike and love the company so much that they tattoo the Nike logo on their bodies.

Are you kidding?

No, I'm not. I'm not kidding at all.

How can someone love a brand so much that they'd want to put a permanent mark on their body?

There are many people who are doing this. I've heard from several people about women in Japan who undergo plastic surgery to look like Hello Kitty. And I've heard it enough that I don't think it's just an urban legend. The women supposedly undergo plastic surgery to their eyes and mouth so that they can look like Hello Kitty. This sounds pretty extreme, but you know what? I live in Los Angeles, and every day I drive around Beverly Hills. I'm living in the plastic surgery capital of the world. I'm living in the capital of transformation.

How is it that we're living in a culture where it's perfectly okay to do this? What does that say?

Look, the fact is that we have the technology now to do this. We have the technology to make ourselves feel younger, to look younger, and to be younger. As a society, we're living longer. People now live into their nineties and hundreds. More people are able to stay healthy for longer periods of time. It only makes sense that we should be able to look younger throughout that time period. It doesn't seem so far-fetched. I do think that some people take it too far. But I'm not opposed to it.

What is it about being young that we find so alluring?
Other people on this planet have their own distinct
criteria for what people should look like. Members of
the Zo'é tribe in Brazil wear a poturu, *which is a long*
wooden plug piercing their bottom lip. Padaung females
wear neck coils from the time they're two years old
because of a long-standing cultural ritual, and some
adult women have as many as twenty coils stacked
around their neck. What is it about the way that we
beautify ourselves in American culture that is telling
about who we are?

> The way you've worded your question makes me feel that, as a culture, we are pathetic.

In what way are we pathetic?

> Everything that we're doing is so medical and artificial! There are no inherent customs or rituals built into our behavior. When you refer to tribal behavior, you're talking about rituals that are a meaningful part of a specific culture. Our behavior is more superficial. Though it's technologically innovative and clinically sterile—in terms of the process we use for this kind of modification—it feels dirty and unnecessary.
>
> Ironically, when humans first started beautifying themselves, we were trying to make ourselves more attractive to God. Now, we do it to feel better about ourselves, period.

But this brings us back to what is considered "cool."
I don't know that we're any closer to defining it, but I
wonder why, as a species, we seek it so ceaselessly.

> It's a way to find community. It's a way of belonging. It's a way to connect. When you find something that's cool that other people like, and you're all drinking the same Kool-Aid, it's a great feeling to have, and it's a way to build your own community. That might not answer your question, but it's the best explanation I can give to describe

our drive to be part of things that make us feel good about who we are.

Do you remember the book Bridget Jones's Diary?

Yes.

In the book, Bridget refers to happily married couples who have children as the "smug marrieds." In many ways, she wants to be part of this club, yet she's also disdainful of it.

Yes. My husband and I use this term all the time to describe couples we know. One of the funniest episodes of the show *South Park* happens to be titled "Smug Alert." The show is about the people who live in San Francisco and drive hybrid cars. In the episode, they're so smug that they smell their own farts. The characters are at a cocktail party, and they literally put their heads between their legs and inhale as they fart. The best part of the program is when there's a "smug alert warning" sent out over San Francisco because of a huge cloud of smug.

This segues perfectly into my next question. After the iPod was introduced in 2001, you could instantly identify anyone who had one because they were wearing the then-distinctive white earbuds. I couldn't help but notice the palpable smugness exchanged between random iPod owners when they recognized that they were wearing the same earbuds.

Yes.

I witnessed the experience and also participated in it. What is that about? What is it about this shared experience that promotes smugness?

Look, you're talking to someone who has lived it. You both realize that you've recognized the same thing about this object and the experience of it. There's something really beautiful in that. Especially when two people are on a subway, mixed in with people from all different walks of life. I see it happen with certain brands that I buy. I remember driving a Prius in Los Angeles and going to a car wash. Somebody else would roll up in a Prius. We would give each other that nod, the nod of smug. And we silently say to each other, "You've got one too, right on. You get me, I get you, and we're not like everybody else."

But why do we feel smug? Why not joy or wonder?

I think people want to feel and be seen as exclusive and special. The fewer people in the club, so to speak, the more unique you are. And if you encounter another exclusive member, you can mirror the mutuality back and forth. It's wonderfully narcissistic.

On Fridays before a varsity football game in high school, all the football players would wear their team jerseys, and all the cheerleaders would wear their cheerleading uniforms. There was a definite smug superiority that they conveyed in the communication of their social status. They happily reflected it among each other, but there was also a harsh judgment against those who weren't in their "club."

My high school posse looked at those people like they were tools. My crew would sit there and say, "Look at those morons." Social status is highly subjective, and depends on your personal point of reference.

Because of your work, you interact with thousands of young consumers online every year.

Yes.

Are you finding any common denominators in the brands or experiences that they seek?

Yes. Young people are talking about "authenticity." Interestingly, if you ask them to define it, they find it difficult to pinpoint what it means. From what I gather, they're talking about brands being honest and transparent.

Is it really possible for a brand to be honest or authentic if the primary goal is to make money?

I think there's absolutely a way of being transparent and honest. Look at Patagonia. This is a perfect example of a company that's able to embody those qualities. If they make a mistake, if they screw up as a brand, they do not hesitate to expose it. Have you ever visited the Footprint Chronicles website? It's incredible. Patagonia tracks the entire development of their products, from design to delivery. If, in the process, they discover that they've inadvertently used some kind of toxic glue that they didn't realize was toxic, they admit it. They're the first ones to expose their wrongdoings and mistakes. It's really refreshing.

If they're admitting a mistake, they're being honest. But how does a brand convey authenticity? What is an authentic brand?

First of all, the word "brand" has so many different meanings, and it means so many different things to different people. So it's very hard to give you a completely objective, textbook definition of what it means. A brand can be the identity of a product, a service, a business, or an experience, and it can include a personality. It can be a logo or a badge or an extension of a person. It can be a sign. It can be a color combination. There's so many different ways that you can define what a brand is. But remember, at the end of the day, it's also a way of identifying livestock. It means so many different things in different contexts, and it can also mean nothing. But I define an authentic brand as one that stays true to the mission of why the brand exists. A company like Patagonia lives and breathes their vision in everything that they do. So does a brand like Muji. Sustainability, recycling, and design minimalism are part of every single thing that Muji does.

Even Nike has stayed true to its mission. They're a performance brand, and they've stayed true and authentic to that sensibility. Everything that they design and develop—from products to marketing to experiences—communicates "performance first." There are many brands that show what it means to be an authentic brand.

You've been at the forefront of working with consumers to cocreate new ideas. Do you believe that cocreation is different from crowdsourcing?

Absolutely. Cocreation may have its origins in crowdsourcing, but it's a totally different concept. I'm not saying that you can't generate creativity from a crowd, but crowdsourcing lacks the deep relationship that exists when brands cocreate with consumers. There is also a process when you cocreate what is missing in crowdsourcing. It's this creative process that occurs between brands and their consumers that takes the experience to a whole new level, and it's what inspires me to do what I do best—which is guide the ideation and realize the innovation.

Creative people and designers are crucial to the cocreation process. They're the link to interpreting what consumers want, need, and desire. They turn consumer insights into product innovations. Back in the days when all you had were focus groups, the creative team would come up with an idea for a product, and then the brand would hire a company to recruit consumers who would judge it. Inevitably, the design had to be changed, and sometimes not for the better. The system was flawed. Often the environment in which the consumer viewed the idea was artificial and had nothing to do with the concept being considered.

There were also issues with how the group was recruited, and, more often than not, one individual would wind up leading the rest of the group in a direction that wasn't helpful.

How does cocreation help companies?

It's not enough to produce great creative work. Consumers won't automatically like an idea just because a brand says so. They need to be part of the creative process—a process that is fluid, organic, and on their own terms. A process like this produces the most useful insights and allows designers to think about products in a whole new way—oftentimes, they're introduced to entirely new ideas. Consumers can be a designer's biggest advocates, but only if designers will let the conversation happen and give consumers the respect they deserve by allowing them to have a say.

I'm very passionate about this subject. Maybe it's because I've seen firsthand how great creative ideas can get killed because the focus group facility had a bad recruit or a moderator was too removed from the process. This infuriates me. Consumers expect a deeper level of engagement with the brands they adore. Why not use this to everyone's benefit? If consumers are already talking about the brand and using the brand, why not allow them to engage on a deeper level?

Are there examples of this that you can point to?

I've witnessed moments when a designer and a consumer click, and really understand each other, and it is truly magical. If you bring consumers and designers together at the very beginning of a project, true innovation can occur. But in order for this to work, it's crucial to find the right people for designers to work with. I consider this to be part of my "secret sauce." I have a database of fifty thousand people who I've selected from all over the world. These are people who are passionate about brands. They're passionate about being involved, and they are engaged with brands in a more meaningful way than others. They want to be part of the entire product development process—they want to talk about why something works and why it doesn't, why they think it's beautiful, and why they think it's ugly. They want to have input. When you bring a consumer into this process, it's almost as though you have a built-in marketing team when you launch the product. You have a group of people who already feel invested in the product and want to see it become successful.

It would be interesting to find out if certain demographics are more open to this process than other groups. But let's talk about young people: Do you think that the young consumer of this era is fundamentally different from the consumers who we were when we were growing up?

Yes, absolutely. They have access to more information. They're more connected. They're inquisitive and curious, and they do their research. And they figure out who's doing what, what products are made of, where their money goes, what their favorite brands are doing, and who the people are behind those brands. This influx of information makes the young consumers of today much smarter. I also think they have better taste than we had.

Really? In what way?

Culturally, I think they're exposed to better design than we were.
A brand like Apple has exposed young people to good design. A brand like Target has helped bring design to the masses and has shown that just because something is inexpensive, it doesn't have to look cheap. It can be beautiful.

That idea is definitely ingrained into the young consumer's mind-set, and I think that's a good thing.

So do you think that this demand for honesty and authenticity is a fad, or do you think it's a longer-term trend?

I think it's a macro trend. As long as we have access to information, these issues are going to be important, and they're going to be top of mind for young people.

What do you mean by a "macro trend"?

A macro trend is something that exists in the culture for anywhere from eight to ten years, sometimes more, and affects multiple product or brand categories: cars, beauty, fashion, technology, and so on. It can also affect the cultural mind-set as well. The need for authenticity in branding is a cross-category trend. It's not just affecting one category. It's affecting multiple categories, and it's affecting the mind-set of the culture as a whole.

Do you think that certain companies are leveraging or exploiting this trend to their benefit? Do you think that they're "authenticity washing" in the same way that some companies are greenwashing?

I think it's hard to manufacture authenticity, and I think people know real authenticity versus phony authenticity. I've seen organizations try to fake it, but I think it's hard. We're much more educated as a culture.

I'm seeing more and more corporations try to reposition their brands in order to provide deeper meaning to consumers' lives—which the brands claim people can achieve through continued consumption of a particular product. Do you think that mass-manufactured brands can really help society and our individual sense of self-worth while simultaneously

providing financial value to corporate shareholders?
Doesn't that feel insincere?

It does, but you know what? I don't mind it very much. If we can utilize the power of big corporations to make the world a better place, why shouldn't we?

I recently had an argument with some folks about Coca-Cola. They were going on and on about how horrible Coca-Cola is. And I couldn't help but counter by asking them if they knew how much water Coca-Cola drops into nations that have no water—and that this is something that Coca-Cola does on its own dime. Or if they were aware that Coca-Cola is helping young women entrepreneurs in its 5 BY 20 initiative. I'm seeing more and more large corporations try to make up for the supposed bad that they're doing in the world. What's so terrible about that?

Some people say they shouldn't be doing anything bad
in the first place.

It depends on how you define "bad." One of the people I was arguing with was blaming corporations for making our kids fat. While I don't think that vending machines should be allowed in schools, I do feel that in general, people drink these beverages because they want to drink them— because they like the way they taste. Nobody is forcing *anyone* to drink a Coke, Pepsi, Dr Pepper, or any other soda! If those companies are using their profits to do good things for needy people, what's wrong with that? I don't think there's anything wrong with that. But I may be in the minority on this issue.

It's great for a company to stand for noble causes, and the companies that I love are those that stand for something meaningful. My whole family buys Patagonia. We support that brand wholeheartedly. Because of what the brand stands for, we're going to spend more and buy Patagonia products, so that we can support the company instead of its competitors.

What about items like cigarettes? I can understand forgiving Coca-Cola for its high-calorie, bubbly beverages when you consider them in light of how much good the company does for the world's neediest people. But what about cigarette brands? Nobody is putting a gun to anyone's head to smoke a cigarette, but when we know that something is so bad for somebody, should the government have a role in regulating it?

No. Again, this is about personal choice, and adults are capable of making their own choices. And either you can buy a pack of Marlboros, or you can buy a candy bar or a soda. As human beings, we have this freedom to choose. If you choose to buy the cigarettes, then that's on you.

What about the perceived "cool factor" that cigarettes can give to someone—which is part of their appeal?

Look, this is hard for me, because I was a smoker. I was a smoker for a very long time. Everybody around me was against it, and they didn't see it as cool at all. But I don't believe that anybody is forcing anybody to do anything, and especially now, since we are all hypereducated consumers. The information is out there, and we're dealing with a very educated group of young people and consumers. I don't believe that people are pawns in this game. I think that they're active, and they participate. But let's also be honest about what we do. There's always a side of me that hates what I do.

Why is there a side of you that hates what you do?

I hate being part of the machine. Don't you ever feel like you're part of the machine?

Absolutely. I oversaw the design of the Hershey's bar
wrapper, and when I see one of them crumpled on the
ground, I stomp over it and think, "I put that there."
But don't you think what you're doing is creative?

It is. It is, but it took a long time for me to come
to terms with working for large companies and
large brands. It took a long time for me to accept it,
embrace it, and love it.

At the end of the day, what makes you continue
working in this field?

I love being able to have an influence on the culture
at large. I love being able to come up with ideas with
groups of people and then see those ideas realized.
And I love to watch people experience and enjoy
those ideas. What we do has a lot of power. We
can change the way things are manufactured. We
can utilize technologies that are greener. We can
affect the way things are made in a very permanent
and important way. We can help inspire people
to realize that they can contribute to making the
world a better place, even if it's making simple,
small changes in their own lives. To me, that is an
amazing gift.

Karim Rashid

Founder, Designer, Karim Rashid Inc.

Talking with Karim Rashid is a little disorienting. Intoxicating. Heady. He is not the design couturier that some take him to be. As he makes evident in this conversation, he is very much an advocate for the democratization of design, which he feels is the only valid way of working now—creating good design that lasts, is accessible, and is affordable. He acknowledges his own transformation over the years, saying, "Look, I've made couches that are very expensive, and they embarrass me now."

With that flavor of self-reflective humility, Karim offers a novel way of looking at his own work or at any design creation whatsoever: If it were buried today and discovered 3,500 years in the future, what would it say about our modern era? Charming in its imaginative scope, the question is meaningful for longtime designers and aspiring Eameses alike.

Rashid has strong opinions about numerous topics. Design versus art, the impact of casual Fridays on the history of design and culture, how creativity is drummed out of us at a young age, the competing cultural inclinations for survival and beauty. He makes a clear distinction between design and art, praising the artistic sensibility on the one hand yet arguing that the art world is now mostly irrelevant. Modern-day artists are "social misfits who like playing with paper," and the real McCoys are those working in the realms of pop culture and other democratic venues. Rashid expresses these and other opinions with an unfiltered audacity; he doesn't blink when calling Massimo Vignelli a fascist or telling a group of Russians that they are clueless about branding.

Rashid's unabashed directness is born from his enthusiasm for design's ability to change the world. Design for him is a way that we come to understand ourselves, and every design created has an impact—aesthetic, environmental, and otherwise—on the world we live in. In this sense, he is insistent that design must fulfill its mandate to be usable for the People, and he continually advocates for design that is substantive, meaningful, well-made. "You could argue that the original intention of design is the betterment of society," he observes. With his enthusiasm for this kind of work and its world-changing possibilities, he suggests that young designers, well-versed in the advantages of design, should skip the corporate commissions and create their own brands instead.

The fact that democratization—"designocracy," as he terms it—is now a hot topic for Rashid is not surprising, considering that he is of the generation that witnessed high-end design go from unreachable exotica to mass-market accessibility. And Rashid was deeply attuned to design very early on—he has a collection of design keepsakes from his youth. An orange Braun alarm clock was the initial icon for a now-much-larger design Hall of Fame.

Like many of us, Rashid has a design fetish. Brands, designers, and iconic designs are for him a source of continual fascination and delight. He is tuned into this craft and its history in a way that few other people are, and his passion and instinct for design is hardwired into him, one that began expressing itself even before he became a teenager. That craft has continued to be refined through his decades of work. "I know how to make people love design," he says.

Debbie, before we start, I want to say that what you are doing is totally necessary.

Necessary?

Yes. Yours are the peripheral professions around designing things, and the design world needs that support.

What do you mean by "peripheral"?

I mean the critics, the people publishing books, the people running design shops, design galleries, design blogs, and so on. This is all completely necessary. I just returned to give a lecture at the college I graduated from nearly thirty years ago. It was so bizarre! I stood in the same lecture hall where I remember seeing Ettore Sottsass, Achille Castiglioni, and Marshall McLuhan speak.

And there I was, speaking to the audience, twenty-eight years later. Twenty-eight years ago, the design profession was completely unheard-of. It was a marginal discipline. Nobody talked about it. The few people who wrote about it were in academia, and it was removed from everyday life. And now, three decades later, everybody is talking about design.

What changed?

Three things. The obvious one has to do with the digital age. Communication is now omnipresent and information is omnipresent. The second fact is that the design of our products has gotten better. There was a time when engineers designed most products. The rest were reverse-engineered, where people would just pull apart other people's products and copy them. The third is that products have become more inexpensive and more accessible. In the past, you couldn't walk into a CB2 and buy a nice, well-made, contemporary chair for $150. You couldn't go to Alessi and buy a well-designed little watch for $75.

These things were just not accessible years ago. Back in the '70s, we had Habitat—that's where we went. My father loved that store. My father was a set designer for television, and he was a painter. He liked design. But he was in a middle- to low-income bracket, so he wasn't in a position to buy expensive things. There were only a few companies making affordable things at that time. There were a few in the kitchen world, but in general, you couldn't really fill your house with nicely designed things even if you were middle-class. Even back then, in 1960, the famous Charles Eames chair sold for $90 retail, which is the equivalent now to $800. We talk about Eames making "democratic" products, but they weren't really. The production processes and technologies weren't sophisticated enough to make things that were truly inexpensive. So, that's the difference. That chair could actually retail now for about $29. I'm not talking about the Herman Miller version—I'm saying you could make a similar chair for about $30–$40 retail.

Well, you've done that. You've created chairs like that for mass production.

I have an obsession with what I call "designocracy." This is because I loved staring at the bright orange Braun alarm-clock radio on my desk when I was eleven years old. I have a shelf full of objects that I've had since I was a kid. You could argue they were more interesting and more conceptual than most of the high-tech products made now. When I first went into design school, I felt I'd be contributing to the world of cool things that everybody would have.

What made you decide to go to design school?

I think the catalyst was probably a Raymond Loewy book my father bought me when I was fourteen years old.

Why did he buy it for you?

He saw that I spent a lot of time drawing objects. I wasn't really drawing families and . . .

Trees and suns and flowers and . . .

Landscapes. I was drawing things in the house and then redesigning them.

A few moments ago, you mentioned the term "designocracy." What do you mean by that?

It's my term for the democratization of design. Honestly, this is the only real way to work in the design world. If you really want to make an impact, if you really want to make people's lives better, if you really want to make change, and if you are concerned about this planet on every level—you have to make democratic things. Because, frankly, if you open up a magazine, or go to a museum, or buy a book, you can see some chair that everybody knows represents a certain image. But no one ever gets to sit on it. This doesn't make sense to me anymore. It's bullshit.

Look, I've made couches that are very expensive, and they embarrass me now. But the reality is that I've learned. I know how to make people love design. The way to accomplish this is by designing democratic things.

Our iconic designers are making things that are inaccessible. This is wrong. Design is not art.

Why not?

An artist is somebody in a particular field who wants to make change, and doesn't use a textbook to figure out what that's going to be. They actually write a new textbook, and they move the profession forward. They evolve the profession. The artist is someone who seeks to do something original.

That's it. For many years, industrial design was a service industry. A company came along and told you how to make things. I came to this profession not wanting to do that.

It's true that the artist in me always tries to do something original. But design is not art. The minute you use the word "design," it signifies that whatever you make has to be used by people. When we say that it has to be used by people, that means you're using technology to mass-produce something. You *are not* making a one-off—that's not design. For me, design has become a democratic art, because it allows everybody to have nice, beautiful things that make their lives more pleasurable, or more enjoyable, or more artistic, or more emotional, or more expressive, or whatever. But this "democratic art" is not art. In fact, art—to me—is an embarrassing world to be in.

How is it embarrassing?

Because it's ostentatious—it's removed. The art world is intentionally doing everything in its power to become more and more elite in order to keep the art business alive. But the reality is this: Art is becoming less and less relevant.

Why? Is it because the art isn't as good?

No. It's because technology has empowered more people to be creative. There's an old saying that goes something like this: "An artist cannot compete with a man on the moon in your living room."

Our real artists are making films in Hollywood. They're making *Avatar*. They're out there shaping the world for everybody. This is where all the real artists are. The artists hanging out in the art world are social misfits who like playing with paper.

On your website, your manifesto states that design has been a cultural shaper of our world from the start of civilization.

I was just in Shanghai, and I went to a museum and looked at beautiful urns from the Ming dynasty. I realized that this is how we understand and dissect our past. We learn through artifacts. We learn about the civilities of the time, the religions of the time, and the sociobehavioral constructs of the time. The objects denote our existence.

How do they denote our existence?

They describe the conduct of the time, the religion of the time, the behavior of the time.

So this is evidence?

Yes. It's physical evidence of our existence. But now that we're in a digital age, I think things are shifting and changing. Yet, historically, these artifacts were the only way we understood who we were, or where we came from, or what we did. I think about this every time I design anything. I imagine burying everything I designed today. If someone excavated it in the year 3500, what would it say about the time in which we live now?

I think the first thing they would understand relates to how we made things. In the last ten thousand years, prior to the Industrial Revolution, we made things by hand, and our tools were very primitive. The future generations would be able to see the evolution of our process of making things with EBM [extrusion blow molding] machines and rapid prototype machines as well as with injection molding and blow molding. They would be able to draw a timeline of our industrial production processes.

What do you think they would be able to determine
about our culture and our society right now?

They'd see that we are living in what I call "the casual age." My theory is that this actually began in tandem with the concept of casual Fridays. Once that became the norm, Fridays then extended into

Thursdays and Wednesdays, and so forth. The next thing you know, people are walking around New York at two in the afternoon, and they look like they just rolled out of bed. Or they're wearing flip-flops in November. I just read that 70 percent of the world's shoe market now consists of running shoes—which is phenomenal. When you go to the airport and you see the shoeshine man with no work, you know why.

The men's tie business has been cut in half during the last decade. Men are not wearing ties anymore. The same dynamic exists in the panty hose business. When was the last time you saw a woman in panty hose?

What do you think this says about us as people?

I think that we now have the freedom to be individuals. And we have the ability to avoid hiding behind uniforms.

But isn't there just a different uniform now?

Not really. If everyone on Wall Street wears a suit and tie, and I go to Wall Street and wear pink, I'm signaling my individuality. Then I'm not lumped into this huge, conforming group. If I wanted to hire a lawyer, I would much rather hire a lawyer who has his own way of dressing and doesn't wear what a lawyer would typically have to wear.

Yes, but that's you, Karim. There's still a uniform for casual Fridays. Think about all those awful beige khakis and horrible polo shirts.

You're right. Look—I'm an idealist. I think the uniform is a form of suppression. But, if I had to guess, I would say that disbanding the uniform for a more individualistic expression allows for a healthier way for humans to evolve. Even the term "act your age" has disappeared. I'm not a typical fifty-year-old, but I know a lot of fifty-year-olds who are listening to dance music and driving around in SUVs. They're wearing ripped jeans, the latest Nikes, and all the rest of it. They're not acting the way that fifty-year-olds are supposed to act.

You've said that every business should be concerned with beauty because it's a collective human need. What does beauty mean to you?

Historically, humans have always been obsessed with beauty on every level. Not only for ourselves, but as it relates to our surroundings, our architecture, our faces. You could argue that we're even more obsessed today. You could look at the plastic surgery that's done nowadays and say that we're becoming so self-absorbed. But even the ancient Egyptians were doing operations to change the shape of people's noses, and there were other forms of implants over the centuries.

Today, beauty is not as much about fitting into a certain sect, tribe, or trend—it's much more about you expressing your own beauty. But to do that, you need to figure out who you are.

Let's put it this way: If we were brought up or educated in a way that supported this notion of being an individual, and that the greatest thing we each possessed was our unique fingerprint and DNA, the world would be a completely different place.

But what do we do? We do the opposite. Think about it. At first, kids are all creative. At three or four years old, they're so perceptive and in-the-moment. And they're so creative! Who gave us this desire, this need to create? It's important to acknowledge that we all draw when we're kids, by the way. We all do! We all finger-painted. When we're young, we all make things. We all grab things. We all start by using our imagination.

And then all of a sudden, conformity comes along, and this conformity continues year after year after year, and all of a sudden, you're just twenty-seven years old, and for some reason you've become myopic about how you should live, how you should dress, how you should behave, and what you should do with your life. And self-expression is not given much priority among those considerations. It has become completely suppressed.

I think beauty is this sense of self-expression. The beauty is that we're all actually different and creative.

The beauty is that we are all completely diverse in every way—in our cognition, our mannerisms, everything. This isn't a superficial kind of beauty.

If humans have this inherent creativity and individuality, why do we have things like the shopping mall? Why do they exist?

At the end of the day, survival will override beauty. The shopping mall is part of our contemporary, pathological need to consume. We live in a world where consuming is a big part of our existence. But let me play devil's advocate for a moment. In the past, there was a time when I had to run around all over a city to find certain things that I wanted. Now I don't have to do that. When I go to the shopping mall, I can get everything in one place. I'm protected from the elements of nature. The climate is right. The air-conditioning is right. That's beautiful, isn't it?

Does it bother you that you can go to almost any shopping mall in the United States and find the same stores selling the exact same things?

That's capitalism. The mall is simply convenient. And frankly, they're not even doing that well anymore. Why? Because of online shopping! I loved shopping in stores, but for the last ten years, I've bought almost everything online. I barely go into stores anymore. Why should I? When I shop online, I have the world at my fingertips. I can shop in the "world mall." I have more choice than ever, and I'm more informed about everything that I'm buying.

What do you love about shopping?

To see what people are making, and to see what the world is offering. I have no issues with consumption. I have issues with consuming things that we don't need and that are badly made. I have issues with things that break down or cause harm. But there's nothing wrong with consuming. A lot of what we consume gives us a better life. Our quality of life is better today than it's ever been in our history. That's a fact. Even if one-quarter of the world doesn't have fresh drinking water, the reality is that the majority of the world is living a better life. Why is that? It's because the things that we have in our lives make our lives better. You could argue that the original intention of design is the betterment of society.

I assume that this is why your motto is "I want to change the world"?

Well, I have several mottos, but yes, I want to change the world. I first said that twelve years ago, and it was primarily because people did not believe that design could change the world. But anything—*anything*—a person puts out in the world has the power to change it. The world we've created and built consists entirely of design. And every other day, there's an improvement on something.

Do you think these views are now part of the "Karim Rashid" brand?

Perhaps. So many people keep talking to me about how I have a brand and how I have this and how I have that. I don't really have a brand—I have an identity.

You used to wear white all the time—now you wear pink a lot.

I wear both. If you walk into my wardrobe, the left side is white and the right side is pink.

Why?

Because that's me. I decided that's me. I knew it years ago. I found a picture of myself when I was five years old, and I was dressed all in pink.

What is it about those two particular colors that you find so compelling?

With white, I feel a sense of liberation—of freedom and autonomy. It's almost like a white canvas: You have no baggage.

What about pink?

To me, pink is the most passionate color there is.

Because . . .

It just speaks about passion. If you have a pink aura, you're known as a passionate person.

When I interviewed Massimo Vignelli, he told me that black, white, and red were the only colors designers should use—all of the other colors were only good for flowers.

Oh, really?

Yes.

He's a fascist—tell him I said that. Every color in the world should exist. And it does exist. In nature, everything from phosphorescent lime to beautiful electric blue—everything exists. I love color. I use a hell of a lot of color in all my work. The human eye can see sixteen thousand colors. Why limit yourself when there are so many possibilities?

Getting back to what we were talking about—how would you define the term "brand"?

A brand is basically a business that has an identity. If it doesn't have an identity, it's not a brand. You should be able to say to somebody, "Shut your eyes and tell me what you see when you hear the words

'Calvin Klein.'" If I shut my eyes and think of Calvin Klein, I see gray, black, and little else. But that's his brand. It's very minimalist, and it's vague. This is always my test for companies. I had a meeting the other day with people from Unilever, and I said to them, "When people close their eyes and think about your brands, what do they see?" And it was really funny, the people at the table did this, and every one of them saw the exact same thing.

Was it something embarrassing?

Somewhat. Last year, I was at the Russia Forum in Moscow to give a lecture on entrepreneurship. There were four thousand people there. I had the audacity to tell the Russians that they don't have any brands. Yet consider a country like Sweden, which has only six million people. I can name ten Swedish brands right now that we all know. And I basically asked the Russians, "Why is that?" The Russians have the know-how, they have the intellect. They're well-educated people, and they have the technology. How come they don't have any brands?

What did they say?

The minister of economic development got very upset and told me I shouldn't be speaking that way. But I told him this could change quickly. You can design three or four fantastic things for an unknown company, and within a year, the brand is known around the world.

Isn't that what you did for Method when you designed some of their products?

Yes. Fantastic example. And Method had no money. This is the new world we live in now. People are realizing the power of design on every level. Look, people invest money to make things, so why can't they be beautiful? Why can't they work? If something has to physically exist in the world, why can't it be uncategorically better than whatever else is on the market?

We should tell young designers not to worry about what they're going to do with their design careers. They should start their own brands. Designers should create their own beautiful brands that can change the world.

Alex Bogusky

Cofounder, FearLess Cottage;
Former Principal and Creative
Director, Crispin Porter + Bogusky

In one of his recent guises, Alex Bogusky was wearing glasses, and with his specs, his boyish good looks, and his newly trimmed hair, he looked to me a little bit like Clark Kent. The appearance seems to be Bogusky casting himself against type, because he has never needed a secret identity. From early on in his career, it has been clear that he was an unstoppable force in advertising and branding. His very start in the business has the ring of myth: While working for his father's Miami-based design firm, he art-directed a project for another advertising agency in the city. Chuck Porter, a partner at the shop, was so impressed that he called the elder Bogusky and asked him who had done the work. The younger Bogusky was hired shortly after.

With that as his origin story, it has been evident throughout his career that Bogusky was capable of performing creative feats that few others could match. In eight years he quickly rose up through the ranks to become partner of the agency he had joined. During his tenure at what came to be called Crispin Porter + Bogusky the creative director invented and created culture-shifting, award-winning campaigns for clients such as Burger King, the Mini Cooper, Coca-Cola, Florida's antitobacco initiative, Volkswagen, Microsoft, Virgin Atlantic, and others.

In 2009, Adweek named Bogusky "Creative Director of the Decade," and his own boss called him the "Steve Jobs" of advertising. CPB won multiple awards from publications and from the esteemed Cannes Lions International Advertising Festival. Bogusky was able to vitalize, revitalize, and transform the companies who hired him, and he shepherded campaigns that triumphed in TV, print, and online, proving that his know-how had few limitations. His work was defined by its radical unwillingness to do anything less than provoke—think Burger King's Subservient Chicken, the Truth antitobacco work showing body bags, or Volkswagen ads featuring a car crash. CPB campaigns defied conventions and generated notoriety for the client while building the brand.

With such stunning successes and such a clear mastery of what he does, it would seem strange that Bogusky would leave the agency world. But there has been an inner voice gnawing at him, and he felt it was necessary to heed the message. His 2008 book, The 9-Inch "Diet": Exposing the Big Conspiracy in America, *which pointed out the dangers of our current eating habits and the food industry's role in encouraging them, was emblematic of the concerns on his radar. He had come to understand the negative impact that corporations were having on our health and the well-being of the planet; he wanted to shift from helping brands to becoming an advocate of consumers. He wanted to do something different. And so, despite multimillion-dollar offers to stay put, he left CPB and put up his own shingle at the Boulder, Colorado–based FearLess Cottage.*

Of course, the move only adds to the mythical proportions of his story: The adman who turned his back on the advertising world to shepherd a new era of consumerism. From the cozy space of the FearLess Cottage office, Bogusky is now devoting himself to a number of world-changing initiatives. With the manifesto dubbed the Consumer Bill of Rights, Bogusky is striving to help consumers assert their power. FearLess Cottage itself is working with companies to help them transform their businesses to come into alignment with the new world order, to ensure that they're working in an authentically sustainable way. Through the collaborative brand COMMON, he is seeking to create an entirely new kind of brand—a cooperative enterprise that would put its imprimatur on the products of like-minded companies based on a foundation of altruism and sustainability.

In our interview, Alex spoke about all this: the dissonance of his current work and past history, his hopes for FearLess Cottage, his philosophy about creative work. If the new endeavors succeed, Bogusky would have yet more milestones to add to his already-astounding legacy. And who would doubt his capability? Throughout his career, he has proved he can do pretty much anything. Alex Bogusky has creative powers beyond those of mere branding mortals.

You have an interesting statement on FearLess
Cottage's website: "Fear is the mortal enemy of
innovation and happiness." Why do you feel this way?

While dabbling with fine art in college, I noticed that if I was ever scared, it came through in my work. I found I couldn't create anything compelling if I was feeling uneasy or frightened. This became nothing more than a "note to self" at the time, but over the course of my career, I found myself in situations where I had to create the culture for an entire creative department. The most important component of this—and the aspect I spent a lot of time on—was creating a culture where people weren't afraid. There's another quote relating to this that I think about a lot: "People are afraid of so many things, but so rarely are they afraid of mediocrity."

Are you afraid of mediocrity?

I think so. Early on in my career, I was definitely afraid of mediocrity, and it helped push my work into a fearless space. If you're afraid of mediocrity, you have to push past wherever mediocrity lives. A lot of people believe that there is a right and there is a wrong, and that there are creative rules. I think that trying to figure out what's the right or wrong way to do things is a form of fear. This inhibits people, and holds them back. In creative departments, you need to create a culture where you can break lots of rules. It probably wouldn't have the same power now because it's so common, but wearing T-shirts and jeans was one way of signaling this idea. It became a very important way of saying, "When you walk in here, the rules are not the same." The idea that you're willing to break that rule meant that you're going to break the rules elsewhere.

The uniform of a T-shirt and jeans has become a part of
the visual language of the creative class.

I've noticed that. Now I wear ties a lot.

So you're breaking the rules that broke the rules. Why are you so interested in rules?

In advertising and design, there are usually two things going on. One is the effort to propel the discipline forward. The other is the effort to refine the craft as we know it. Both camps are important. I think you can look at people's work and identify which camp they're in. There are those who refine the craft as it exists, and they create, in many ways, the most beautiful work. They make the work that is the easiest to like.

Those who are trying to undo the craft or destroy a piece of it—or push the discipline into a new place—that's important too. And as soon as this type of work is successful, then the craft gets applied to what they've done.

Which camp were you in?

I was more in the "pushing it forward" camp. My hope was that, at the end of my career, people could say there was advertising before Crispin Porter + Bogusky and there's advertising after Crispin Porter + Bogusky, and it changed because of us. And I feel like we did that.

I've read that you didn't really like advertising—that it wasn't sacred to you. What made you decide to go into advertising in the first place?

In many ways, it was just a fallback. I grew up with design and designers—my parents were both involved in the field—but I wanted to be a professional motorcycle racer and a windsurfer. But those things didn't turn out so well. I fell back into the family business, the design firm that my dad was running with his brother [the Bogusky Brothers], and wound up getting a job in the agency. I didn't really know anything about advertising, but I actually did like advertising. Ultimately, for me, what I loved most was the additional impact the copy provided. I found design was often very implicit. Bringing in words made for a more explicit communication and more immediate feedback. I really like that.

Crispin Porter + Bogusky created numerous groundbreaking campaigns and absolutely changed the face of advertising. Why did you leave?

I was having less fun in advertising, and I wasn't leaping out of bed in the same way that I had for most of my career. I think that it was a very, very good fit for me for a long time, and yet at the same time . . . I'll tell you something about the way my mind works: I make decisions and I put them in the back of my head. I don't go back to refer to them, but I know they're there. One of those decisions related to where I would live—I decided that I would move out west when my kids went to junior high. That's what compelled us to move to Colorado.

I just don't think I was a "lifer," even with my own company. For me, there was something that didn't make sense about doing one job forever. I felt I had to try some other things.

Was it about trying something new in your life and having another chapter in the arc of your career? Or did you lose your sense of the purpose or intention of advertising?

Well, when I got into advertising, it was a different time in the world.

In what way? Was it more like Mad Men?

I miss the *Mad Men* era, and I miss the two-martini lunches. When I first got into the business, there was a copywriter at the agency who would close the door and get stoned so he could write copy. Everyone understood this was his process. I miss most of that stuff. But no, that's not why I left. The world was different because, at the time, we weren't aware that we were bumping up against the physical boundaries of our ecosystem.

That's the big change that has occurred. People have become aware of this at different times. Al Gore has known it for thirty years. For me, it's been five. I realized that the current processes of capitalism are not going to provide a happy outcome. And yet people are beginning to redesign many aspects of business and industry. I felt that advertising was not in the center of this change—in fact, it was clearly outside where these changes were being made. I tried to take that kind of thinking to our clients, and our best thinking was not finding a very receptive audience. Actually, I shouldn't say "our best thinking." I felt like my best thinking wasn't finding a receptive audience.

Why? Why do you think that your best thinking wasn't finding a receptive audience?

I felt like I was the tail trying to wag the dog. The work that advertising people and agencies can do is really important. But in the traditional relationship, I found it was getting frustrating. So in some ways, I felt it would be more important to leave and try to agitate the industry. When I say "agitate," I mean in a good way. I didn't want to annoy—I wanted to begin to move certain issues a bit more to the center. And I felt that leaving the industry would give us an easier pulpit to do it from.

On FearLess Cottage's website, you say that you want to be "an insurgent in the new consumer revolution." How would you define "insurgent"? And what do you mean by "the new consumer revolution"? Was there an old consumer revolution?

Our society has a very short memory, and I love to go back and look into our cultural history. One of the most interesting things I like to look at is the term "consumer." People actually don't like being labeled a "consumer." Nevertheless, I use the word a lot— I have yet to find a synonym that I can replace it with. People say, "I'm more than a consumer!" And yes, of course they're consumers, but where is your power to change things when you're a consumer? And many people say, "Well, I'm not a consumer, I'm not okay with that label." In a recent tweet to someone, I said, "I'll stop calling you a consumer when you stop breathing and eating." Obviously, none of us can stop consuming. It's just part of what it is to be human. But "consumer" has become a bad word despite the fact that "consumerism" actually began as a title for a consumer movement. It really was!

Consumerism was the movement to protect consumers. Now it's become the definition of overconsumption.

But historically, that's not the original definition of the word.

Words get corrupted, changed, and moved around, but the idea of consumers being empowered actually began with the term "consumerism." When I started thinking about this, I went back and looked to see if there was a consumer's bill of rights. I not only found that one existed, but I also discovered that John F. Kennedy wrote it in 1962—in *1962*. There was a lot going on at the time—the Cuban Missile Crisis, Vietnam, and civil rights battles. Yet, somehow, he thought this was important. He authored the Consumer Bill of Rights, and it is amazing. Its principles are dated now, but the reality is the relationship between company and consumer has evolved and can evolve further. But we need to have more democracy in the relationship—in most cases, we're talking about putting more democracy into capitalism. It's not a democratic system right now.

Corporations now have more rights than most people.

Yeah, they have limited liability that we don't have, and they have the right to give in unlimited ways to political campaigns, which we also don't have. They have many more rights than people do.

What do you feel needs to come out of the new consumer revolution? If the new consumer revolution is successful, how will it change us?

Well, I wrote the new Bill of Rights. I want companies to sign it, and I've met with a few that seem willing to do so. Truly progressive companies will sign this. And then consumers can start to think about what isn't democratic in the relationship they currently have with corporations. This relationship is just like anything else: whatever you're used to seems to be the way it should be. At one time, it was acceptable to have kings. You'd have one person with unlimited power who could do whatever he wanted. The people of that era thought, "That's fine, and anything else is going to throw us into anarchy." The first time we experimented with democracy was a total leap into the dark. We *thought* it could work, but no one in the history of the planet had ever tried it. Then the new system becomes part of our awareness, and it subsequently creates new expectations on both sides.

In order for something like a Bill of Rights to be broadly successful, it seems to me that corporations would have to give up a lot. This is particularly true for the giant companies selling fast-moving consumer goods. Why on earth would they want things to change, given how successful they currently are?

I've been trying to understand this, and I've been using physics to look at it. Throughout history, we've refined our theories and models of physics because the old theories didn't fit what we observed. That's how we got to quantum physics The old ways and the old principles that corporations used for capitalist purposes are not working as well as they used to. There are new sets of rules that are beginning to outperform the old set of rules.

I'm not exactly sure how these "new rules" might be impacting corporations. But it seems to me that the companies selling fast-moving consumer goods are trying to reposition their products so that they might be seen as, for lack of better term, good for consumers. But the ultimate goal still seems to be "sell more product." For the most part, corporations are not saying, "Let's try to do things in a different way, or let's try to establish new rules in an effort to make the world a better place." Their behavior is still targeted to pleasing Wall Street.

Correct. There's very little discussion about selling less of anything.

I recently had a conversation with Milton Glaser, and he said the same thing. He told me that those of us in branding must figure out how to get people to stop buying things. People shouldn't have to buy certain things over and over. They should be made well enough to last longer, or even last forever.

I think that that discussion is beginning. All of this is about awareness, unfortunately, and the awareness of these issues has not yet permeated our culture. There is no way that there are going to be laws created that are going to protect us from ourselves. Because—as you mentioned— corporations have a "suprademocracy," they don't need to listen to anyone. Their influence on democracy means that we won't be able to change these things with an edict from us alone. It will need to be through awareness. The conversation around sustainability has just reached a certain level of awareness. And what Milton is talking about is design instructing culture. We can't get there until we go through what we're going through now, but this conversation is starting to happen. I recently interviewed two people on my Internet show, *FearLess*, and we were talking about the Eco Index. The Eco Index measures everything about a production facility or a product and calculates a sustainability score. It's an open-source index that anybody can use.

When we started talking about scoring design, it became apparent how difficult this is. "Trendy design" is obviously not as sustainable as more classic design. For people to realize this, design has to instruct culture, and then culture makes the change. Nowadays, if I walk down the street with something trendy and new, people might look at me and think, "That's cool." If design begins to influence this space, then the reaction would be very different, because that same trendy thing will no longer be cool. It will not be cool because it essentially says, "I'm using something that I won't be able to use next year or the year after. It's going to go out of style." To choose something that will quickly go out of style would become uncool. Design could reframe fashion and what's cool in a way that could change people's behavior. But you can't do this without awareness. The power of design is that it can start to create the awareness. The people working on the Eco Index are beginning to be able to determine how they would score the "designing of things" by assessing everything from carbon dioxide footprint to how zippers are made and how much nylon a product contains.

Do you consider this part of the new consumer revolution? Is this the kind of work that you want to be part of?

Yes, but I want to play on both sides. With FearLess Cottage, we play on the consumer side. We're trying to build that awareness for the consumer, and we're trying to generate higher expectations from a relationship with a corporation. The current relationship can be described as "I'm going to give you this dollar. And in exchange for this dollar, I get these goods."

We want to change the equation to "In exchange for this dollar, I not only get these goods, I get a completely transparent look at how you behave and how you created this product. I also get a complete and transparent look into what you believe politically. If you don't want to do that, I'll take my dollar elsewhere."

If that were the expectation, people would have a very, very powerful impact through their consumption.

How do you think that could happen? How could that model be implemented?

That's why I need to work this from both sides. At FearLess, we are working on what the consumer expects in a way that puts pressure on the company. When I say pressure, I don't mean pressure that takes the form of "the stick," but that takes the form of "the carrot." Corporations are really good at stiff-arming government. But we've worked in the business, and we know they're also passionate about knowing what "wind" the customer has this week. We have to begin creating these winds for customers, and corporations will move in response, because they want to pursue the dollar. There's no doubt about that—we've seen that over and over.

With FearLess, we're working on consumer awareness. With our initiative COMMON—which is a community, a business incubator, and a collaborative brand—we're working on prototyping new corporate structures and relationships. This work came out of the realization that a lot of people wanted to get involved with FearLess and didn't know how they could. So we created something that involved designers in an effort to reimagine the world and reimagine capitalism. I don't think designers necessarily feel like they have permission to do that.

Tell me about COMMON. You just described it as a collaborative brand. How is it collaborative? What are your hopes for it?

Let me step back at bit. One of the big questions we need to ask and answer is, "How can we all have enough?" To Milton's point, we are moving into a time where we just can't keep buying more stuff. Here's an example of this: You probably own a drill, right?

Yes.

How often do you use that drill?

Not very often.

Almost everyone has a power drill, right? Other than people who work in the construction business, we collectively don't use them very often. There's an abundance of drills that is not necessary. Up to now, society hasn't been particularly good at collaborating and sharing. I live in a really high-end neighborhood in Boulder, and yet three of my neighbors all chipped in to buy one lawn mower. They did so not because they can't afford one individually, but because they realize how dumb it would be for each person to have a lawn mower. When you collaborate, you unlock value. Where there was once value for one individual, there's suddenly value for three.

Many companies are beginning to do this with their own collaborations. The Eco Index is a version of this—the Wal-Mart Index, which Wal-Mart is using to assess the sustainability of their suppliers and products, is as well. And the company moved from squeezing value out of their of suppliers to beginning to invest in them by making their shipping space available in what would otherwise would be empty Wal-Mart trucks. There is tremendous value within organizations that we can unlock. There's a lot of "more" there. In essence, we can consume less but have just as much. This is a very important, fundamental notion.

When I first looked at this—as an ad guy and a marketing guy—I saw that when assessing a company and its total market value, often half of its value is made of this thing called "brand." The truly progressive companies are working on that half of their company to figure out how to be more collaborative and efficient in order to create better value for themselves and others. They wouldn't normally be able to access their brand value. Now they can.

How do you feel about brands? Why do you think that they're so important to people?

There is a "badge" value to brands that is probably both good and bad. I was originally going to suggest it might be all bad, but I'm not really sure it is . . . But maybe it is. If you take a very Buddhist perspective on this and notice that you have this inclination to badge yourself in order to feel worthy, then that is certainly a problem. You may still be able to take a Buddhist approach and consider badging yourself only with things you're a fan of. And that would be okay, I guess. Then again, thinking about Buddhists—they wear the robes. That's basically . . . a brand. It's an impossible irony to avoid.

Do you think there's something hardwired in our brains that compels us to visually signal that we belong to a specific group with certain values? I recently read about a study at Oxford University that examined cultures all over the world and determined that religion comes naturally—even instinctively—to humans, and that we see an unseen agent at work in the world. The idea that God exists is prevalent and deep-rooted. I often wonder if branding is something that is also "prewired" in us, given our need to project what we believe, where we belong, and who we are.

I think that branding is very, very much intertwined with religion. If we are wired by a higher power for religion and for God, then I think we could be wired for branding as well.

Why do you think that?

In all these cases, they seem to work in parallel in terms of the way we badge ourselves, and each one of them is a little mini–belief system.

Let's return to the question I asked earlier: What is your biggest goal for FearLess Cottage and COMMON?

My goals are pretty easy to attain. I remember the first time someone said congratulations to me for all my success in advertising, I was really offended by it.

Why?

Because I had been creatively successful for a long time prior to that, but it just wasn't as evident financially. I was offended that they used money as a gauge of success.

Do you think you would have left Crispin Porter + Bogusky and made this dramatic change in your life if you hadn't been as successful financially?

That's a good question. How can I really answer it? Early in my career, I didn't care much about money because I didn't think I would ever have a decent job, so I didn't think I'd ever own a home. All of this has been incredibly surprising to me.

Why did you feel like you would never be able to attain those things?

My family was essentially lower middle class, and I didn't go to college. I started working, and I couldn't comprehend how I would be able to afford a home. What I wanted most from my career was to have a good time working with people that I really liked. That was it. That was my goal for my career, and I was able to achieve that pretty early. And after that, it was just a matter of "Can you keep that going?" Then it transformed into other kinds of success that might fit other people's definitions, but I had already achieved the fundamental piece for me. When I think about success for FearLess, I already feel that it's been successful in many ways. I feel that my goal of bringing attention to ideas that are important for designers and marketers is happening. It's not one of those "finish line" things. Success and being "finished" for me are two different things. Success is something you can carry with you through a career. I would rather think, "I'm being successful," than "I'm going to achieve success."

When you were working at Crispin Porter + Bogusky, you created campaigns for Burger King, which is also a client I've worked with. Do you ever feel guilty for any of that work, or any of the commercials you've worked on throughout your career?

I don't feel guilty. Burger King is a Miami company. As a Miami kid, my feeling was, "Burger King: Yeah! McDonald's: Screw them!" I grew up eating Whoppers. When I got the chance to work with Burger King, it was more about helping a company that had been laying off people for eight years and trying to turn things around for them. What I didn't realize until the last couple years is that the Whoppers I ate were not the same Whoppers that are served now.

What do you mean?

The industrialized food system has changed the food for everybody in it. The problem is not necessarily McDonald's or Burger King, or anyone in the food system. It's the system itself that has subsidized the overfarming of corn and soy. Now corn and soy get cut up, sliced up, diced up, and turned into all sorts of different things. These kinds of transformations have also changed our beef system. So the beef that I ate as a kid isn't anything like the beef that we eat now. As those realizations came to me, there was a values conflict. But that process only started about two years go.

So today, I couldn't work on it. But when I started, it was very much in my sweet spot. As I evolved, the things that I could work on evolved. This has bigger implications. As I looked at trying to bring the agency in line with where my values were moving, I couldn't do it without firing two hundred to three hundred people. I didn't feel that people should lose their jobs because my values had shifted and theirs hadn't. That didn't seem right. Particularly since I wasn't 100 percent certain that I was correct.

So I can't say that I feel guilty. You know what I feel guilty of?

I feel guilty of not working harder to understand things earlier, when I could have.

Maybe I just got too excited about the growth of the agency. And I lost that critical eye. I want to be honest with myself about it. I don't want to kid myself. To answer your question: No, I never felt like working on Burger King was a mistake. I actually felt that working on Volkswagen was a mistake. We resigned working on the Mini to work with Volkswagen.

Of the decisions I made, that one was the hardest. I understand why I made it: I made it purely for financial reasons. We felt we were at risk by having only one giant account—Burger King—and we needed to balance it. But it was a purely financial decision, and it went against my heart, because I so loved working on the Mini. Most of the decisions we made, we made with heart. The only things we screwed up were decisions where we only used our head.

Tom Peters

Author, Business Consultant

---

*In 1982, Tom Peters and Robert Waterman wrote the
book* In Search of Excellence. *The book presented
case studies of businesses that were thriving and
outlined eight principles of how to lead and build
businesses effectively. The book—which debuted when
the United States economy was ailing and American
businesses were in desperate need of management
help—flowered into a full-grown movement, a
business big bang. Business leaders had lost a sense
of the value of innovation, of integrity in mission, and
how to create a thriving business culture.* In Search of
Excellence *helped business leaders to reorient.*

*The book gave Peters a platform for critiquing
ideas and business models that had been getting
him "pissed off" for over a decade. He had become
increasingly incensed about the prevailing approach
to business management during his work as a
consultant at the firm McKinsey, where he had been
since 1974, and in the research he had done prior to
that for his PhD in organizational behavior at the
Stanford Graduate School of Business. Following the
success of the book, Peters became a management
guru nonpareil, the A of the A-list in the management
consulting world.*

Part of his impetus in writing In Search of
Excellence *was his certainty that a business—much
less an economy—couldn't be assessed through the
lens of the numbers and statistics that business
leaders, consultants, and economists would often*

obsess over, to the detriment of other aspects of what makes a business—or a brand—sing. Businesses couldn't be led through a top-down, autocratic strategy that didn't allow for innovation and the vital contribution of the people in the organization. Customers needed to be acknowledged and revered. Emphasis needed to be placed on true innovation and on making quality products.

The overobsession with numbers remains one of Peters' main critiques and an issue that, as he says, still pisses him off. His point is that there is a lot of psychology involved in both business leadership and in the brand choices we make as individual consumers, and the numbers don't reflect any of it.

Brand, too, is one element of a business that remains beyond calculation, that can never be fully conveyed or explained. Part of Peters' work, of course, is brand consulting, and he offers up some important thoughts about what brands mean in the contemporary day and age. He emphasizes the importance of design and considers the connection between brand and "story."

Speaking of brand, Peters is well-known for coining the idea of "Brand You," a catchphrase concept that has earned him both devotees and enmity. His identification of the individual as brand was a recognition of cultural trends that had seemed to reach an apotheosis in the '90s. Brand thinking had become pervasive, as had the use of media as a form of personal expression and business tool alike. In our conversation, Peters bemoans the fact that the "Brand You" idea is often misinterpreted. It is related to the concept of the individual as brand, yes, but it is not the narcissistic raison d'etre that some critics say it is.

Peters has a lot to say about brands, history, innovation, and management. He has an irrepressible energy, and he'll segue from Quaker Oats to Deng Xiaoping, from Gutenberg to containerization. He is very happy to ruffle feathers, and he is not one to

censor himself. Tom himself embodies that healthy—
if animated—mix of rationality and irrationality that
he sees so lacking in others.

He has continued to write, offering his pointed
views on business and strategy in books like The
Little BIG Things: 163 Ways to Pursue Excellence,
Liberation Management, and Thriving on Chaos. As
much as he has assailed the downsides of corporate
culture, he has continually advocated for the
collective good we can accomplish. "An enlightened
view of any profession can result in a potentially
significant contribution to society," he says.

*I was recently reading an article about Snooki, the 4'9"
star of MTV's* Jersey Shore. *Apparently she's hoping
for a career beyond the reality show, and she is trying
to set herself up as a brand.*

Jesus.

*I'm wondering what your thoughts are about the
"person as brand" phenomenon. I think the idea comes
from your late '90s* Fast Company *treatise about "the
brand called You." Not that I'm assuming that Snooki
has read or been influenced by it . . .*

Oh, I'm brokenhearted. [*Laughs.*]

I'm trying to picture her with an issue of Fast Company
from the late '90s.

Alan Webber and Bill Taylor started *Fast Company*,
and I was a supporter. I was a supporter long
before it actually became a magazine, when it was
just a dream.

*Well, there's no question you helped put the publication
on the map.*

Well, I don't know about that. I think it was a perfect
fit for the '90s. I always saw it as a response to a
changed economic reality. And of course, there were
social commentators like Dinesh D'Souza who said
Seinfeld and I were emblematic of everything that
was wrong with the '90s. Now, don't get me wrong.
I was delighted to be considered a cultural icon and
mentioned in the same sentence as *Seinfeld*. But it
really bugged me, because he missed the point.

Why did it bug you?

It bugged me because it suggests that Brand You was
a product of a me-centric, egocentric world gone
awry. I would never for a minute deny that when
you're thinking about Brand You, you're thinking
about yourself in the world. But my point was that
it has developed ten times more as a result of the

outsourcing of human labor and the use of modern software, which replaces human labor. People like my father, your father, and people who worked in the tall towers of Manhattan and Chicago were fundamentally—except by their three closest friends at work—not known by their name. They were known by their badge. You used to be able to survive as "Badge 129" in the purchasing department, as long as you came to work regularly and didn't rock the boat. That was the survival tactic.

In the post–World War II environment, thanks to the GI Bill—which I think is one of the most enlightened pieces of legislation ever passed—you were able to get a college degree from a good school. You were a reasonably intelligent human being. You were not necessarily hardworking, but you were not not-hardworking, and you were a reliable person. That was enough for lifetime employment. That is gone.

In today's environment, you've got to stand for something. You might not have to do this if you're a nineteen-year-old shift manager at McDonald's, and we certainly aren't talking about those folks who are working at Google. But the guy who was the faceless person in the faceless purchasing department is either going to be outsourced to India or outsourced to software. The great race is between the two. To stay employable today, you've got to have some sort of signature. It pissed me off that Brand You was simply seen as a younger generation's deterioration into egocentrism. Look, I'm not an idiot—I'm not advocating narcissism. But it's true that you've got to think more about yourself now. But let's explore this further, because there is a paradox to Brand You.

Yes, you have to think more about yourself and how you're positioned, but you can no longer survive by sucking up anymore, because the boss you were sucking up to has been laid off. Now you're more dependent than ever—by reputation and otherwise—on your horizontal network of peers. Now you have a national or international group of people, for whom you've done good and reliable work, and this group has become your professional family. So you have to have a greater degree of loyalty to your peers and be a significant member of a group more than you ever have had to before. So it's a paradox. You have to think, "I've got to be more 'me,' and I've got to be more of a thoughtful member of an extended family than I was before, because solo doesn't survive either."

Writers are probably one of the few professionals who have always had to depend on horizontal reputations. You've had to take care of relationships with the guy who gave you the opportunity to do your prior book, or the person who knew you when you were working at the *Spokane Herald* and then recommended you to a job at a better paper. I'm arguing that the person who wants to be a purchasing professional now has to depend on horizontal reputations as well.

Do you think that people really aspire to be purchasing professionals?

Read David Foster Wallace's *The Pale King*, and you can find out whether IRS agents want to be professionals or not. I think they do.

If you're really good at something, your obsession can become societally useful.

Presumably, if you're a purchasing professional at Safeway or at Deloitte & Touche, and you're a rabid believer in environmentalism or global warming, you can use your purchasing job to demonstrate to your company that if you buy green products, you'll not only be building a better relationship with your consumer, but you'll be helping your company and yourself in the world. An enlightened view of any profession—even the job of a prison guard—can result in a potentially significant contribution to society. We can't all be writers and management gurus, for God's sake.

Speaking of management gurus, The New Yorker *has often been quoted as saying, "In no small part, what American corporations have become is what Peters has encouraged them to be." I have two questions about this statement. First, what have you encouraged them to be? Second, what do you think you've encouraged them to be?*

[*Laughs.*] And the third question you need to ask is this: "After the great crash, is that a recommendation or a condemnation?" And I'm not sure which would be the correct answer.

Do you really think what you've encouraged them to be was the reason for the crash?

[*Laughs.*] No, neither my arrogance nor my self-abdication is that extensive.

The book *In Search of Excellence* was researched in the late '70s and published in 1982. Having lost World War II, the Japanese were in the process of winning World War III by knocking out our car companies, our shipping companies, and so forth. The Carter-era recession/depression—which at the time was considered as bad as the economic situation could get—brought on interest rates of 20 percent, inflation of 15 percent, and 11 percent unemployment. These numbers were worse than what we currently have. And then we had the Reagan revolution.

The fat cats always took businesspeople seriously, but now "regular" people started taking business seriously. *In Search of Excellence* was one of the first business books to move from the back of the bookstore to the front of the bookstore. It not only became a best seller, but a top best seller. In many ways, it spawned a whole generation of authors who are now sitting at the front of the bookstore.

The timing of the book was perfect, but my coauthor Bob Waterman and I had no way of knowing that. We spawned everything—including

Brand You-ism—among professors at Harvard and
Stanford, in Chicago and Wharton, as well as a jillion
other places. All of a sudden, there was a movement
to think about organizations more self-consciously,
and that happened to coincide with a situation where
we were getting nailed by the Japanese on the basis
of quality. The emerging movement meant that
people were thinking. Because the ultimate "quality
logic"—the reasoning that relates to quality—is if you
have the desire to improve the quality of something,
that's a noble intention in and of itself. But if you're
really going to improve quality, then you have to
pay attention to your workforce—whether you're
managing a retail bank branch or an automobile
company. Organizations became a bit more people-
centric. Another important influence was when
significant computerization began to further
influence our behavior, and suddenly you didn't need
seven levels of management.

So if there is—and I'm not necessarily willing
to acknowledge this—but if there is a postmodern
corporation, I and two hundred people like me
in the "talker business" and two hundred people
like me running consulting companies have
benefitted. But even if we can't conclude that there
is a postmodern corporation, we can certainly say
that something did happen, and despite the many
remnants of hierarchy, it's arguably something
that's different from the organizations we had
in 1947 or 1957. So yes, I will acknowledge that
I became associated with this movement more
than most people, though I will not acknowledge
having contributed more than a whole bunch of
other people who were also involved. It was truly
a community of us who, for better or worse, made
the contribution. When I say this, there is no
false humility at all. There were suddenly dozens,
hundreds of bloody business books, good, bad, and
indifferent that were housed on the front shelf of
Barnes & Noble, or the late Borders, or wherever.

Why do you think In Search of Excellence *changed business so much? What was it about that book that has resulted in a magazine like* Fortune *saying, "We live in a Tom Peters world"? Why?*

As a reasonably good student of the history of innovation, I can tell you that timing is everything. Period.

A lot of people have ideas that are ahead of their time, but as we say with the introduction of a new product, there are "three times": too early, too late, and lucky. I was lucky. I really believe that. I don't believe that there is a lesser or greater number of interesting ideas now any more than in the era of the railroads, when we were making such phenomenal breakthroughs.

Really?

Look, there are shelves and shelves of books with titles like *Empire of the Air*, which investigate the radio equivalent of the Internet age. I've got ten books on the transcontinental railroad and railroads in general, and the stories are hilarious. If you read the commentary of the people who were around then, you can find out about the guy who rode halfway across the Midwest on a train and described how his head was swirling and how things were too fast and the world had come unglued. He actually didn't think his head worked anymore.

I read that after the railroad was invented, people thought that if you travelled faster than forty miles per hour, the pressure on your body would be so intense that you would break up or explode.

Absolutely. In thinking about railroads, another thing consistent with today is how one invention spawned a plethora of ancillary innovations that wouldn't have been possible otherwise. Two of the great breakthroughs inspired by the railroad were the invention of standard time, or time zones, and the invention of the bill of lading. Before that, people didn't know how to ship goods across the country and keep track of them. And suddenly we were able to ship jillions of tons of things and know exactly where they were. I also find the history of containerization to be absolutely spellbinding. There are always going to be some things that every generation tends to think is unique only to them. But the railroad changed war, peace, technology, enterprise, and families. When the railroad came to England, the Duke of Wellington—the guy who won Waterloo—said, "We should not leave the railroads untrammeled, or the hoi polloi will be racing around the country." Can you imagine? Wouldn't that be terrible? That's just as bad as the bloody Chinese shutting down the Internet, for God's sake.

It's fascinating to look back over the trajectory of innovation and invention. What can seem like a minor contribution can ultimately have a tremendous impact on the way we live. Look at the plastic bag. I was recently reading an old Harvard Business School case study about the 1974 disposable diaper wars between Kimberly-Clark and Procter & Gamble.

Back in the day, you had to dispose of what was in a cloth diaper by flushing it down the toilet. It was unsanitary to put it with other household trash because paper bags couldn't contain the excrement, and it was against the law to put it out on the street for garbage pickup. I find it so interesting that something as benign as a plastic bag can change the way we sanitize, the way that we handle our infants, and the way we reduce hazards to our health. It's extraordinary.

I just read an article suggesting that Gutenberg's printing press was not that big of a deal. The big deal was the industrial production of paper so that you could use the damn press. We went a long way from the monk's parchment to the availability of paper for the hoi polloi.

But this brings us back to my point about luck. There were probably at least fifty well-formed iterations of containerization, but there was no place to unload the containers. It wasn't until you invented and built the infrastructure that suddenly the container could change the world. But who's the person who invented containerization? We have no idea who it is because nobody cares.

It reminds me somewhat of the current state of the rock 'n' roll business. These days performers aren't making money from ticket sales. They're making money from merchandise. So now a rock band goes on the road to sell T-shirts.

The way I read the situation, they started making money from ticket sales when they stopped making money from records and CDs. Now we're at another iteration of that: The ticket sales are irrelevant and the rock star branded T-shirts are relevant.

So branded merchandise is fueling the music business. Why do people care about branded items? What do you think it does for the human psyche?

One part of it—which is less relevant today than it was in the past—is once they got connected with companies like the Unilevers and the Kimberly-Clarks and the P&Gs, a brand was a guarantee of reliability. This did not exist in my grandfather's store in rural Virginia. Have you read Thomas Hine's book on packaging? One of my favorite examples from his book focuses on Quaker Oats. Hine talks about how, in 1870, oats were something you fed to an animal. And suddenly, you had a cardboard box with a Quaker on the outside, and oats became a human delicacy—due entirely to packaging—in the short space of twenty years.

First, branding was about safety and reliability, but let's also acknowledge that human beings are an emotional species. I was in China for the first time in 1986. As soon as Deng Xiaoping took the lid off of regulation, women went from wearing gray, shapeless Mao jackets to sporting colorful wardrobes nearly overnight. This need to express our individuality and vibrancy is obviously a fundamental, basic human need.

Why do you think it's a basic human need?

I have no idea. It may be that giraffes are colorblind, so they have patterns on their bum that other critters don't. I assume at some point, in some sense, it's a version of peacocking. I assume that there was probably an aspect of Darwinian selection to it. My bet would be it has something to do with this, though I do have a proclivity for being fairly Darwinian in my beliefs. Frankly, I have no idea what the history is.

Let's assume that we are hardwired to want to be attractive to each other for some deep-seated procreational need. How is this connected to oats transforming into a delicacy when the food is put in a package decorated with the image of a Quaker?

In Darwinian terms, we're suckers for stories. Stories are the way that humans have always communicated. The Quaker Oats box is not only visually attractive, but it's a story.

Since Aboriginal times in Western Australia—and I'm sure if one goes back thousands of years, or hundreds of thousands of years before that, you'll find the same dynamic—a good story has always been a good seller. A brand is a story. Period. Frankly, I would rather dump the word "brand" and use the word "story." I think we're in the process of wearing out the word "brand." At some level, when I'm a brand, I'm more commercial. When I'm a story, I'm more human.

So what do you think the Quaker story was at the turn of the 20th century?

I presume that—to your point with plastic bags and diapers—as late as the beginning of the century, sanitation sucked. The pharmaceutical companies should get none of the credit for our life expectancy going from fifty to seventy-five during the 20th century. The two things that account for 90 percent of this improvement are sanitation and diet. So here comes a cereal that's reliable and clean and that you could buy for your dearly beloved children without any fear they would get sick when they ate it.

How was the Quaker telling that story? What did the Quaker represent?

Doesn't a Quaker, in theory, stand for reliability? If it's good enough for a Quaker, then it's got to be good enough for my little Martha.

One of my favorite stories revolves around the Morton Salt Girl. She is all about metaphor. Morton chemically alters a salt crystal so that it won't stick to other crystals when it's wet or humid outside. The Morton Salt Girl is holding an umbrella while the salt is pouring freely. So when it rains, the salt pours. But you don't have to read a word—it's all expressed by a visual puzzle that you have to figure out. I think this is why people like it so much. People love puzzles—they feel better about themselves when they correctly figure them out. That's why people like the "I ♥ New York" logo so much. It's a puzzle made out of a word, an abbreviation, and a symbol.

I remember reading an article about a social psychology experiment relating to this and being totally unsurprised, as I imagine you would be. Two sets of subjects are given two lists of the same words to memorize. One of the lists is of the words "farm," "basement," "bar," and so forth. The other list is the same, except that random letters are left out, so instead of basement, you've got *B-A-S*, underscore,

M-E-N-T. In terms of subsequent recall, the people who had the list with missing letters outperformed the people with the full words by a dramatic margin. Cognitively, you had to work your ass off, so it stuck in your mind.

Yes, the experience of figuring out the words creates a deeper neural pathway in the brain.

It's extraordinary the way the brain works . . .
I hate economists.

Why? Why do you hate economists?

Because they're impersonal bastards. They believe in the rational model, which makes them dumb. When the great recession of 2007–2008 descended upon us, it was not an economics issue. It was a psychology issue.

How was it a psychology issue?

The behavior that got us there was herd behavior. The government has convinced people of the emotional need to own a house. If you look at the economics studies, in many respects the housing market doesn't go up all that much over a long period of time. There are a million studies that will tell you that renting makes more sense than owning. But psychologically, owning a piece of turf is incredibly important. So I understand why people—who had no money and were given the chance to borrow money—were total suckers for it. And I use "sucker" not in an abusive sense, but in a realistic sense. Then again, you've always had herd behavior on Wall Street.

They're now saying Silicon Valley is the "green" crash. The current punch line is that any human being, including you and me, can put together a business proposal tomorrow morning. And as long as we use a computer and include the word "green" a sufficient number of times in our proposals, the venture capitalists will be showering us with money by dawn the day after.

I'm obviously using hyperbole, but that's where we're seeing more of this herd behavior. In terms of the rational-mindedness, I've trained in that. I was trained as an engineer, but now I'm a reformed engineer, a "born again" engineer. The reliance on rational models—or models in general—to me, makes economists highly suspect. I don't believe anything they say. That is very close to not being hyperbole. In the 1970s, when I was getting my PhD, my classmates and I read books by psychologists Amos Tversky and Daniel Kahneman. Tversky and Kahneman invented "behavioral economics." This is the hottest branch of economics right now, the "Freakonomics" branch.

Kahneman won a Nobel Prize in Economics, but he was a social psychologist, period. I am royally pissed off that these effing economists have appropriated psychology and now call it the coolest thing in economics. Screw them. These straightlaced, rationally thinking economists have appropriated social psychology, and it pisses me off for reasons that are totally childish on my part.

Why childish?

Because it's stupid. **I'm delighted that the irrational realities are beginning to seep into economics. The rational me is delighted that irrationality is seeping into the rational profession, because maybe they'll get some things right.**

Look, I have a very strong smart-ass streak. I have learned to be "appropriate" and politically correct on many scores over the years. To the extent that I must, I guard my "smart-assery" when I'm giving speeches to middle managers from financial services companies. But the smart ass lurks no more than one glass of chardonnay below the surface.

I'll remember that when I need to get your honest opinion on something. In the past, you've said, "Design is so critical it should be on the agenda of every meeting in every single department in the business." Why do you believe that?

The term I've used for twenty years—and maybe I stole it from somebody or maybe by the grace of God they've stolen it from me—is "design-mindedness." Design-mindedness is about bringing an aesthetic dimension into a discussion of anything. I am a great fan of Carly Fiorina. A lot of the reason was that she—kicking and screaming—brought a design aesthetic to Hewlett-Packard. I know this because I lived next door to Lew Platt, Carly's predecessor, in college. Prior to Ms. Fiorina, Hewlett-Packard ranked 200 on a list of 199, in terms of design sensibilities. When she left, they were a significant consumer goods company, and that was Carly, pure and simple. When they gave her successor, Mark Hurd, the credit for having a great design team, it made me want to barf. Carly was not a good chief operating officer, and she probably needed to be let go at some point. I don't deny that for a minute. And she had an ego that was a little bit out of control, and I don't deny that for a minute either. But she brought about a cultural change at Hewlett-Packard, which makes the work that Lou Gerstner did at IBM and Jack Welch did at GE look like chump change by comparison.

Do you think that anything can be successful now without being highly positioned?

Yes.

Really?

Well, we obviously would have to spend the next two weeks defining "highly." As the ethos of quality that began to bubble up in the United States during the 1980s took root, the major fast-moving consumer goods companies started having significant problems going up against store brands. Once store brands became reliable, they began to market and brand themselves. Then Wal-Mart came along, and the average American started saving something like $900 a year, which isn't small cookies for people making $45,000 annually. The things they're buying at Wal-Mart might be much less sexy, but as long as they're quality products, this is perfectly acceptable. The recession obviously has pushed people even farther toward this model.

Look, I own a Subaru. I own a Subaru because they're perfect for Vermont. But the quality revolution has taken such root that, in terms of quality, I'm probably just as well off with a Kia as I am with a Subaru or a Mercedes.

Do you really think that the quality is that comparable?

Yes.

So it is really just branding and positioning?

Well, branding, positioning, and people who like to have sex with their car. The electronics in BMW and Mercedes cars allow you to do a whole lot of things that you really don't need to do. But in terms of a vehicle that can travel thirty thousand miles without ever having to go into a shop, I would bet that a Kia is very, very close to these other brands.

Malcolm Gladwell

Author, Cultural Critic,
New Yorker *Columnist*

---

*Malcolm Gladwell, the author of several books
that I revere, is a staff writer for* The New Yorker.
He is a genius.

The first thing that I want to talk about is a common denominator—or a lack thereof—in three of your books: The Tipping Point, Blink, and Outliers. None of the books have the word "brand" in the index.

No, they don't, do they?

No, they don't. Is this something intentional, or is this discovery a surprise to you?

Well, there isn't much of an explicit discussion of business strategy in any of those books. In that sense, I suppose it's not surprising. Those books tend to approach the issue of branding sideways.

Yes, they do. But the word "brand" appears numerous, numerous times. You talk about Levi's and Clairol, and ketchup and mustard, and the Beatles, and as I reread the books before our interview, I couldn't help but wonder what the index would show for the subject. I was very surprised to see that it wasn't in any of the indexes.

This is not meant as a snub of your world. It's such an amorphous word—maybe I've shied away from it.

Why do you think it's amorphous, and why have you shied away from it?

I think I have the same feeling toward the word "brand" as I do toward the word "Africa." "Africa" is an incredibly problematic word for me. It's a word used with great frequency to describe an intricately complex area made up of people, countries, and cultures that have no more in common than we do with Uzbekistan.

But because it's a convenient word, and a well-known word, and a geographically defined continent, we use that word to sum up and generalize everyone who lives within the continent. In a way, it really is unfair. But we've inherited that framework, and I think we'd be better off if we banned the word entirely.

Getting back to "brand," the word has similar implications. Yes, it's of much smaller consequence—it's a trivial example of the same problem, but it *is* a problem. The word gets thrown around so recklessly that I wonder whether we wouldn't be better off setting it aside. Instead, if we could use more specific words that zero in on what we're really interested in discussing, it would help the conversation.

If we were to ban the word "brand," or use it only in specific instances, what words could we use instead?

I would start by trying to distinguish the different dimensions of "brand," because there aren't an infinite number of them. "Reputation," for example, is a large component of "brand." But very often, it's the part of brand that you can do very little about. Reputation tends to be very stable.

I'm thinking about this at the moment because I'm writing about college rankings, and this presents a beautiful example of the drawbacks of the notion of brand. If you look at the *U.S. News & World Report* rankings, for example, a quarter of a college's rank is based on peer assessment and reputation—which is basically a brand score.

Harvard's got a great brand. In the category of reputation, it gets the highest peer evaluations. But this can be very problematic, because you can quickly get into areas where you see that different organizations' reputation scores don't correlate well with more objective measures of their performance.

So what exactly is reputation if it's not something that actually corresponds to how well an organization performs in the marketplace? We have the word "brand," and a big chunk of it is this thing called reputation, and this thing called reputation is disconnected from notions of quality. This makes me think that I should treat reputation separately from the other elements of brand.

*Is that because you think that reputation is
more subjective?*

Yes. But it's more complicated than that. I've
been thinking about this because in addition to
writing about schools, I've also been writing about
hospitals. And the situation is even more complex
with hospitals. The measurement of a hospital's
reputation or brand value is heavily uncorrelated
with the hospital's actual performance. Everyone
says that Sloan-Kettering is a great hospital, right?
But this is essentially a meaningless statement.
It doesn't tell us whether or not a person would
be better off going to Sloan-Kettering than to a
different hospital. And that makes me strongly call
into question the usefulness of some of these terms.
I'm actually more interested in the idea of what's
left in a brand after reputation is removed.

What do you think is left?

I'm not sure that I have a useful answer. But I
wonder where the very, very personal idiosyncratic
experience-based reactions to a service, product,
or institution reside. In that sense, maybe I'm more
interested in the residue.

The residue?

Yes. I don't have a specific answer to your question
about what's left over after reputation is taken
away—I would say the residue is what remains.

*But, getting back to where we started, why do you
have trouble with the word "brand"? Aside from
the subjectivity of reputation, what is it that bothers
you most?*

First and foremost, the overuse of the word.
For example, when people started referring to
themselves as brands, I began to roll my eyes.

Why?

Because we're now using the word in every conceivable context. The more broadly you use the word, the less useful it is as a way of distinguishing or describing complex phenomena. I object to its lack of precision.

How do you feel about the word "love"?

I suppose it's mildly problematic in the same way, except that I feel we're quite expert in understanding the various ways in which the word is used. We've thought long and hard about when that word is used in a meaningful way and when it's superficial. By the time you're fifteen, you've thought about the word "love" in a way that you haven't thought about "brand" or "Africa."

We might have spent more time thinking about love, but I don't know if there's a way to gather empirically precise data about what it means.

True. But if we were as sophisticated in our use of the word "brand" as we are in the use of the word "love," I'd be happy.

That's interesting, because I feel the opposite—I feel there's probably less mystery to the concept of brand than there is to love.

That's funny . . . Maybe you're right. I haven't thought that much about it beyond the last minutes of this conversation.

In your essay "Listening to Khakis," you investigate "what America's most popular pants tell us about the way guys think." How do you think brands can telegraph how we think?

My answer to that is a little indirect—have you heard of a site called Svpply, spelled with a *v*?

No, I haven't.

It's just a start-up. It's one of those sites where people sign up, and the software then allows them to go to all kinds of other websites and drag products onto their personal pages. It's like a Facebook page, but it isn't filled with your friends and musings, it's populated with the products that you like. I think it's rather cool. You can also follow people, so if I find someone whose tastes I like, I can follow them and observe their other marketplace choices. And the site can also find people for you, so if you liked five particular things, it stands to reason that you will like a person who likes the same five things. It's a collaborative filtering algorithm meets Facebook.

Or Match.com.

Or Match.com, yes. But what I find interesting is that the site is very explicitly making a point about how our personalities are in part a function of the collection of objects, ideas, and things that we surround ourselves with. It picks up on the work that psychologist Samuel Gosling has done in which he goes into your room and has people rate your personality on the basis of what's there. He's found that those ratings are as good as or better than ratings that people create after they've met you.

I don't think that kind of assessment would have been as valid fifty years ago, and this shift is tied to the task we have of constructing our identity in our world. But it's not just an expression of how brands contribute to our collective identity, it's also related to how we impose our own notion on brands. The user is now helping to define the brand, and this fact and the sorts of conversations that now go on between user and brand are fascinating. It's not a trivial matter, and in some cases, it can be quite meaningful.

*If you look back fifty years ago, you can see how
people began associating themselves with brands
that telegraphed specific movements or political
views. Even something as benign as a Volkswagen car
projected certain values that went beyond the basic
necessities of transportation. The speed in which
these associations have become integrated into the
construction of our identities is staggering. What are
your thoughts on why we do this?*

There was a really lovely piece that the novelist
Zadie Smith wrote for *The New York Review of
Books*. She reviewed the film *The Social Network*,
and in the review, she's quite critical of Facebook.
She describes how the constant broadcasting
of your likes, your friends, your thoughts, and
your things to the world has robbed people of an
interior life.

Zadie teaches at NYU and she describes
the way her current students are different from
her students of previous generations. She's struck
again and again by the kind of emptiness at the
core of people's ... "existence" is too strong a word
for this, but it's enough to say that everything
is on display, and there's nothing that is "just
yours" anymore.

*But everything people put on display is simply what
they want to display.*

I think her argument is that the things people put
on display inevitably generate a kind of inertia. In a
world where we now have extraordinarily efficient
ways of communicating and displaying, the question
of who you are becomes incredibly complicated.

I think that brands are a part of this. When
you surround yourself with certain kinds of objects,
they become a public statement about who you are.
There are hundreds of choices that are necessary to
fill out your life with objects and things, and I think
that requires an inner logic as well.

BRAND THINKING AND OTHER NOBLE PURSUITS

Maybe the modern version of introspection is the sum total of all those highly individualized choices that we make about the material content of our lives.

You spoke earlier about new forms of social media. Why do you think that Facebook and Twitter are so popular?

As someone who writes for a living, I totally understand the impulse. It's the same impulse that led me to go into writing, except that in my generation only a select few got to stand on a stage and tell the world what they were thinking.

What do you think that impulse is?

It's the desire to share your thoughts. This, I think, is universal.

Why?

Why? I don't know why. We're fundamentally social creatures. Our brains grew because we wanted to communicate. That's why we're not apes, I suppose. This is essential to what makes us distinctive creatures. But before social media and the Internet, there were serious logistical constraints on people's ability to share. Now, there are increasingly fewer. So it's not just professional writers and artists who can do this—everybody can.

Another important part of this is that these forums are available to teenagers. Never before have we had these kinds of communications technologies in the hands of those who have the greatest desire to communicate.

But I also think that when we look at these new technologies, we're confusing two things. We're confusing age-specific preferences with long-term technological changes. A lot of what we see on Facebook and Twitter is specific to the lives of teenagers and young adults. It's a phase that we all went through, and that everyone will always go through, but it's being magnified in the current young generation because they've got this extraordinary tool they can use to communicate.

But just because someone is a massive Facebook user at seventeen does not mean she will be one at forty. To my mind, the jury is still out about what will happen to our desire to use these technologies as we get older. I was on the phone nonstop when I was fifteen. Now I barely use the phone at all.

I feel bad for the teens who are using Facebook to reveal their thoughts so publicly. If anybody were to get their hands on my diary from when I was a teenager, I'd be horribly embarrassed. It was so ridiculously girlish, unsophisticated, maudlin, and obsessive.

The incredibly complex process teenagers once had for working out their self-identities has now become even more fraught with emotion, excitement, and danger because everything is so public. In the past, you could have worked out all that angst inside your own head privately. Teenagers nowadays will rue the permanence of some of the stuff they post.

Do you think the way we're communicating on the Internet is an evolution of the way we once communicated on the telephone? I remember that right after the iPod came out in 2001, there were quite a few articles written about how it was causing today's youth to be totally isolated. There seemed to be a real concern that the iPod was encouraging social anomie. But the introduction of social networking sites has countered that trend. Do you think social networking is just an evolution of our limbic needs?

I would say that the introduction of the telephone was far more socially transformative than the introduction of the Internet. I think these are all points along a kind of evolution. They are all extraordinarily meaningful. But this is a process with very, very deep roots.

We've been upending, reshaping, and redefining the norms of social interaction for 150 years.

Do you think that it's just part of human evolution? Do you think we're finding out anything new about ourselves? Do you think that it's profound in any way?

Well, each time we change the norms of interaction, there's a refocusing of those norms. Each technology has its own implicit biases, and each favors one kind of interaction over another. They're not necessarily dramatic changes, but we tilt the lens in a different way each time.

I believe that we're currently tilting in favor of weak ties that have become quantification tools. They provide a quantitative measurement of impact, and not necessarily a qualitative measurement. Previously, letter writing and diaries were very qualitative and not quantitative. Those particular forms of social expression tilted in favor of strong, deep, meaningful ties and the formulation of really powerful, close-knit friendships.

Right now, we're focused on scale when it comes to the realm of sharing information with people. In previous generations, the focus was on intimacy. So, there's been a trade. The kind of information sharing that we have now is really, really great for innovation, for the adoption of new ideas, and for forming new coalitions.

Each era has its own specialty, which is neither better nor worse than the one before. They're just different. And it may be that the next iteration in this ongoing revolution turns back to a previous norm. I suspect it will turn back toward close-knit, intimate ties.

Really? In what way?

> I have no idea. We have no idea what the next
> iteration is. We didn't see Facebook coming. We
> didn't see cell phones coming. We didn't see any of
> this stuff.

*Do you think that there's more superficiality in the way
that people are interacting now?*

> I wouldn't use that word. It's a trade. If you're
> interested in having large numbers of contacts,
> and if you're focused on things like innovation and
> broad-scale social organization, then it's wrong to
> use the word "superficial." Those are incredibly
> important aspects of cultural interaction. And
> they happen to be what is best suited to the kind
> of technologies we have now. The trade-off is that
> the interactions you have tend to be thinner and
> weaker. But that's just the other side of the coin. It's
> not a judgment. I'm very, very hesitant to use value-
> laden language.
>
> I recently wrote an article about social media
> that featured a scenario about a man who formed
> a group on Facebook to find and match bone
> marrow transplant donors. Facebook is beautifully
> adaptive for that kind of task. It's an extraordinary
> feat to be able to canvass that many people in an
> incredibly short period of time, with no money,
> and still solve a discrete, difficult problem. This is
> new technology at its absolute best. And it happens
> to be a superficial tie that is used for a profoundly
> important end.

*In this same article, you talk about how social networks
are based on weak ties and that they're ill-suited for
activism that challenges the status quo. You say that
for that type of revolution, you need strong ties. What
about the Obama campaign?*

> Actually, the Obama campaign was a good
> illustration of weak ties on a number of points. In the

grassroots organizing, social media was an adjunct to an existing and incredibly well-organized, on-the-ground, precinct-by-precinct movement. Social media was used in a secondary role to raise money and to supplement the far less efficient phone trees and mass mailings that have defined previous campaigns. It did not replace the nuts-and-bolts, neighborhood-by-neighborhood activation that has been part of every campaign since political campaigns began. People were recruited via social media to go door-to-door. The campaign used the incredibly efficient tools of connection to mobilize people for real work. And when I say "real," I mean face-to-face, on-the-ground work.

What social media also provided for Obama was support that was a mile wide yet only an inch thick. The minute there was the slightest unsteadiness, everybody abandoned him. I have never seen a bigger group of fair-weather friends for a candidate. This doesn't make me feel better about digital forms of organization. From the vantage point of three years out, there is nothing in the way that social media provided support for Obama that makes me feel better about social media.

In one of your earlier pieces in The New Yorker, *you wrote about the Clairol hair color slogan, "Does she or doesn't she?" You wrote, "All of us, when it comes to constructing our sense of self, borrow bits and pieces, ideas and phrases, rituals and products from the world around us—over-the-counter ethnicities that shape, in some small but meaningful way, our identities. Our religion matters, the music we listen to matters, the clothes we wear matter, the food we eat matters—and our brand of hair dye matters, too." Why do these things matter so much?*

One reason is that our material choices as consumers are no longer trivial. They are now amongst the most important choices we make.

They have consequences well beyond our own selves—they have global consequences. They have consequences on our economy, on the community we live in. When you eat a McDonald's hamburger, you are casting a vote for a certain kind of agricultural system, and for a certain kind of climate. In a sense, everything we do casts a vote for a certain kind of world. And this isn't true in the same way it was one hundred years ago, or if it was, we weren't aware of it. We weren't forced to make that connection because our world wasn't being driven on this macro level by the sum total of consumer choices—at least not in the same way. So it makes perfect sense that when you decide what car you're going to buy, you think long and hard about the choice, and when you drive a Nissan Leaf, or a Chevy Volt, you're saying to the world, "These are my values. This is the kind of world I want."

When we do this over and over and over again, we will find that it can address some of the problems and crises in our world.

The declarative value of consumer choices and the public statements made by consumers in their brand choices are an enormously powerful tool.

If we were to tally up the votes cast for the various possibilities of our world, what do you think we could say about the kind of world we're creating right now?

We're in transition. The fascinating elements of the consumer space right now are the macro choices implicit in our micro choices. We're suddenly much more interested in things that are green and sustainable, and we're much more interested in the longer-term, broader implications of our choices. People are beginning to see that when they buy a pair of jeans, they're making a choice that extends well outside their own borders.

At the beginning of this interview, you seemed to be
quite dismissive about the idea of "people as brands."
Why is that?

Well, I don't mean to be dismissive. It's just that a
person is not a company or a product. Can we talk
about the kind of abstract dimension of someone's
appeal? Yes, absolutely. Is Madonna selling a
product—which I would say is her and her music—
the same as General Motors selling cars? Maybe.

What about Martha Stewart?

Or Martha Stewart. Yes, clearly, there are cases
where it's a useful term. But what I was reacting to
was the "everyone is a brand" movement that I felt
was in vogue a year or so ago.

The Tom Peters, "the brand is you" kind of thing?

Yes. At a certain point this takes us *further* away
from meaningful human interaction, not closer. I
have the same reaction to that as I have to people
who take the Myers-Briggs test, and then declare to
the world that they're an "INTJ." It's not useful or
helpful to define oneself according to this crackpot,
incredibly narrow, restrictive personality typing
system, and then tell the world, "This is who I am."
No. It's not who you are. Human beings can't be
reduced to four letters. Fast-food franchises can
be reduced to four letters because they're selling
the same burger over and over again, in the same
context, and in the same kind of building, according
to the same kind of rules.

Human beings aren't that way. The beautiful
thing about Facebook is that it allows people to
express themselves in their full complexity. I've
seen some of the lists of people's likes and dislikes,
or of the things they listen to, and these lists can run
on and on. *That's* a meaningful contribution to our
understanding of each other, not "I'm this kind of
brand." It's simply an oversimplification.

*So why do you think those personality tests are
so popular? Why do you think they're given so
much credence?*

It gives people a superficially appealing
"understanding" of each other. I think that we
should be fighting pigeonholing, not enabling it.

Do you think you are a brand?

No. I hope not. I am a person.

Acknowledgments

A very special "thank you" to Tad Crawford for believing in me from the beginning.

Thank you to Bob Porter and Delia Casa for their keen eyes and kind spirits.

Thank you to my dear families: the Millmans, the Feinmans, the Parneses, AIGA, The School of Visual Arts, *Design Observer*, *Print* magazine, *Brand New*, the Institute for International Research, *The Dieline*, and Sterling Brands.

Very special thanks to Lisa Grant and J'aime Cohen.

Big love to my homegirls: Susan Benjamin, Katharine Umsted, Marian Bantjes, Susan Milligan, Emily Oberman, Bryony Gomez-Palacio, Joyce Rutter Kaye, Christine Mau, Moira Cullen, Carin Goldberg, Paula Scher, Olga DelaRoza, Amy Brusselback, Helen Stringer, Karin Lippert, Ilene Feinman, Alissa Walker, Laura Victore, Jennifer Giannotti-Genes, Irma Lunderman, Amanda Bach, Virgina Sanchez, Megan Taylor, Ellen Leikind, Ruth Spudic, Esther Ginsberg, Ruth Spudic, Maria Anthis, Margie Butler, Jane Naillon, Darralyn Reith, Sharon Reiter-Lindberg, Kim RIvielle, Krista Vazquez, Pamela DeCesare, Petrula Vrontikis, Tina Roth Eisenberg, and Lisa & Louise; and to the boys:

Gregory St. John, Simon Lince, Cary Liebowitz, Mark Kingsley, Aaron Kennedi, Andrew Gibbs, Mark Dudlik, Mike Bainbridge, Peter Mundy, Chris O'Rourke, William Lunderman, James Schultz, Chip Kidd, Paul Sahre, John Fulbrook, James Victore, Stefan Sagmeister, Stefan Bucher, Jay Gould, Rob Edelstein, and Armin Vit.

Thank you to Steven Heller for being Steven Heller.

Thank you to Rob Walker for his foreword, and to Kurt Andersen and Jonah Lehrer for their incredible generosity.

Thank you to David Rhodes, Tony Rhodes, and Richard Wilde for allowing me to teach.

Thank you to the brilliant people that let me interview them for this book: Malcolm Gladwell, DeeDee Gordon, Seth Godin, Wally Olins, Dan Pink, Virginia Postrel, Karim Rashid, Tom Peters, Brian Collins, Joe Duffy, Phil Duncan, Alex Bogusky, David Butler, Dori Tunstall, Dan Formosa, Cheryl Swanson, Sean Adams, Grant McCracken, Bill Moggridge, Stanley Hainsworth, Margaret Youngblood, and Bruce Duckworth.

Thank you to the singularly talented team that assisted me with this book: Rodrigo Corral, Jeremy Lehrer, Curtis Fox, Jen Simon, Steven Attardo, Cindy Peng, Martha Depenbrock, and Sarah Burningham.

Thank you to Edwin Rivera for everything.

Index

Books from Allworth Press

Allworth Press is an imprint of Skyhorse Publishing, Inc. Selected titles are listed below.

How to Think Like a Great Graphic Designer
by Debbie Millman (6 x 9, 248 pages, paperback, $24.95)

Emotional Branding: The New Paradigm for Connecting Brands to People, Updated and Revised Edition
by Marc Gobe (6 x 9, 352 pages, paperback, $19.95)

Design Thinking: Integrating Innovation, Customer Experience, and Brand Value
by Thomas Lockwood (6 x 9, 304 pages, paperback, $24.95)

Brandjam: Humanizing Brands Through Emotional Design
by Marc Gobe (6¼ x 9 ¼, 352 pages, hardcover, $24.95)

Branding the Man: Why Men Are the Next Frontier in Fashion Retail
by Bertrand Pellegrin (6 x 9, 224 pages, hardcover, $27.50)

Design Firms Open for Business
by Steven Heller and Lita Talarico (7 3/8 x 9 1/4, 256 pages, paperback, $24.95)

Branding for Nonprofits
by D.K. Holland (6 x 9, 208 pages, paperback, $19.95)

POP: How Graphic Design Shapes Popular Culture
by Steven Heller (6 x 9, 288 pages, paperback, $24.95)

Design Disasters: Great Designers, Fabulous Failures, & Lessons Learned
edited by Steven Heller (6 x 9, 240 pages, paperback, $24.95)

Green Graphic Design
by Brian Dougherty with Celery Design Collaborative (6 x 9, 212 pages, paperback, $24.95)

Designers Don't Read
by Austin Howe; designed by Fredrik Averin (5 ½ x 8 ½, 208 pages, paperback, $19.95)

Designers Don't Have Influences
by Austin Howe (5 ½ x 8 ½, 224 pages, paperback, $19.95)

Designing Logos: The Process of Creating Symbols That Endure
by Jack Gernsheimer (8 ½ x 10, 224 pages, paperback, $35.00)

Advertising Design and Typography
by Alex W. White (8 ½ x 11, 220 pages, paperback, $50.00)

The Elements of Graphic Design, Second Edition
by Alex W. White (8 x 10, 224 pages, paperback, $29.95)

Creating the Perfect Design Brief, Second Edition: How to Manage Design for Strategic Advantage
by Peter L. Phillips (5 ½ x 8 ¼, 240 pages, paperback, $19.95)

To see our complete catalog or to order online, please visit *allworth.com*.